DEAR SANDY, HELLO

D0595243

Dear Sandy, Hello

LETTERS FROM TED TO SANDY BERRIGAN

by Ted Berrigan

EDITED BY
SANDY BERRIGAN AND RON PADGETT

COFFEE HOUSE PRESS
MINNEAPOLIS
2010

COFFEE HOUSE PRESS books are available to the trade through our primary distributor, Consortium Book Sales & Distribution, www.cbsd.com or (800) 283-3572. For personal orders, catalogs, or other information, write to: info@coffeehousepress.org.

Coffee House Press is a nonprofit literary publishing house. Support from private foundations, corporate giving programs, government programs, and generous individuals helps make the publication of our books possible. We gratefully acknowledge their support in detail in the back of this book. To you and our many readers around the world, we send our thanks for your continuing support.

LIBRARY OF CONGRESS CIP INFORMATION

Berrigan, Ted.
Dear Sandy, hello : letters from Ted to Sandy Berrigan / edited by
Sandy Berrigan and Ron Padgett.
p. cm.
ISBN 978-1-56689-249-0 (alk. paper)
1. Berrigan, Ted—Correspondence. 2. Poets, American—20th century—
Correspondence. 3. Berrigan, Sandy—Correspondence. 4. Psychiatric hospital
patients—Florida—Miami—Correspondence. 1. Berrigan, Sandy. 11. Title.
PS3552.E74Z48 2010
811'.54—DC22
2010016258
PRINTED IN CANADA
1 3 5 7 9 8 6 4 2
FIRST EDITION | FIRST PRINTING

ACKNOWLEDGMENTS
Tom Veitch • Patricia Padgett
Dick Gallup, who was there for Ted during those difficult months
Maureen Owen • Carla Harryman • Bessie Citrin
Alice Notley, Executrix of the Estate of Ted Berrigan
The Estate of Joe Brainard
Columbia University Butler Library Special Collections
Coffee House Press staff

This book is dedicated to
Carla Harryman and Maureen Owen,
friends and supporters in life and poetry,
and to friends and strangers who have written me letters.

—SANDY BERRIGAN

EDITOR'S NOTE

In the interest of focusing on this pivotal time in Ted and Sandy's relationship, some letters, images, and poems have not been included here (missing text and images are indicated by †). In addition, while every effort has been made to sequence accurately the undated letters, several could be ordered only through educated guesswork.

The letters presented here, particularly those in Sandy's section, have been edited very lightly in order to preserve Ted and Sandy's voices.

—Coffee House Press

CONTENTS

Preface

BY SANDY BERRIGAN

Since being unexpectedly separated from my husband was the catalyst for these letters, I thought it would be useful for the reader to know about the circumstances that led up to this correspondence, perhaps the longest and most intense sequence of letters Ted ever wrote.

In the fall of 1960, on my first day alone in New Orleans and waiting for my freshman year at Sophie Newcomb College to begin, I got linked up with a group of engineering students and their professor. They toured me around town, and then in the evening I walked out with the professor. He was older and very restrained. Nothing compromising happened, but that experience intensified my curiosity about life and men.

A year and a half later, when I met Ted, I was still a very innocent Sandy Alper. I had the habit of hanging out in the Student Union with different types: students from South America, older guys who liked to gape at college girls, philosophy grad students. One of the people, a friend of the philosophers, was Dick Gallup, a junior at Tulane. Was he looking for girls? Dick was rather shy. I wasn't shy and I liked unusual people (one of my other friends was a guy who would sing bits of Mahler over the phone to me).

In February 1962, Dick said that a good friend of his, Ted Berrigan, was coming from New York to visit and that he was a great guy and he wanted me to meet him. Soon Ted arrived. He was eight years older than me, handsome, experienced, and interesting. I remember the two of us trying to get into Dick's locked apartment and how Ted swung up on a post or a drainpipe to try to get in a window. In those days he was fit enough to do that. I was swept off my feet.

Ted was in New Orleans for about a week, during which time it became clear that there was a sexual attraction between us. Being a virgin, though, I wouldn't let myself get carried away. One evening we were horsing around in the Student Union when I found myself on the floor on top of Ted saying, "Would you marry me?" Ted was game. He said yes. For me this meant I'd have to run away from college. My reasoning was that living with Ted would be far more educational than staying in school.

Around the tenth or eleventh of February, I lugged a big suit-case out of the dorm, announcing that I was taking some props to the drama department, and we got a bus to Houston. We could stay with Ted's friend there, Marge Kepler. In Houston we had a blood test and I pawned my watch to pay for the marriage license. We bought Ferlinghetti's *A Coney Island of the Mind* as a wedding gift to ourselves. That afternoon we made love (I for the first time), in Marge's bed. It turned out that she had been his lover in Tulsa. Later the three of us had to sleep together because there was only one bed in the house.

Ted had a dream of the perfect young innocent girl who would believe in him, trust him, and admire him. The "Chris" in his *Sonnets* is such a figure. I think Ted hoped that I would be that person. But he always needed more: more people to love and to listen to him. I was too inexperienced to know that.

After two or three days in Houston we went on to Tulsa. One of the motives for Ted's entire trip was to deliver his master's thesis to the University of Tulsa. We stayed with Ron Padgett's parents, Lucille and Wayne, who were very hospitable. (Ron's father gave me a wonderful wedding ring.) I managed to drop Ted's thesis in a mud puddle but it was salvaged, and Ted received his degree.

Meanwhile I had called my parents. I wasn't trying to escape them, I was just looking for a different life. I'd always been out of it in high school and I hadn't wanted to join a sorority in college or to date college boys. My parents, wanting to see me and to meet Ted, sent us tickets and we flew to Miami.

Things went poorly there. Dick and another friend of Ted's, Tom Veitch, soon arrived. My Aunt Rose and Uncle Bert noticed what they felt to be the strange behavior of these two, such as nosing around in the medicine cabinet. Ted tried to reassure my parents that he would do his best to support me, but now, thoroughly suspicious, they looked through our things, where they found a letter to him from Ron, talking about drugs on the Columbia campus. They also noticed that we were taking coins from my coin collection. My parents became frightened and irrational, and the next evening the police showed up and carted me off to the Jackson Memorial Hospital mental ward. With no income and no friends in Miami, and menaced by the police, Ted took a bus in the direction of New York City.

I hadn't expected anything like this to happen. I was freaked out. Ted began to write me letters to cheer me up and to keep me from giving in to my parents, who wanted an annulment. He wrote once a day and sometimes twice, till he was able to sneak back to Miami. After two months in the hospital, I had been granted a pass to go to the public library downtown. We met there, and we fled.

* * *

At one point the publisher of Coffee House Press told me that he was taking his time with setting a deadline for this book because he wanted me to be sure to have the book I dreamed of. In thinking about this later, I saw I did not have a dream other than to get these letters published before I died. Now, I also realize that I wanted the book published in order to validate my presence in Ted's life. It was a pivotal and passionate time for us both, although perhaps not for the same reasons. Compared to Ted, I was voiceless, as I had married him at such a young and unformed age. I have never told this story because basically I am not a writer, though I have written hundreds of letters—these being the first and simplest—as well as a body of unpublished poems.

Another reason for this book is to reveal what Ted was thinking, reading, and doing at this time in his life. It also makes public what could happen to a young woman in the early 1960s who went against the prevailing norms of behavior. Some young women of the time experienced similar treatment. I was lucky not to have been given shock therapy or heavy drugs. These letters give a sense of what it was like for a sane young woman to be put into a mental hospital.

The letters also contain some repetitions. I have not omitted them because they emphasize the intensity of the situation. Ted and I were both totally embroiled in the circumstances, though he did have a life in New York that included poetry, friends, intimate relations with women, and complex daily problems. My life was limited to Jackson Memorial Hospital in Miami, Florida.

This is a book that can be read slowly. There is no beginning, middle, or end. It is not the complete story of my life with Ted, but it gives a clear picture of the start of it.

Dear Sandy, Hello and The Sonnets

BY RON PADGETT

D EAR SANDY, HELLO can be read in a number of ways: as the
emotional high drama of a young married couple, as a
fierce battle between social values, or as the self-education
of a poet laying his heart bare, but for those who are interested in
the poetry of Ted Berrigan it can also be read as the prelude to his
masterwork, *The Sonnets*. In these letters we find not only references to poets, poems, and even particular lines of poems that
influenced him, but also much of the emotional turbulence that
helped infuse *The Sonnets* with such energy and drive.

Ted left evidence of all this not only in the letters, but also in
his private journals, which are now publicly available in The Rare
Book and Manuscript Library of Columbia University's Butler
Library, in thirteen volumes.[1] The first volume (January–July
1961), which predates the letters in *Dear Sandy, Hello*, discloses his
problematic relationship with his girlfriend, Pat Mitchell, his
pursuit of other girls, his first use of Desoxyn (a form of amphetamine that was to become his favorite), and his unstable living
conditions, along with his literary interests.

Although volumes 2 and 3 are not in strict chronological order,
it is easy to piece together the sequence of events in them. During
late 1961 and early 1962, it became clear to Ted that he needed a
change. He was sharing a one-room apartment with Pat and me.
His relationship with her was worsening and he was unable to

---

[1] Selections from the journals were published in the magazines *Shiny, Nos. 9/10*
(1999) and in the hard-to-find *Tremendulate* (n.d. [2009], n.p. [Shutesbury, Mass.]).
The library also houses most of Ted's letters in the current volume.

sleep during the day, since I was up and about. Enrolled in an Ancient Greek class at Columbia, he soon fell behind in the course work. Although he was adamantly opposed to what we called bourgeois values such as duty, he must have been struggling to justify to himself the fact that Pat was supporting both herself and him by trudging off to work in an office all day. Ted was reading and writing, but he felt he was at an impasse. His journal entry for February 1, 1962, tells of his making love on that day to Anne Kepler, a Tulsa high school classmate of mine who had come to New York. It also says, "Off tomorrow, I hope, for Florida, New Orleans, Houston (to see Margie [a former girlfriend]) and Tulsa to take examination for Masters."

In New Orleans he met Sandy Alper, an innocent undergraduate at Sophie Newcomb and friend of Dick Gallup, and only a few days later, on February 13, in Houston, Ted wrote, "I was married today at two o'clock in the afternoon to Sandy Alper of Miami Florida. She is nineteen. I am twenty-seven."

The newlyweds spent their honeymoon in Houston and Tulsa, and when they went to Miami to visit Sandy's parents she was forced into a mental hospital and he was run out of Dade County by the police and warned never to return. Thus began the separation described in *Dear Sandy, Hello*. During that separation the letters take on the function of Ted's journals, except that they are addressed to a person other than himself, a person he wants to tell everything to. In them we learn a great deal about Ted's philosophy of how to survive in a society that is hostile to unconventional people; about his emotional ups and downs; and about the literary, artistic, and personal influences on his poetry. The letters fully document this stormy, anxious, gestational period that led, like an inclined plane, up to his writing *The Sonnets*.

The letters end shortly before Ted returned to Miami and whisked Sandy away, going on the run through Tulsa, St. Louis, Denver, Chicago, and Tulsa again before alighting in New York

City. There, through the persistent efforts of her parents, Sandy spent several weeks in the mental ward of Bellevue Hospital—her parents still assuming that she must be insane to have married someone like Ted—awaiting a court hearing, the first of which took place on July 11 or 12, 1962,[2] in Brooklyn.

Journal entries for July and August have numerous references to Ted's collaborating with Joe Brainard on art works and little handmade books, such as "Made a sonnet sequence with 19 sonnets in it... Joe did the cover" (August 20, 1962). I recall that the poems mentioned here were well-made, traditional sonnets, stylistically conventional. Ted had been absorbed in Shakespeare's sonnets at least as far back as early February of 1961. I remember that he had them in his pocket when we were erroneously arrested by the police (for armed robbery!) when we visited Providence that month. Ted was trying to learn how to make a large work out of small works, trying to see if Shakespeare's sonnets were simply a collection or in fact an ordered sequence. In any case, working with Joe simultaneously on the same surface, with words and art interacting, encouraged Ted to write more spontaneously, to accept what was to some degree a chance interaction. On October 17, his seeing *Stones,* the collaborative poem/lithographic suite by his hero Frank O'Hara and Larry Rivers on exhibit at the Tibor de Nagy Gallery, must have confirmed Ted's growing willingness to loosen his compositional habits.

Two weeks earlier, in his journal, he had quoted Ezra Pound ("The sonnet occurred automatically when some chap got stuck in his effort to make a canzone") and mentioned writing three new sonnets: "Seems the sonnet still interests me."

And how! But it was all about to take a momentous turn. On November 16, Ted asked Sandy to pick her favorite lines and

---

[2] Ted's journal says the twelfth, his "Personal Poem," written on the day of the hearing, says the eleventh.

phrases from his nineteen old sonnets, out of which he created a new one, arranging the fragments somewhat by chance. He added: "The result was very good for a beginning. But I am still confused about the AMOUNT of control the writer should have over his writing (or CONSCIOUS CONTROL)."

Four days later (at 5:15 a.m., the signature time of *The Sonnets*), he wrote: "Wrote (?) (made) five sonnets tonight, by taking one line from each of a group of poems, at random, going from first to last poem then back again. . . Wrote by ear, and automatically. Very intersting results. . . All of this was partly inspired by reading about DADA but mostly inspired by my activities along the same line for the past 10 months (or since reading *Locus Solus* two and seeing the Assemblage show [at the Museum of Modern Art] and working on collages with Joe)."

Ted, with Sandy's help, had set in motion the creative machine he had been assembling over the past two years, the machine that would enable him to create a "big" work, *The Sonnets*. The letters in *Dear Sandy, Hello* are an intimate self-portrait of the poet who aspired to do just that.

Letters from Ted

TELEGRAM TO JOE BRAINARD

Tuesday, February 13, 1962
Houston, Texas

*I was married today at two o'clock in the
afternoon to Sandy Alper of Miami Florida.
She is nineteen. I am twenty-seven.*

—Ted Berrigan

[Savannah]
February 27, 1962

My darling Sandy,

I love you very much. Have faith and courage. They've separated us for now, but we are and always will be husband and wife. Not fathers and mothers nor doctors and annulments will ever change that. Come to me when you can. Call my mother if you need me. I had to leave Miami but I'll never leave your heart.

All my love,
Ted

March 1, 1962

My darling Sandy,

I want very much to make this a love letter. I've never written any
kind of letter to someone I love as much as I love you. Although
words are my name and my game, I doubt that I have the words
to express the depth of feeling, of love, that I feel for you. My
every fiber of being aches for you. Everything I do is less because
you are not with me, and yet more because I know you, love you,
and am married to you. I love you very much.

But other things intrude into my personal letter to you. So let
me get them out of the way fast. Here is what has happened to me
since I left you:

I took my suitcases from your room, leaving most of my books,
and some clothes, and a deputy took me to the Norfolk Hotel. On
the way he searched me, and of course found nothing sinister in my
possession. At the hotel I roused Dick, and he and I walked the five
or six miles to the Jackson Hospital. There we were refused permission to see you. They wouldn't tell me how to get permission. I called
your father, but he offered nothing. So, I returned to the hotel, and
after thinking as best I could, I decided the only thing left for me to
do, the only way I could help the situation any, was to come to
Rhode Island. I was broke, had only your box of pennies and no
place to stay. We all left, and drove to New York. Dick and I are now
here in RI at my mother's. I've called you every day, and written to
you twice. They wouldn't let me talk to you, but your doctor, whom
I talked to tonight, said you could receive mail. I just sent a telegram
to you, and will send this letter special delivery tonight.

Sandy, I don't know what's going to happen. From every angle
they have us cornered. But no matter what they do, confine you,
restrict me from seeing you, even annul the marriage, they can't
change the fact that we love each other. And our marriage was

made long before any legal papers certified it, and no legal papers can end it. We shall be married to the end of our days. I could never do anything in life other than love you. I am new and better for knowing and loving you. My dearest, don't let them shake your faith in yourself. You are the best, most healthy, most sane, most good person it has ever been my good fortune to know. They can't change that.

Please don't blame your parents too much. If they are misguided, and too blind to see you, nevertheless I think they love you. Let us be honest and good and generous, even if no one else is. We shall be together again. Whatever they say, they won't keep me from you. Don't let anyone keep you from me.

The doctor has promised to let me know when, if at all, that I may talk to you on the phone, or see you. When that time comes I shall come to Miami immediately. But he warns that it may not come. They say you are disturbed. Everyone should be that disturbed.

Ed Kaim tells me that you are a very special girl. And Tom still thinks you are the very best person he has ever met. As for me, I love you, which is more and better than I ever dreamed love could be.

If they let you write to me, I am at my parents' house, 53 Gordon Avenue, Providence. I may go to New York, but my mother will send me your letters immediately. My mother has written to your parents, begging them to allow us to be together.

To some extent we are helpless. But our love, our spiritual marriage, is more than anything they can do. A truly great person once wrote to me, when I was in the depths of despair, to have faith and courage. Once more I send you the same message. Have faith and courage. It's Sandy and Ted Berrigan forever and ever. I love you.

Good-night, and all my love,

your husband
Ted

March 2, 1962

My darling Sandy,

your letter was waiting for me when I came back to New York after two days in Rhode Island. By now you should have my letter from there. I nearly cried for joy to see your handwriting, read your words. Honey, I had a lot of words prepared to write to you from here. I thought of them all the way back from Rhode Island while Dick drove. But now I can hardly write. I just want to take you in my arms and hold you.

Sandy, get out of that place. If it takes a month, a year, years, get out of there. Lie, steal, cheat, do anything, but get out and come to me. I will be trying every way I know how to get you free. But they have us where they want, they think. I am sure they are going to have this marriage annulled. They are going to find you "disturbed," and have the marriage set aside. Well, we don't need to care about that. Our marriage can't be set aside, no matter what legal authorities say. What is important is that we be together again. We can't fight them their way. What we have to do is do anything they say, resisting only when we feel we have to. Don't sign anything. We'll do what they say, but when their backs are turned, we'll be gone. Come here any way you know how. If you think I can help by coming there, tell me, and I'll hitchhike there tomorrow. Once we are together, we'll vanish from their sight until such time as they recognize our love, our marriage, our dignity as human beings. Honey, don't ever let them make you think you are sick, or disturbed, or anything of the kind. We are all sick, and disturbed, but if you ever believed anything I said, believe me when I say that you are the best, the healthiest, the most good of all of us.

I think of you all the time. I will write every day, trivia or deep feelings, just to feel near to you. Have faith. Have courage.

I wrote the first poem that I have written to you last night. I think it is good. It seems true to me, and that is the best criterion I have to judge. You are my god, my lady of the lake, my white goddess. Without you I am nothing.

Sandy, I believe in Mozart, in Beethoven, in Wagner. I believe in Walt Whitman. I believe in Rembrandt and Leonardo, in Jackson Pollock, in Frank O'Hara. I believe in Margie Kepler and Dick Gallup and Tony Walters and poor Jim Sears and even in Leslie. I believe in the Communion of Saints. I believe in the forgiveness of sins. And I believe in life everlasting.

I believe that marriages are made in heaven. I think that all the choirs of heaven and all the saints rejoiced when we made our marriage vows in the park in New Orleans when you first looked at me seriously, and I first touched your arm. Your father and mother have forgotten that kind of truth. All the people around you have forgotten it. The clouds of glory clustered around them at birth have all been wiped away by the outside world. You aren't that way Sandy, you remember in your heart how it was when the world was new and good and Cain hadn't yet been provoked into unnaturalness by his mealy-mouthed father and brother. I tried to tell your father that you were naturally a way that I have been constantly struggling to get back to. You are a child. Pray God I can become such a child. Saint Francis was such a child, and Henry Miller, and Thomas Wolfe, and Jesus, and Teresa of Avila. These people around you will of course discover that you are sick. Sick. The best of people are always sick, or sinners, in the minds of the majority. The best and the worst have a certain understanding, but the mediocre, sold-out, fearful majority, afraid to risk a step for danger, will always point an accusing finger at you and me, and say, "sick."

Honey, I'm a hard-nosed son of a bitch. They can't get at me. They can put me in jail, keep us apart, do whatever, but they can't get at me. I know them. I don't even dislike them or hate them.

My heart and spirit are protected from them simply because I don't believe in them. I know they would be good if they could. I know that you and I will love, will be married, even if they keep us apart forever. I have faith that they can't keep you from me, nor me from you.

But I'm worried about you. You are so loving and trusting. I fear they will get at you with kindness and then twist you. I know you have more strength and soul and integrity than any of them. Beware their wiles. Stay innocent, and trusting, and loving and good. But don't let them twist you, hurt you, change you. Flee that evil country. Come to me, come to me.

I'm staying now at Joe's, where I shall remain until I hear from you. Dick is also here. My sister and mother are writing to you. Dick is writing. Joe wants to write you. I am sending you our goddess. Do you want books, anything? My family already loves you simply from hearing your voice, seeing your picture, hearing my words. I have sent an announcement of our marriage to the Providence papers. I'll send the clipping. I am also in correspondence with your doctor, but I have no hope that he will do anything except declare you "disturbed" and have our marriage annulled. If they manage this don't let the actual annulment upset you too much . . . it will be meaningless. In New York, where the legal age is eighteen, we will vanish from their sight if only you can get here. I love you so very very much. Every poem I read, everything I see and hear and feel, is you. Dream of me, please. We are, we shall be, more than happy. Let them be rational and calm and legal. We shall be Shelley and Mary Godwin, Elizabeth and Robert Browning, Petrarch and Laura, Dante and Beatrice, Shaw and sweet Mary Morris. They cannot triumph. We cannot fail.

My dearest, your poem, your words were beautiful beyond words. I am your spouse, your husband, your lover. You are my wife. I never understood that word before you. Now I know I shall never do anything higher or better than marry you. As love is so much more than words, I love you. And as it is words, I love you better still.

Here is my poem. I have tried to say that whatever comes, my heart will not be destroyed, will love, will break, will love again. And will only love you as wife. I

[Remainder of letter missing.]

March 3, 1962

Dearest Sandy,

it's five o'clock in New York City, by your grandfather's watch, which I'm wearing on my left wrist. Dick and Joe are asleep. I'm tired, but wide awake, and thinking of you. What good goddess brought us together? Nothing can change the fact that we came together. I love you so very very much, miss you so much.

I've contemplated writing to your parents, begging them to let us be together: they can't deny what their eyes saw: we were happy together. You, their daughter, were happy. But I don't think it will do any good. They met me. We talked. They talked to you. They are having me investigated by a private detective agency, and time will tell what will happen. There is nothing that anyone can find that will make me an unworthy husband for you. I am not a narcotics addict. I am not an alcoholic. I am just a poet, living in relative poverty, from a normal American background, trying to live a good life. But I fear they won't see it that way. We'll see.

Honey, I don't even really know if these letters are reaching you. Perhaps they are being censored. If so, I hope at least they let you know I am writing, and that I love you. Your doctor said he would tell you that much.

Are you all right? Tell me everything you can. What's happening? What are they telling you? Are you reading? Can you keep a journal? It would be a good thing if you could write down all that is happening. Good for you, good to read in the future.

I'm reading Henry Miller (*Tropic of Capricorn*), poems by John Ashbery, Joe's notebooks, and a novel by a writer named Clellon Holmes called *Go*. Dick is reading the newest book on the pre-Socratics, Tom is reading a book by Edward Dahlberg (who wrote the poem Dave said is very great, remember). Tom and I wrote a collaboration today called "O'Hara's Sources." It's a fourteen-line poem using ground rules. I'm saving all these things for you in a notebook, for you to read when you come here, when we see each other again.

I wonder what Mimi thinks about this. And Leslie.

Out my window here on the fifth floor I see new buildings going up, people bustling in the streets, the sun going down far across the island. It's cold and crisp here, exciting as always, full of color and noise and winter. I love NY but it is all empty without you. At the Museum of Modern Art there is a series of Roberto Rossellini movies, and playing now is one called *The Flowers of Saint Francis.* It is a masterpiece. We'll see it when you come, it will always be playing in NY. Saint Francis was a jongleur de Dieu, God's wild man, God's jester. How good. Hooray for Koch and O'Hara and Miller and Shaw.

Ed Kaim, who I haven't seen yet, told Ron that you were someone very special. He said that he called you Cassandra. He sent Dick and Tom and me seventy-five dollars to get out of Florida with. Honey, Mrs. Padgett was right. Kaim, and Tom, and Tony, and Dick, and Anne, and Dave, and Joe: you have friends you don't even know yet. I want you to meet Lorenz Gude, a ripped-out-of-his-mind young boy from Bellows Falls. And Bill McCullam, a suited, dress-shirted, conservative complete genius who came to see me at three a.m. the day I left New York for New Orleans, to say good-bye, and tell me about his thoughts on love and poetry and human beings. And Harry Diakov who knows everything about Ezra Pound, studies Russian, is a student of India and all about it, impossibly cultured and intelligent. And Tony Powers, the world's most competent, ruthless, powerful Irishman ever seen. He's a throwback to Jonathan Swift and Wolfe Tone and Parnell.

Pat hates me it seems, but not really. Anne is her very good, sweet self, and wishes us the best of everything possible, after her initial (and healthy) rage. I want very much for you and her to like each other, to love each other. Ron is hung up on Pat, thinks maybe I am a villain, but isn't sure. He's a good fellow anyway.

There are so many things I want to send to you, but I don't even know if you are getting my letters. I want to send you our goddess, and a notebook Joe made for me while I was gone, full of his ideas about art and poetry, and prints from magazines, and wild humor, and a telegram which says "Married today 2 p.m. to Sandra Alper in Houston, Texas, etc."

New England is clear as crystal, covered with ice and snow, glinting in the sun, diamond-hard and beautiful. The drive from RI to NY was beautiful, more beautiful I think than any trip I've taken without you. Only your absence made it tragic. We went through New Haven, and New London, and down the Saw Mill River Road, through Mystic, Connecticut, magic names, almost magic places. You and I will go to those places, Sandy.

Sandy . . . . you know, I hardly think of you by name. I have to reach to call you Sandy, or honey . . . . I hardly think of you . . . really it's more that I feel you, that I sense you, almost that I am you. Words, names, seem almost to come between. I feel your mouth, your hands tickling my back, your sweet breath, your breasts, your beautiful hair and mouth, the flesh of your thighs, your presence everywhere even when you were out of the room. Sometimes at night when I could feel you watching me, looking at me, when I knew you thought I was sleeping, I laid there in the warmth of your gaze and loved you so much all I could do was go to sleep, for fear that I would die of love if I even opened an eye, or moved. Sometimes when we talked in the Padgetts' kitchen, and other places, I had to make jokes or else I would have cried for loving you so much. Only tears could have said what I felt. And my darling, my love, I tried very hard to show you that feeling, to tell you by being honest even if it meant raging, to tell you by joking, by reading, by being myself, by making love to you even through your first tears, by touching your breasts, with my legs, arms, genitals, mind, soul, everything. I never came to a girl as I did to you. Only with you was I most what is good in me. For you I would give up my poems, get haircuts, wear suits, be "respectable," "honest," "healthy," anything. But I love you more than that. I love you so much that I can never be dishonest or small again except that I beg you to help me overcome that smallness by touching me. I love you so much that for you I will be the highest, the noblest, the most beautiful person I am capable of, even that I may be worthy of your love. Together we will be so fine, so good, we will be radiant in the eyes of everyone, and even doctors and lawyers and Indian chiefs and bail bondsmen and poets will have to love us. Even in their insecurities they will have to love us. Honest, everyone loves you. Do you know that? Even those who seem to be harming you love you. It is through ignorance they hurt you. That is why I can bear them no malice, even though I am heartsick over what is happening. You are so beautiful, so right, that everyone loves you. Even your doctor, who calls you disturbed, loves you. He wants to help you. It is his petty intellect, his shallow understanding which makes him think he can "help" you. He should watch you, and be helped. I know I am a great man, for how else could I have gained your love? I love you, I love you. Have faith. Have courage. Don't let them make you hard.

My dear, my love, my soul, I don't want to stop talking to you. I want to reach out to you. I am reaching to you. I send you this poem, written by someone else. I'll write the finest love poem to you one day, on paper, and all days through my living, my life.

THE GOOD-MORROW

I wonder, by my throth, what thou, and I
Did, till we lov'd? were we not wean'd till then?
But suck'd on countrey pleasures, childishly?
Or snorted we in the seaven sleepers den?
T'was so; But this, all pleasures fancies bee.
If ever any beauty I did see,
Which I desir'd, and got, t'was but a dreame of thee.

And now good morrow to our waking soules,
Which watch not one another out of feare;
For love, all love of other sights controules,
And makes one little roome, an every where.
Let sea-discoverers to new worlds have gone,
Let Maps to other, worlds on worlds have showne,
Let us possesse one world, each hath one, and is one.

My face in thine eye, thine in mine appeares,
And true plaine hearts doe in the faces rest,
Where can we finde two better hemispheares
Without sharpe North, without declining West?
What ever dyes was not mixt equally;
If our two loves be one, or, thou and I
Love so alike, that none can slacken, none can die.

Sandra, Sandy, my wife forever, for now good-night. John
Donne's words I send you, and these, my own: I love you.

Ted

[March 4 or 5, 1962]

Sunday afternoon on the East Side of New York and out the window kids are playing on a giant fifty-foot mound of sand in a building area. I want to go play too. I wish you were here. I wish, I wish you were here,

Dear Sandy,

I found a picture of a beatnik today in a history book. What do you think?

He's the captain of the *Montior* which fought the *Merrimac* in the first battle between armored ships. Probably wrote his poetry between battles or during. (He must be a poet, look at his hair and beard. Probably was a horrible narcotics addict too.)

I wish I knew what a beatnik was so I could be one.

I've written three poems in the three days I've been here. O happy New York. And all the time I feel you. My writing is new, and better, and I know it's because of love. Which means you.

Last night I saw a bad opera based on Goethe's story *The Sorrows of Werther.* Do you know it? It's the story of a tragic love ending in suicide. The opera was bad, but Goethe is great. Werther was the first romantic, or something like that. These days though, we who feel, who live, who love romance, understand it through John Wayne's eyes. Which is good. (What am I saying?) I'm not really incoherent. I'm in a kind of trance from reading Henry Miller's *Tropic of Capricorn.* It is so great I have to stop every few pages and wonder. After speaking of killing birds to eat (a fantasy) he writes:

> If I killed a little bird and roasted it over the fire and
> ate it, it was not because I was hungry but because I
> wanted to know about Timbuktu or Tierra del
> Fuego. I had to stand in the vacant lot and eat dead

birds in order to create a desire for that bright land which later I would inhabit alone and people with nostalgia. I expected ultimate things of this place, but I was deplorably deceived. I went as far as one could go in a state of complete deadness, and then by a law, which must be the law of creation, I suppose, I suddenly flared up and began to live inexhaustibly, like a star whose light is unquenchable.

Sandy, my beautiful, innocent wife, Miller has just said simply much of what I have been struggling to tell you. If I eat dead birds in vacant lots, it is not because I am hungry, but because I need to discover Tierra del Fuego, the land of fire, the fiery earth. I people my poems with nostalgia. They are in part my bright land. And through the past few months, and most of all through loving you, through marrying my soul, my self to yours as was preordained, I have now flared up like a burning rose, like a dove, and begun to live inexhaustibly, like a star whose light is unquenchable, good to eat a thousand years. Thank you.

I send you this picture of a man. The faces of saints shine with a light that reveals them to you, and to me, and to whoever has eyes to see.

Camus has been dead for two years. Dead at mid-life.

Tonight Dick and I and Joe are going to see *Breathless* and *L'Avventura* in a double bill. You and I will see them again when you are here. *Breathless* is so frantic, so nervous, so controlled anyway. So alive. *L'Avventura* is like a dying life. Days take minutes. Seconds sometimes last for hours. In both pictures, from opposite sides of the coin, marvelous things are done with time. To rip out of the mind of human beings the dead concept of time as mathematical . . . time is not arithmetical. Nor is it geometrical. It is magic. It is unexplainable, like the force of life, the élan vital, the primal drives. The revolutions of the earth deceive us. Time is Space is Life. Einstein is the supreme poet. Korzybski is his prophet.

Bergson and Whitehead went to the desert, and came back to show us the way: where? To our own desert, so we could find our own way. Everyone does everything himself. All those who are going to make it will, all those who aren't won't. Miller writes:

> And now here I am, sailing down the river [life] in my little canoe. Anything you would like to have me do for you I will do—gratis. . . . [In this land, the bright land,] the spermatazoon reigns supreme. Nothing is determined in advance, the future is absolutely uncertain, the past is nonexistent. For every million born 999,999 are doomed to die and never again be born. But the one that makes a home run is assured of life eternal. Life is squeezed into a seed, which is a soul. Everything has soul, including minerals, plants, lakes, mountains, rocks. Everything is sentient, even the lowest stage of consciousness. Once this fact is grasped there can be no more despair. At the very bottom of the ladder, chez the spermatazoa, there is the same condition of bliss as at the top, chez God. . . .
> The river starts somewhere in the mountains and flows on into the sea. On this river that leads to God the canoe is as serviceable as the dreadnought. From the very start the journey is homeward.

Honey, keep faith. They can't touch you, us, after all.

I'm writing, waiting to hear from you, to hear what is going on, what is happening, what is going to happen. I am at an impasse, because I can do nothing until I hear from you, or your doctor, or your parents. I have no money, only New York, and Dick and Joe and always and ever our love. And because of that this life is all good. The hospital, your mother and father, the deputies, the Negro clerk at the Norfolk Hotel, the private detectives, the people outside I have not met yet, it's all somehow good in spite of itself. We have love, you and me, and that makes even separation be good. To be together is the same as to be separate when there is love that is love. No one can touch that love. We are never apart. I am with you, you are here, even when we are not thinking of each other. Love is before thought, beyond thought. No one can understand that we ran off after five days. How can we expect them to understand that we loved each other before we even met? I love you in Pat, and in Anne and in Dick, and Dave Bearden and Jim Sears, and in my mother, and in Rilke and Whitman and Mozart and Harpo Marx. You knew me as Dick and as Lenny, and as Leslie, as your father, as Stone, and Doris, and Antoine St. Exupéry, as Ed Kaim, and as Hayakawa, and John Wayne, and Khachaturian. When we met we knew each other, had known each other for a million years. When you feel pangs for Lenny, it is because he is me, and I am him, and yet we are two different husks of body and to have one seems to be to lose the other. But it isn't to lose the other. I love him because he knew to look at you. My small mind may be jealous, but the me that is me knows that we are all one another and one soul. I love you, because to me you are everything, everybody, the world. And I must love the world if I love you. You are the best of everything, the good that is in every-thing. My sweet, my dear, we, the world, are all in love with you.

For now, good-bye. Forgive my wordiness, my rhetoric, my inability to tell you without words that I love you. I am still small and weak, still fearful that no one can know me unless I talk. If I could never write another word, never utter another syllable, never see or speak again, to you, to anyone, I know you would know that I am loving you, that I will go on loving you, that I loved you before my life, and will love you beyond any death.

Forever, your
husband

March 6, 1962

Dear Sandy,

enormous snow and rain are swirling around outside in cold New York, and it's cold inside this room, without you. I've said, and thought, a thousand times these past few days, "I wish Sandy were here." There are good things here, but they would be so much better if we were seeing them together.

Dick and Joe and I and Anne went to the Museum of Modern Art yesterday, and saw a tremendous show of works by Jean Dubuffet. Do you know his work at all? He works mostly in a texture that looks like earth, and lava, and stone, and sand, the very essence of the stuff of the earth. His style is called "Art Brut," which means something like Brute Art. He is Paul Klee as King Kong, kind of. His representational work, paintings of fantastic cows and women and people, resembles children's paintings, or the world of the insane. It's all really good. His world picture, his weltanschaung, evolves partly, I think, from Bergson, and White-head, and the philosophy of organism, which believes that every-thing is alive, everything has soul. I don't want to talk about it too much, because I want to show these things to you soon, but, for example, one of his paintings, done in oil and sand, on a scraped canvas, looks like a rock surface, and nothing else. It is flat, plain, something like the coral we saw in the Keys, but darker. It is called "Lesson to be learned from the earth."

Here's a couple of his things that I cut out of a book of Joe's for you to see. These are not too recent, but still fairly typical. Honey, you'd really love this show. I hurt when I saw it, because of my love for you. †

† Indicates missing or deleted text or image.

I don't remember the title for that one, but it's something like "Slaphappy Cow." This next one is a kind of metaphysical landscape. †

I haven't gotten any letters from you since the first beautiful letter, which was here when I got to Joe's. Maybe you've sent some to Rhode Island. My mother said she would forward any that came. But I'm worried, fretting, afraid of any number of things. Maybe you aren't getting my letters. Maybe you are sick with despair. Maybe any number of things. I hope you are getting these letters, I hope you are strong, and unoppressed. Sandy, I love you so very very much. I have a hundred plans for us, a thousand things we must do, a million things we must talk about, and all I really want right now is just to see you, even a momentary glance . . . or just to talk to you . . . to know you are well, and that you love me.

Joe and I are making a book for you, of poems that I love, that are by poets who are somewhat obscure, poems you don't see too much, and prints that he loves that are the same way. I've typed out three or four so far, and it should be finished soon. Have you heard from Kathy (my sister)?

Tom came by last night, and read the collaborative story Dick and I wrote, and then Tom and I wrote two. One was bad, but the second one, called "The Return of Jesus" (title given beforehand by Joe) was pretty interesting. Each of us wrote two sentences at a time. I can't wait to have you read these things.

Also, Joe and I are working on a series of poem collages based on the American flag theme. Each one is the same size, about the size of a ten-cent American flag. Joe pastes materials together to make a variation on the stars and stripes and then I write poems on the whole thing in red ink, or blue, or crayons. The effect so far is interesting, and something may come out of it all. It's good to be working hard, too. Goddamn it, I wish you were here.

I'm going tomorrow to see a play by O'Hara, and one by Kenneth Koch. I wrote to O'Hara last night, and sent him five poems and asked him if he'd like to go have a beer somewhere. And, speaking of poetry, *Time* magazine has written the worst article I have ever seen anywhere on poetry. It is horribly banal, patronizing, dishonest, and completely wrong. I never thought that even *Time* could be so stupid, so evil. But at least they published a couple of good pictures. Here's one of a fellow un-goy of yours, which is fine. Does this look like the Antichrist? Like a horrible beatnik? Or like a good person, a young, sincere, serious, slightly bemused poetic fellow?

Honey, if I don't hear something soon about what's happening down there I'm going to round up the NKVD and invade Florida on white horses. I miss you terribly.

> All my love,
> your husband
> Ted

March 8, 1962

Dear Sandy,

yesterday, my second letter from you. It made me feel very good, and at the same time very sad. Things there for you are just about the way I pictured them. Goddamn! Honey, those people are trying to get at you in the most dangerous of ways, through all that is good about you. You are not "sick." You are not "disturbed." They are entirely and 100 percent wrong. Any psychiatric treatment is only as valid as the system of values upon which it is based. In this case the system of values is not even clear to the holders of those values. They are trying to make you healthy by imposing all that is sick on you. Shaw says in *The Quintessence of Ibsenism* that "Duty is the primal curse from which we must redeem ourselves if we are going to progress any higher." These people want to make you more "stable," more "responsible," less "impulsive," and more "sane." They don't know what they are talking about. If you ever believed anything I said, believe this: it is most important that you get away from there as soon as possible. If there is any way you can come to Rhode Island, to New York, come as soon as that way is open. I'll send you the money if you need it. Call my mother at ST 1-3606 and tell her what I said and how much you need. Or telegraph me and I'll call you. Sandy, in a letter to your mother, my mother, referring to our supposed impulsiveness in running off, told your mother that I have "never done anything impulsive in (my) life." I didn't realize she was that perceptive, but she told the exact truth. Your doctor and your parents cannot understand that my running off with you was far from impulsive. For us, you must get out of there.

But enough of lectures. It's seven-thirty in the morning here, and the sun is shining. Yesterday Dick and I went up to Columbia, and met Tom, and walked around seeing different people, and looking at books. I have some new good books of poetry, and I'm reading a lot, not writing too much, except for the series I'm doing with Joe. I've read *Go,* a novel by Clellon Holmes about New York in the 50s, finished Henry Miller's *Tropic of Capricorn,* read a lot of poetry by a lot of people, and am now reading Federico Garcia Lorca's *Poet in New York,* and the selected poems of Vladimir Mayakofsky, the young Russian poet. Dick has finished a book by William Styron called *Lie Down in Darkness,* and is reading Styron's second novel, *Set This House on Fire.* Styron is a young Southern writer, and he is very very good. Both those books are as good novels as have been done in America since *A Farewell to Arms.* Dick has also written three poems. New York agrees with him. At the moment, he is waiting for his check for tuition refund to come from Tulane, and so is sleeping on the floor at Pat and Anne's. So all his production is under wearying circumstances. Tom is the same as ever, walking around like a three-toed sloth, peering out from under the hood of his red jacket with suspicious eyes at the world. He found a book by Blaise Cendrars, whom Henry Miller talks about all the time. It's one of the three Cendrars books translated into English (from French) out of more than fifty written. I'm going to read it when Tom finishes.

[Remainder of letter missing.]

March 8, 1962

Dear Sandy,

two letters from you this morning, after I mailed one to you. I don't know whether to cry or what to do. It's so good to hear from you, so wrong that you are a prisoner. For that is what you are, a prisoner. Meanwhile, they, meaning your mother and father, are cementing the whole structure very nicely.

The letter Ron wrote to me about the investigation will make very nice legal evidence for them that I am mixed up in a sordid narcotics affair. The truth of course is very different. Every university, especially in large metropolitan areas, has its dabblers in marijuana, Benzedrine, etc. More than half the students I know take Bennies, or Miltown, or sleeping pills. Everybody knows that, too. This particular investigation centered around marijuana. I had nothing to do with the whole business. I hardly know the boy, Ed M——, who was a main figure in it. My name was not mentioned. I never received marijuana from anyone involved, nor ever gave any to anyone involved. I don't even like marijuana, it makes me sick, because I don't smoke. The one time I ever tried it, I found it uninteresting, perhaps because of my own inability to take it into my lungs. At any rate, I had nothing to do with the investigation. Let me try telling that to any judge of whether our marriage is to be annulled or not. Hah! This case was open and shut before it even began.

Meanwhile, the detectives showed up today at Pat and Anne's.

Honey, about my mother, and your mother's remarks. My mother has worked hard for her kids. That's the kind of person she is. But she's not gaunt, starved, poverty-stricken, needy, or anything of the sort. She needs no help from me, nor does she want any. She'd be insulted. She had a happy marriage, and she loves her children. She has a nice home, with plenty to eat, good clothes, a daughter and son and mother with her. She works approximately forty hours a week, a normal working week, and is in fine shape. She definitely isn't working her fingers to the bone for her son, me. Don't kid yourself, or let anyone kid you on that score. She's a fine, healthy, good woman, who is happy to have you for her daughter, and happy with her family, even if we get on her nerves sometimes, as she gets on ours.

Your doctor, and the nurses, and everyone concerned, most of all your parents, are horribly at fault in this whole matter. They are more ignorant than malicious, but that does not make them less evil. I have no hatred for them, but I am contemptuous of them. Try not to cry over their ways, they are worth tears, I think, but they will only use your tears against you, as you have already seen. If only it was me they had locked up there, instead of you. Goddamn.

But enough of my ranting. I love you, I miss you, I grow angry for you, weep for you. Most of all I love you. I wonder if they (meaning anyone) read my letters to you. Do you know? It doesn't matter, anyway, but I am curious. I almost hope they do. Every day I chafe against this inactivity towards our situation. The sad fact is that love doesn't always win out. In fact, it rarely wins. I don't want us to be another Heloise and Abelard, nor another Romeo and Juliet. I want us to be together. But there is nothing to do here. You must wait. Or you must somehow get away. If you can get to New York, and we have a five-minute start on them, they'll never get us again. But for now I am powerless to release you. Honey, I wish I could write you only sweetness and light, but I can't.

This letter is being written on the same day as the letter with the picture of Shaw in it. Dick is still asleep, Joe is working on his collages. Bill McCullam is lying on the floor reading Bochenski's *Contemporary European Philosophy*. The sun is shining brilliantly outside, and it is warm again in New York. I'm drinking a Pepsi. In a few minutes I'm going to wake up Dick, for sport, I guess, and we'll go over to Anne's to see what the detectives have been up to. The walk down through the Village is one of the best things about New York. I wish you could go with us, and that we were going to see how Anne is, or what Tom or Ron is doing, and that all of this was nonexistent. But it isn't.

I'm going to send the goddess to you tomorrow, and I hope it gets there safely. Have you been getting postcards from Joe?

Quit eating so much candy! You fat thing.

Tom sends his love, and he says he is going to write. I'll write again later, and later, and later, and again and again. Do you hear from Karen, or Leslie? How is Mimi? I love you very much,

your husband forever,

Ted

March 9, 1962

Dear Sandy,

it's three in the afternoon, I just woke up, after being up most of the night talking to Joe and Dick about this and that, love and books and detectives and J. D. Salinger and new poems. A letter from you was waiting when I got up.

It's ironic and funny, but almost sad about the Negro maid who ran off with her husband when she was twelve. If you tell the doctor about it, no doubt he will dismiss the fact, as if Negro maids were not people. The cold facts are always insignificant when you have your conclusions figured out before you make your tests and analyses. They "knew" beforehand that you were "sick," "disturbed," and all the rest, and they knew exactly why. Now, no facts are going to change their minds. Everything you do or say only proves to them that they are right.

The detectives arrived on the local scene yesterday, and talked to Pat and Anne separately. They asked the girls such questions as was I homosexual, a drug addict, did I love you, was I after your money, was I honest, serious, how did I earn a living, how would I support you, were any of my friends drug addicts, or homosexuals, etc. What an evil mind someone has. Didn't those parents of yours use their eyes when we were with them? *We were happy*. Anyway, the detective really got an earful. I sure would like to read his file. Both girls asked him why he didn't come and talk to me, but he begged the question. They told him I'd be happy to talk to him.

I'm re-reading Henri Bergson's *Creative Evolution*, which is really a fine book. Also, and incidentally, I made some arrangements yesterday to pay all the money I owe for the return trip to NY from Miami and all the rest. Lorenz Gude, a friend from Columbia, brought me down an assignment to write two papers for a worthless rich student, one an architectural comparison of two churches, Romanesque and Byzantine, and the other a paper on labor and management relations. The first is ten pages, the second twenty, and I'll be paid fifty-five dollars. I only owe fifty, so things are good. I think it's dumb to have people write papers for you, but I'll be happy to write them. It gives me a chance to do some work on things I'm interested in, but wouldn't normally do research on at this time. And you can be sure they will be good.

Joe is sitting over on his bed writing a postcard to you. My fingers are sore from pounding the typewriter. When I first get up my hands are not as loose as later in the day, and I miss the keys sometimes and bang up my fingers. But it's not anything, anyway. I love you so much, Sandy, and I'm so happy when I get a letter from you that I run to the typewriter to answer. Please don't grow despairing or resigned about this situation. We must remain militant about it, even if we have to be quietly militant. Our only chance is to hold out, to resist.

We are making hot coffee now, and preparing to work on our collages some more. We're still working on our religious one, although Joe has done two of his own, without writing, since I wrote yesterday. Meanwhile. Dick moved in with Tom last night, uptown. He's there now, will probably be down later. Joe got money in the mail today, so tonight we all go to the movies, to see the Marx Brothers in *The Big Store*. We are all secretly the Marx Brothers ourselves.

Please don't stop reading Shaw after *Man and Superman*. Shaw is the kind of writer who contains infinite variety. If you want to go and read Ibsen next, try reading Shaw's little book, *The Quintessence of Ibsenism*, first. It's the kind of book to read before reading Ibsen, and it's a great book. Shaw wrote it before writing any plays. In fact, I'll send it with this letter.

My darling, my wife, I love you so, I hate to end letters. It's as if I stopped talking to you and left the room. But for now, goodbye, and all my love, "The Snake."

> All my love forever,
> your husband.
> Ted

Honey, the book is at my old place—I'll send it later. Love you. Ted

March 9, 1962

Sandy,

here is a print[1] I bought for you at the museum—Joe put a mat around it. Today is our anniversary. We've been married three weeks.

I love you—
Ted

[1] This was a print of Chagall's *The Wedding*. —Ed.

March 10, 1962

Dear Sandy,

it's Saturday night in New York, and I'm sitting in Lorenz Gude's room at Columbia. Gude and Dick are playing cribbage to see who goes out to get Pepsis. I have a towel wrapped around my newly washed head, and I look like Lawrence of Arabia.

It's been a tough day. I had to move out of Joe's today. He just can't work when there are a lot of people around and there are a lot of people around when I'm around. So, Dick and I are walking the streets, waiting for his check, and reading our books. I'm reading *Big Sur and the Oranges of Hieronymus Bosch* by Henry Miller and Dick is reading *Tropic of Capricorn.* I want to send this (my) book to you as soon as I finish.

I wrote a five-page letter to your mother and father last night, but threw it away. It was just a waste of time. I can't change their minds. I just want them to please get out of our way and let us be happy. I love you very very much.

I'll still get mail at Joe's until Dick and I get a place, which should be next week. Meanwhile, we're in flux and can't do much except read. Did you get the two books I sent? *Suzuki Beane,* and later, *The Quintessence of Ibsenism.*

No letter from you today. And no mail till Monday. But don't let the news in this letter fool you. I'm strong, I feel alive and good, I love you and nothing can really touch me as long as we love each other.

I wish this wasn't such a bland letter, but I've no more paper, and no desk to sit at nor typewriter to type on. I write to tell you how much I love you. My words are all of yours. I am your husband, your brother, your father, your child, your lover forever. I love you. Ted.

March 11, 1962

My darling Sandy,

it's a Sunday evening now, and I'm writing this from Tom's place in uptown NY. I spent the night at Columbia last night, and tonight I'm going to stay with Ed Kaim, whom I saw today for the first time since I got back to NY. He said you were a very special girl (someone else had already told me he said that about you), and he said he had once written a poem about you, called "Cassandra." While I was at his place I met a fellow named Bill Gross, who also knew you, and who walked around in a kind of daze when he found I was married to you. He, too, said you were something special. You know I am right, honey, everyone who ever met you loves you. Ed told me to mention a girl named Carol to you, I don't remember her last name right now, who was either a friend of yours, or in school with you. She went with Harry Diakov, a friend of mine here, for about three months last year. Do you know who I mean?

Today I felt so terrible that you aren't here. Dick and I and Lauren walked around the Village, watched the folksingers in Washington Square, went and ate some of Joe's birthday cake, and it was a fine day. I ached for you every minute.

Detectives continue to harass my friends, and to stay away from me. They've talked to Lauren's mother in Tulsa. They seem to be claiming in part that I am the ringleader of a gang of young kids who all take narcotics of one kind or another, and who are all under my evil power. They have concocted elaborate stories that Lauren and Dave went to Mexico to get "stuff" and then Lauren brought it here to me. Good God, what melodrama. It is almost but not quite funny. Meanwhile they've scared Lauren's mother out of her wits. They've got Pat and Anne and Ron and some people I know at Columbia completely jumpy. The only ones really not bothered are me and Dick, who haven't done anything, and could care less about the whole business. All I want is to live with my wife and have the good life that we can have. I love you. I want to be with you. I want all this to stop. It's just silliness. But what can I tell them to make them stop, nothing.

This isn't what I want to write to you about either. I want to tell you how much I miss you, how often I think about things we did and things we will do, how I yearn for your presence, your body in my arms, our mouths pressed together, filled with each other and love. It will be. It must be.

Please forgive these short letters. I'm jumping from place to place, immobilized by the whole situation. If they would only do something one way or another, and let us know where we stand. I'll write better letters as soon as Dick and I get a place and I have time to call my own. For now good-bye, and I love you.

> Forever your husband,
> and all my love,
> Ted

I love you very much.

March 13, 1962

My darling Sandy,

We've been married a month today. What a fine present I received for our anniversary: three letters from you all at once, and two pictures. You look so soft, so warm, so beautiful. I love you more than ever, more than I ever thought it possible to love. We will be together. If you are released from the hospital and can't get away from Miami, I'll come there. I don't need anyone to put me up. I can take care of myself. If you are released, and there is any possibility that you can run away, you must do so quickly. Here are some alternative plans: first, money. I'll send you money, a little at a time, or a lot at once, if you think you can use it to get away. I'm not being watched by detectives. They are investigating me, but not by surveillance. If you could get out of Florida, I could join you somewhere, and we could run away to Mexico, or to anywhere, and live our own life. You could go to the airport, and fly to the first place you get a flight to, and send a telegram to Tony Powers, 601 W. 160th Apt 6C, telling him your address. He would tell me and I would join you there within a day or two. You could go to Houston, to Margie, who is at 1116 Lehall. Or to any city and put up at a hotel for a couple of days. Don't worry about clothes or anything. Just go in what you have on. Or, if you could get to NY, go to a pay phone and call Tony Powers (Anthony Powers) at Johns Manville Inc. in Manhattan, tell him who you are, and that you need to find me. He'll tell you what to do, and I'll come to you. We could easily hide in NY. And if none of that can be accomplished, well, we'll come up with something else. When they finish the investigation we should know one way or another what they are going to try to do about the marriage. If they don't get it annulled they can't legally keep us apart, and I'll come there immediately. One way or another we'll be together. About the doctors and the tests et cetera: honey, just be yourself, and continue to be aware of their insensitivity and their stupidity. The deck is stacked against us, and they will come up with decisions about you that they have already decided long in advance. It is criminal that they should be allowed to proceed like this, but they are allowed. Just be yourself, don't let them get at you too much, they aren't fit to even talk to you, let alone "treat" you.

Time goes by here, and the weather changes from rain to warmth and back to rain. I'm still at Ed Kaim's, which is in uptown Manhattan near Columbia University. Dick's check will be here soon, maybe tomorrow, and he and I are going to get a place. I'm not doing anything about a job, because I don't want to get one, and then quit because I have to go to Miami, or something like that. I'm simply waiting for things to develop.

Yesterday Lauren and I went to the Museum of Modern Art. We went in the pouring rain, and were both soaking wet when we got there. My shoes have holes in them and my feet were warm and squishy with water. We walked around the museum, looking at the Picassos, the Gauguins, the Pollocks, and it was great. I showed him my favorite paintings by Juan Gris, a marvelous Spanish Cubist, and we had a long talk about Sabi.

Sabi is a Japanese word for which there is really no English equivalent. It is a feeling one gets at times for a kind of life where everything is like it seems to be when we think of the "good old days" which of course never really existed. It is a kind of nostalgia for a life which is called to mind when you think of trains speeding in the night, and great American names of cities and towns, and old cars, and October in the "Railroad Earth." Thomas Wolfe is full of it, and so are old cowboy movies, and even old gangster movies, and poems by Frank O'Hara sometimes and many many other things, such as the paintings of Andrew Wyeth (there is one particular one called *Christina's World*). Do you know the feeling I mean? Marcel Proust writes about it a lot, particularly in *Swann's Way*.

And Lauren and I talked a lot about you, and I let him read one of your letters, and today I showed him your pictures, and he wants very much to meet you. He says you are beautiful. He is a good person, and I feel that he is my equal. We have much good feeling about each other.

Dick came over to Kaim's last night to get me, and he played the guitar most of the evening, and everyone was enchanted. Harry was here, and his girlfriend, and Kaim, and Lauren. Harry is a fencer, and we all fenced awhile, and it was unbelievable. I want to learn to fence, and be another Errol Flynn. Everyone said my style of fencing was straight out of Douglas Fairbanks, just like my style of everything else, but I told them it was really John Wayne.

I finished Henry Miller's book called *Big Sur and the Oranges of Hieronymus Bosch* today, and it really was a good book. Miller continually fills me with the joy of life. Right now I am living like the fox lives. All my senses have become sharper, and I smell, see, taste, and hear much more acutely than before. Food tastes marvelous, because we eat little. The weather is simply exciting all the time. We walk up and down all the streets. And all the time I think of you. I want so much to touch you, to lie with my eyes closed and feel you watching me. I do love you so.

Dick is asleep on the couch now, having been awake for about thirty hours. Lauren is reading *Time* and Ed is prowling around the house in his bathrobe pondering man, God, and the cosmos. I'm wearing Dick's red charro jacket, and black pants, and I look like the Irish Pancho Villa, writing the complete poems of Adolf Hitler on the flugelhorn. (That's a Henry Miller flight of fantasy made up by me.) Ed just decided to go to the library, and is going to bring me abstruse obtuse books on architecture for the paper I'm writing for pay. In a few minutes we are going to eat. We have apples and eggs and of course Pepsi-Cola. And we have some cookies, too.

I sent the goddess today. I couldn't send it earlier because of moving, but I sent it airmail and you should have it by the end of the week. Don't read Daphne du Maurier, you dope! Actually, read anybody you feel moved to read. That's what I do. If you feel like it you might read *The Grapes of Wrath* (or did you tell me you did already?). It's a fine book. I'm glad you read some of *The Daring Young Man*. I read a story in it while we were in Tulsa, that Bearden gave me, remember? It was called (I think) *One Two Three Four Five*. It was very good. Another book of Saroyan's that I liked very much was called *The Adventures of Wesley Jackson*. Shall I send you some books? What would you like? I'll get whatever you want and send it. I'm going to send this Miller book as soon as Dick finishes it. I think you might really like it. I made a few notes in it to you.

I hope that I'm going to see *Saint Joan*, Shaw's play, put on by the Old Vic players of London tomorrow night. We haven't raised the money yet, but we will, somehow. Shaw is so great. He has one of the best pieces of writing I've ever seen on the Gospels in his preface to his play *Androcles and the Lion*. Honey, pay particular attention to what Jesus says, in the Gospels. Much of the rest is the workings of the minds of lesser men, but Jesus' actual words are always inspiring. The Kingdom of Heaven is within you, he says. Ask and you shall be received. You must love the Lord thy god with thy whole heart, thy whole mind, thy whole soul, ... Jesus is really a great man. He got what great men get, too.

Your friend who prays sounds very sweet. It is very fine that she prays for you, and prays for us. We will pray to each other, Sandy, you and me, for her. We shall pray to our gods, ourselves, us, for her, and for us.

My mother wrote a thank-you note to the Padgetts for us, and got a note in return saying that you were a wonderful girl. My mother says your letters are really nice, and that she hopes you will continue to write to her. She is behind us all the way, and is in contact with your family, too. I don't want to tell you to "nag" your parents, but I don't want us to let them forget that we want to be together, too.

Dear, that's all for now. Time for supper, and a shower, and some reading. I dream of you every night, and all day, too. I pray we will be together very soon.

All my love,
Ted, your husband
forever

March 14, 1962

My darling Sandy,

it's 5:30 p.m. in New York City, and I've been sitting in Ed Kaim's
house reflecting upon the past twenty-four hours. Lauren
and I and Dick had a long talk about the dimensions of
the mind, and the individual differences in ways of seeing,
and the possible differences in the ways the world has of
appearing to each of us

and outside it was crystal clear and shining, and all the profiles of
buildings leaped out at the sky as we walked down
Broadway this afternoon, on our way to the University
Library to read about the Abbey Church at Cluny, and
the Hagia Sophia

and at the library I checked out *Imitations* by Robert Lowell and
a long philosophical poem called *The Dragon and the
Unicorn* by Kenneth Rexroth

and when I returned to Kaim's Tom was there waiting, and we
talked about Arthur Rimbaud and Tom Wolfe and Tom
said that he didn't think all men were searching for a
father, but that the mother problem was something else,
and he also said that "what if the wood woke up one day
and found itself a violin?" and that pretty much summed
up the way we all felt about the dimensions of the mind

because every day I wake up and find myself a violin, or a trumpet
or a snare drum, or some days a harmonica, or a well-
tempered clavier, someday I hope to wake up and find
myself a string quartet playing the last quartets of
Beethoven.

Last night after writing to you, and then sitting around playing
cribbage to see who made the coffee, we all suddenly
decided to go to the Brooklyn Bridge, and so we put on

our beatnik costumes, charro jackets, big cowboy boots
and fake beards, and stalked off to the 2 a.m. subway, and
roared down the island to the giant spiderweb that is the
Brooklyn Bridge. There we forgot all metaphors and
simply stood in awe. And I thought of you. How much
you would enjoy these days and all of this. We will be
together, we will do all this, we will, we will, we will.
And then Lauren and Dick and I and a strange fellow named
Dana wandered down the steel and concrete jungle that is
lower Manhattan: Wall Street, the stock exchange, the
courthouse Federal Hall where the Stamp Act Congress
and the Congress of the Confederation met, and where
George Washington was inaugurated
and where the Bill of Rights was adopted, and I thought of you
locked in that hospital. And then we went back home, to
read books, Henry Miller, and Erich Neumann, and
Blaise Cendrars and then to go to sleep
To wake up today and think of you, and dream, and go tonight to
see *Saint Joan*, and then to come and write to you and wait

and wait.

I love you oh so very very much

your husband forever

Ted

March 16, 1962

Dear Sandy,

I just finished a long letter to you telling you about the play (*Saint Joan*) and what everyone was doing and that I love you very much. But now something new has come up.

I just talked to Dr. Skigen on the phone. Also to your parents. Here is the situation: the doctor is going to recommend that you undergo prolonged treatment in some kind of hospital situation. He also is going to say that your "trouble" dates from when you were a little girl, and that this particular situation, meaning our marriage, has little to do with it. This of course means that your parents will have grounds to annul the marriage, claiming that you didn't know what you were doing, et cetera. Your parents wouldn't tell me anything, but they indicated that they were in consultation with attorneys. The whole thing points to the fact that they are going to end the marriage, and confine you in one way or another. The doctor was very brutal when talking to me, obviously with the idea of getting me to stay away from you. He told me not to tell you what he said, and when I asked him if I could see you he said maybe, but he'd have to think about it.

Honey, as far as I can see, we are powerless before them. They won't pay any attention to the fact that we love each other and are married. I have no money, and that is very important. I am going to go to the Legal Aid Society tomorrow, or as soon as I can, but I already know that the poor have no rights when they contest those who have money.

Here's what I think is the only thing we can do: you must cooperate with them as far as possible, in order to allay their suspicions. They will not pay any attention to you when you tell them what you really think. Don't ever sign anything, under any condition, not even seemingly innocent papers. If they annul the marriage, don't let that worry you at all. We're married, and nothing can change that. No doubt they will annul the marriage. Write me as often as you can, and try not to let them deny you that privilege, but if they do, it's all right. We'll be in touch spiritually, always. The main thing is that you must get away from them as soon as you can. Go anywhere, as long as you are free from them. Then get in touch with me through Margie, or Tony, or my mother, or directly. We will go to Mexico or hide somewhere in the u.s. If they send you to a hospital somewhere besides Florida I'll come to a nearby city. We will get together, we will.

Sandra, never let them convince you that you are sick, that we have done wrong, nor that they are at all in any way right. We are good, and we have done a good, right thing. We'll fight this out if it takes forever. Meanwhile, try to understand everything that goes on around you. Watch everything, learning everything, let your mind grow. Read and think, and try try try not to despair. The world is a very sick place in many ways.

I want to come to Miami and see you, but I really don't know if they will let me when I get there, and I suspect that your parents will find a way to put me in jail if I do come there. So, I can only stay here and wait. Write me and tell me what is happening to you if you can. The doctor said to not tell you all this, so the only way you can answer me about it is through secret letters. They may not let you receive my letters anymore if they find out.

Honey, this is the worst, wickedest thing that anyone has ever done to anyone else. I don't understand it at all, although I know people are capable of such things. We must continue to be loving, to have love, but yet we must fight this all secretly. Silence and cunning are our only weapons. We just wait, and wait, and then move quickly when we have the chance. Try to get your money and I will send you money.

Perhaps the Legal Aid Society can help. But I doubt it.

I love you very much. I look at your pictures all the time, and I want to cry when I see them, you are so good and so beautiful. That you love me is more honor than I ever could deserve. The title of husband to Sandy is the proudest thing I have ever had. I shall love you forever and ever as long as love exists. Let them try to change that! I am at the depths of despair right now, because of my insufficiency and ineptness in this situation, but your love shall keep me strong and good. Pray for me, and I shall pray for you, and to you. Remember the men and women who have been through this already, Shelley shall serve as our model. Our love is stronger than all the evil in the whole world. If these people would only learn from you, they could not do such a thing. I love you, I love you, I love you.

All my love forever,

your husband,
Ted

March 17, 1962

My beautiful darling wife,

three letters from you tonight, and I am raised from despair to the heights. Also a clipping from my mother of the wedding announcement in the Providence paper. I'm so happy, so proud that people will read that you and I are married.

And Ann's song was fine, and beautiful. I'm glad she is there with you. I'm glad you can be silly sometimes, and I'm glad sometimes you get tired of all the empty voices around you.

And more news, good things, something to make me feel good, something for me to brag about to you: Frank O'Hara sent me a card today in answer to the letter I sent him. Isn't that good that he answered? I told him I would understand if he didn't. Here's what he wrote:

Dear Ted Berrigan:

Boy you certainly know how to cheer a person up.
Thank you very much for your letter and for the
poems which I like a lot especially "Traditional Manner,"
"Biographers," and "Words of Love." Forgive this card,
I thought perhaps you could give me a call
at work during the weekdays (CI 5-8900) and
we could meet for a drink or something. Also
do you want to meet K Koch? He's great. Anyhow, if
you want the poems back before we arrange to meet,
let me know and I'll mail them. Otherwise I'll give
them back when I see you.

Best,
(signed) Frank O'Hara

I'm really thrilled very much. It's like having Picasso tell Joe he likes his work. I'll write and tell you what we talk about and all the rest when we meet.

It's 4:30 a.m. on St. Patrick's Day. Everyone just came in from a party, Dick, Lauren, Harry, and a fellow named Johnny. So much for them.

Honey, I am going to make this a short letter, although I have much to tell you. I am going to write to you from now on of poetry, of plays, of movies, of Greek, of everything we would be doing together if you were here. I'll tell you what I've seen, what I think, and you can tell me what you think of what I think. But for right now, tonight, I want to tell you this:

I've thought a lot about getting a job and being respectable for the sake of making your parents relent and help us be together. But it's no good. They can never approve of us. I can't talk about it too much, because it isn't something that can really be talked about. They and all the other theys will always be against us till the end of time. Playing the game only makes it worse. Once I wrote

> These days I burn, and I cannot be still, / Burn I
> must, for with fire must I kill, / those griefs in me
> make me hurl my rage / upon those whose griefs I
> would most assuage.

These days I burn, and I cannot be still. My dear beautiful clean healthy loving sweet wife, my Sandra, my Sandy, I am powerless to cope with these monsters on their own battleground. My only weapons are those which they do not even recognize. But I make these vows to my heart, which is you. I vow upon my life and my love:

that I shall burn hotly and never turn back from the flame of anything in the world or out, until I have purified myself and become worthy of the great love between us.

that I shall write and write and write, speaking the truth as I know it, all for you and for myself, as long as I have strength in my bones and flesh and blood.

that I shall not compromise, I shall not sell out, I shall not be less than myself ever, except that I feel shame and dishonor when I do so. Then I shall repent in your name.

I need make no promise that I shall love you forever and ever, for I loved you before I ever knew what love was, and my love for you is not something dependent on my willpower, nor my flesh and bone. It is my all, my mind, my heart, my soul that loves you, and always shall.

These things I shall do in your name, in our name, in the name of love. And if I don't have the stuff to write great poems, no matter, for I do have the stuff to be a great poet. And having it, I have it more because of you.

No power on earth can keep us apart, even should they keep our bodies apart. And I feel that they cannot long do that, even if they keep us separate for days and weeks and months.

Remain Sandra Berrigan my love, and laugh in their faces for joy. If we have the stuff, and I know we do, we can never be defeated. I love you, I love you, I love you.

> Your husband forever,
> Ted

March 19, 1962

Dearest Sandy,

it's seven thirty in the morning, and I'm sitting in one of the study rooms at Columbia University. No one else is here, and through the window I can see an empty campus. I feel good. I just had eggs and corn beef hash for breakfast, and in an hour I'm going to take a paper on comparison of the Hagia Sophia Cathedral of Constantinople with the Abbey Church at Cluny to the fellow I wrote it for, and he's going to give me twenty dollars. And I'm thinking about you, and I love you very much.

I haven't written for two days. I'll try to tell you about those days, but I'm not sure I can fully describe the way they were.

I've been staying at Ed Kaim's, and Lauren and Dick and Eddie were also staying there. In addition, we had many visitors all the time. One or the other of us usually stayed up all night, so the place was never dark. From time to time I slept, but not often, in the past week.

I've been saying these past few days that I've felt I've reached a stage in my life where nothing can beat me into submission. Well, I still feel that way, but I had to undergo a severe test in the last few days. My faith is still strong, but my body is weak.

Everything began at around 5 p.m. on the sixteenth when I talked to your doctor. He didn't say anything I didn't expect, but to hear the words which confirmed all my worst expectations threw me into a severe depression. That night, however, I got three letters from you, and the marriage announcement from my mother, and I began reading Henry Miller's book about Arthur Rimbaud, and so my depression was lifted somewhat, into fierce dedication, to you, and to life.

I went to sleep about 4 a.m. that night, and I woke up the next day at 2 p.m. to the noise of Tony Powers calling for a St. Patrick's

Day celebration. I thought I felt good, and Tony and Dick and Lauren and I went and drank a few beers, and talked, and then we all went to Pat and Anne's, and played records, and drank a few more beers, and danced. I actually had very little to drink, since I was either talking or dancing most of the time. I thought I was enjoying myself. Then, about 12:30, while I was talking to Pat and Tony about nothing special, I suddenly felt very serious, very solemn, and I had a feeling that I didn't belong with those people, and that I was seeing them intimately for the last time. Then the situation of no place to stay, all the chaos, and most of all the loss, the absence of you, overwhelmed me, and I started crying. I cried for about ten minutes, silently, while Pat tried to explain to me why she and Joe and Ron and Anne hadn't offered to let me and Dick stay with them as long as we needed to. In the middle of her speech she said that I would have let them stay with me if the situation were reversed. Something snapped in me and I grew calm, and got up, and washed my face, and left. Everyone seemed to sense some sort of finality about my leaving and Anne ran after me and asked me to please stay—but I couldn't even answer, I just left. I was in a daze, and I found myself in the bus station, after a while, but I realized that I didn't want to leave NY except to find you, and that I couldn't help you any more anywhere other than I could here. Next I found myself wandering around Times Square, crying again, and saying over and over, "I don't know what to do." After a while I went back to Eddie's, but I couldn't get in, no one was there, and again I broke down. Somewhere along here Lauren and Dick and Tony came, but I broke away from them and went back downtown. Somehow I stumbled into a hotel finally, after about two hours of aimless wandering and fits of crying. I went into a room and fell into bed, and cried myself to sleep. All the time I was detached, and observing myself, and wanting to pull out of it, but I just didn't have the strength.

Well I woke up weak, but not beaten. I went to Columbia, got great books, read them, wrote an eleven-page paper. I resolved not to go back to Eddie's and not to get bogged down in trivia again, but instead to collect the twenty dollars, get a room for myself, and get back to work, which gives me a point of order upon which to focus my life.

I feel strong. To know I can break down is good for me. It means I have depths of feeling I was afraid I did not have. I could not have fallen into tears without you. Loving you has released me from chains which I imposed upon myself long ago. The chains of showing only strength, never weakness. I felt cleansed, washed in my own tears, and still on my feet with renewed strength.

We can't fail, honey. They can't beat us. We can take their worst, and come up on our feet. Pray for me, and I shall pray for you. It doesn't matter to whom you pray—pray to yourself, to Ann Lyons, to me—just pray. I shall pray to you and me for us.

I love you more with every moment.

Your husband forever,
Ted

March 19, 1962

Dear Sandy,

two letters from you today, and a picture. I feel so good when I get
your letters that I am exhilarated for the rest of the day. But tonight
I feel sad that your father had to upset you so. Honey, I don't want
to talk against your dad. I deplore his actions, but his motives and
conduct are something for him to live with and nothing I say will
change him. About me, about us, evidently his mind is made up.

But I beg you not to worry about those things which need not
be doubted. There is never in the world a chance that I could stop
loving you. And I love you as a husband loves a wife, as a man
loves a woman. Being with you has made my life whole. I have no
need of another woman, now that I have known you. I honestly
don't know what is going to happen to us. Only time will tell. But
I know that I am faithful to our love, faithful to you, to the fullest,
in every word, thought, and action. You need never doubt that I
love you now, and that I will go on loving you as long as I may go
on loving, which means forever. Your father feels that he has
reasons to doubt that I love you. Well, let him doubt, if he must.
I do love you, and God help me I suppose I even love him,
although I despise him a little, too. He simply doesn't understand.
He has ideas about love and its external signs. Can he understand
that I love Margie, that you and I and Margie slept three in a bed
on our wedding night? Can he understand that I felt love for poor
bitter young defenseless Leslie? Can he understand how you and
Sue got along so well, and how I love Dave Bearden? If he
distrusts us, and distrusts these things as evidence of my bad character, how can he understand that you and I love each other? If he
thinks that there was something sinister about the friendship
between you and me and Dick and Tom, and if he thinks it
impossible that we could in all innocence plan to drive to NY

together, how can he understand our love? I feel sorry for him. But I am very angry that he should come and upset you as he did. Honey, cry that we are apart, but not for the possibility that I will be unfaithful, or that I will grow tired of waiting. You are burned into my heart and mind. I recognized you at first sight. The first thing I said about you was that you were great, remember? I love you, I love you, I'll be waiting beyond the grave. I love you.

Ann asks you what I mean when I say have faith. Faith in what? Dear, I mean faith in God. We are God. You are God, I am, she is, the rocks in the field and the trees are. Have faith in the God in you, and in all of us. Have faith that if you work as hard as possible to bring yourself nearer to the God you are, that the God you are will help. Have faith in yourself, is what I mean. Have faith in me. Have faith that your mother and father will do what is really good sometime. But don't let your faith deceive you into waiting for all this. Faith is what makes one work. Work. I believe in God. I believe in working towards the God in me. If I work towards the God in me, and you work towards the God in you, we will naturally come closer and closer together, for the more godlike we become, the more spiritually bound to each other we will be. We can not do anything for others except make ourselves as good as possible, in whatever way seems right to us. We must continually question ourselves to be sure we are still going forward. And we must trust our sanity and we must have faith in ourselves, even when, and especially when, all but little children and the insane say we are ourselves little children and insane. Well, so we are. So we are.

My beautiful sweet lovely wife. When I think of you, when I think of you as wife, as lover, as cook, as walking in the street with me, in movies with me, and on buses, and in bed, and in Chinese restaurants, and in your room, I am so overwhelmed with love I am nearly faint. I promise you again I will be good, and for you.

I repeat what I said before about the court hearing, and all the rest. We cannot defeat them, nor make any gain, through legal conventional normal procedure. I am not normal, nor are you. We are poor. I want to pursue a life that in all probability will not pay money. I want to tell the truth, whether it be that I experiment with such things as LSD or peyote, or pills, or whether I am totally against the educational system, and glad when girls or boys quit schools like Tulane or Sophie Newcomb. I want to be myself, and live my life. I want to proudly say I. I do say I. Who else may I speak for more with more accuracy. I scorn those who are afraid to say I. I love you. I want to support you. I don't need money from your parents. I would take it if they offered it. I want you to do what you want. I want you. You have said you want me. Therefore, I for either one of us, after that, is We. I asked you to run away. You decided to. They wanted us to come to Miami. We decided to. I wanted to decline my degree. I asked you first. Of course I did. I want to write poems, and not idle my time away in some job I care nothing about. We need to eat. You want to be a teacher. So, of course, of course, I decide to get a job. We thought they might offer help with your education, they didn't. Did we ask them to? Of course not. We are married. I want you to do what you want, as I want to do what I want. What is a job to me, if I am helping you? I *wanted, I want* to work for you, in whatever way our life together calls for. I. I. I. I. I. Can they understand that? We can, you and I. Don't let them shake you, honey. I may be "sick, sick, sick," but before you and I decide that we are "sick" let them tell us just exactly who are the healthy ones they are comparing us to in order to determine our sickness.

Themselves? They saw we were happy, and they put you behind a locked door. The doctor? When I asked him what I could do to help you, he advised me to "bow gracefully out of the (marriage) before it was too late." He knew his diagnosis before he made it, before ever talking to me. When I asked him if he thought that if I cooperated with him and advised you to cooperate it would ease your mind about us being kept apart, he said he didn't think all that had happened to us had anything to do with your "disturbance." Of course they didn't give you any tests to see if you'd been taking drugs. They know better. When the policeman talked to me in Miami he said, "Dr. Alper is a big man around Miami." And you and I are little. We don't have a chance with them, honey.

· Except that they can't make us stop loving each other. They can't take you from me, nor me from you. They can't destroy us if we continue to have faith in ourselves and each other. We are sane. They are sick. We are right. They are wrong. The majority is always wrong. The minority is always right. Nietzsche is a great man. Freud is a great man. Shelley is a great man. All the Dr. Skigens and Dr. Alpers are little men. And you and I are on the side of the angels. No wonder that everyone in the hospital except the doctors would let us be together. Who has anything to gain but the doctors? Who has self-importance to uphold except the doctors? But I don't even want to go on about it.

I'll write to you about the Theater of the Absurd tomorrow. I have a book about it, and there is a series of plays running in NY now under the heading Theater of the Absurd. Kenneth Koch is one of the playwrights, and some of the others are Samuel Beckett (an Irishman who was once James Joyce's secretary), Ionesco, a young American named Edward Albee, and another named Jack Richardson, an Italian named Arabella,[2] another American named Jack Gelber, and there are really a lot of others. Their plays are what are now considered the most "modern" as far as both style and content go. The Giraudoux play we saw in Miami was a link between the old theater of Shaw and the new Theater of the Absurd.

---

[2] Ted means Arrabal, the Spanish writer. —Ed.

Jean Genet, a Frenchman, is one of the most important new writers, too. They have very much interaction with the audience in their plays, often using deliberately insulting and provoking remarks to stir up the emotions of the audience. The idea is to involve the audience even more than before, to extend the boundaries of the stage. Sometimes characters sit in the audience. Sometimes some of the lines are improvised, depending on the audience response to taunts. Not all the playwrights have this direct approach. Some are "members" more because of content than style. Beckett is like this. The plot is either nonexistent, or else upside down and backwards. The idea is to make the audience view the old tireless problems with new eyes, a fresh approach. The major theme of all the plays is the same as the major theme for Shaw: how to live in a world not ready for goodness. And also, how to live, why to live, in the face of imminent death. Also how to face with honor the injustice of the world as reflected in its poverty, its racial prejudice, its downright callousness to love and dignity. Williams (Tennessee) has been writing about these things for years. The new writers are attempting to bring a fresh approach to the presentation. Your father was able to do us in, and at the same time claim that he liked *The Madwoman of Chaillot.* The new writers don't want people to be able to be like that. They want them to either ignore their plays, or else be moved by them, and be affected by them. Art must move someone. It must.

Henry Miller, in *The Time of the Assassins,* his study of Arthur Rimbaud, says that this era is one in which the artists are ignored. And when the artists, who are true prophets of the future because they see more clearly in what directions we are headed, when they are ignored, then the world is heading for a period of destruction the likes of which it has never known. I myself am not sure the world ever heeds its artists. The nature of many is to acquiesce to comfort, to routine, to habit, in other words, to death. The nature of the few, the artists, whether they write or paint or play or not, is to live, to fight comfort in order to be more alive. To keep their senses sharp and their minds expanding. The many are against expansion of the mind, because it is painful, and they would rather give up the reward of enlarged vision and understanding rather than undergo the pain of growth. The many think they are adults. They want to grow no longer. They are against everything that expands man's consciousness. The people who are Freudians now, convinced Freudians, are those who crucify people like Wilhelm Reich, and who are against any use of narcotics in spite of their proven ability to give man increased knowledge of himself. These people would have crucified Freud, indeed many of them nearly did, had they been born a few years earlier. They like Giraudoux, but hate Henry Miller because he uses words which all twelve-year-olds know, and talks about things which their hero, Freud, said should be talked about. What Henry Miller will they be crucifying next year? Maybe me. They like Walt Whitman now, although they never mention that he was bisexual, or perhaps predominantly homosexual, and they like Shelley, although they don't mention his life much, but they hate Allen Ginsberg, dismissing him as immature, or trivial, and they seem to be totally against us, you because you committed the heinous crime of loving me because I have life and spirit, and me because it is my very life and spirit which causes me to live the way I do. Does your father think I'm stupid? Oh no. Sick is the fashionable word now. They used to say that Byron and Shelley were "Diabolical" because they seemed not to believe in the Christian God. Well, this year, in this season, I am "sick" because among other things I scorn their new God of analysis. But they know better. It is not analysis I scorn, but the analysts. I would love to be analyzed by Freud, or Otto Rank, or Carl Jung, or Wilhelm Reich, or even Alfred Whitehead or Bernard Shaw or Walt Whitman or Allen Ginsberg, or Sandy Alper Berrigan, but I am not about to be analyzed by Dr. Jack Skigen or Dr. Louis Alper whose home and swimming pool are symbols of the very things which I need to repudiate *for myself* so I can be like Freud or Whitman or the rest. Did Freud have a swimming pool? Or a practice in Miami? Did Whitman, or does Carl Jung?

I seem to be unable to get off the same old subject. But it's our subject, and we are stuck with it. I want a good life for us now. Pity poor Ann Lyons, for she is willing perhaps to believe in a good life in the hereafter, but I feel I know better. Honey, I have as little patience as you, for I want us to have our youth, our good life now. This life is ours, and I bitterly resent the loss of every minute. If I could make them all vanish I would. But we can't. And maybe I wouldn't if we could. I want them to have their lives too. But why doesn't your father let go of your soul?

Honey, I'm enclosing two very great books. I got them tonight for you. Don't think about extravagance or expense. It gives me great joy to show my love in the small way of sending you books. Please ask me for any and all books you want, please. It makes me feel near you, and useful to you, to be able to send them. If you have to leave them all behind later it's unimportant. Only that you and I come together is important. I love you so very very much. I am your husband, your lover forever, Ted.

March 20, 1962

Dear Sandy,

it's now 6 a.m. in the morning on the twentieth. Last night I saw a movie called *The Gunfighter*, with Gregory Peck and Karl Malden, at the Columbia Film Series theater. It was an old movie, made about ten years ago. Gregory Peck played Jimmy Ringo, once one of the "fastest guns in the West." He made an attempt to quit gunfighting, but too many kids wanted to get famous by gunning down the great Jimmy Ringo. So, sooner or later, sooner in the movie, he was killed. The film was in very stark black and white, and was one of the best examples of Sabi I've ever seen. Jimmy Ringo represented the legendary American hero, tough, competent, heart of gold, nerves of steel, doomed to die, but living resignedly and heroically while alive. The Wild West version of Hektor. He never killed a man except in a fair fight, etc. It may never have been that way, the age of heroes may never have existed, but we all have nostalgia for it anyway. The white knight. Who never even went to the bathroom.

> but it's no use you love Alan Ladd he's Shane he's
> the last of the old-time gunfighters and
> what am I to do?

I wrote once. Sabi is a real thing, and a good thing. It is only superficial idealism that is bad, because it is dangerous, and makes us forget that even Jimmy Ringo goes to the bathroom, even Hektor can be killed, even Ulysses runs sometimes, et cetera.

Harry is asleep on Ed's bed, Lauren on the couch, Dick is reading an anthology of French poetry, and Eddie is cleaning his pipe after reading mythology all night. Another night among the intellectuals. I couldn't find a room last night for myself, but I will this morning. Meanwhile I spent the night trying to write lines, images, poems, with no success, but at least I did some work for you. Here are some quotes[3] from a book called *Theatre of the Absurd* written by a man named Martin Esslin.

(A play of this type may be compared) to a piece of jazz music "to which one must listen for whatever one may find it in." There should be some meaning in it for each member of the audience.

If a good play must have a cleverly constructed story, these have no story or plot to speak of; if a good play is judged by subtlety of characterization and motivation, these are often without recognizable characters and present the audience with almost mechanical puppets; if a good play has to have a fully explained theme, which is neatly exposed and finally solved, these have often neither a beginning nor an end; if a good play is to hold the mirror up to nature and portray the manners and mannerisms of the age in finely observed sketches, these seem often to be reflections of dreams and nightmares; if a good play relies on witty repartee and pointed dialogue, these often consist of incoherent babblings.

It must be stressed, however, that the dramatists whose work is here discussed do not form part of any self-proclaimed or self-conscious school or movement. On the contrary, each of the writers in question is an individual who regards himself as a lone

[3] Actually a combination of quotations and paraphrases. —Ed.

outsider, cut off and isolated in his private world. Each has his own personal approach to both subject matter and form; his own roots, sources, and backgrounds. If they also, very clearly and in spite of themselves, have a good deal in common, it is because their work most sensitively mirrors and reflects the preoccupations and anxieties, the emotions and thinking of many of their contemporaries in the Western world. . . .

In the *Myth of Sisyphus* Albert Camus discussed the absurdity of life from a rational standpoint. Everyone must die. The purpose of life is death. From the standpoint of reason this makes life absurd, since its end is to defeat itself. There is no hope for a promised land. There is only death. Ionesco adds to this that "Absurd is that which is devoid of purpose . . . cut off from his religious, metaphysical, and transcendental roots, man is lost, all his actions becomes senseless, useless, absurd."

This sense of metaphysical anguish at the absurdity of the human condition is, broadly speaking, the theme of the plays of the writers in the theatre of the absurd. But it is not merely subject matter which defines the theatre of the absurd. These playwrights attempt to present the absurd situation as it is, without resort to the tight rational form of the drama of their predecessors such as Shaw, Wilde, and even Sartre and Camus as playwrights.

The theatre of the absurd does not argue about the absurd, it merely presents it.

It tends toward a radical devaluation of language, toward a poetry that is to emerge from the concrete and objectified images of the stage itself. The element of language still plays an important part, but is subordinate to the actual happenings on the stage. Often what happens contradicts what is being said, and for example, in Ionesco's play *The Chairs* the poetic content lies not in the banal words but in the fact that they are being said to an increasing number of empty chairs on stage. The theatre of the absurd is thus allied with the anti-literary movement which has found its expression in abstract art, plotless novels and poems, et cetera *(note: like some poems of mine, notable the one which ends "Signed, The Snake.")*.

The public, conditioned by experience and criticism, to a certain type of play, finds the absurd absurd. But it has an internal logic of its own, available to all those who approach it freely and openly.

Eslin lists Beckett, Adamov (Russian), Albee, Genet, Pinter (Eng.), Simpson (Eng.), Ionesco, Arrabal, and one or two others as the major writers of the Theater of the Absurd. I'll send you his book if you want it, but it isn't too good to read it without reading about thirty plays first.

So much for the Theater of the Absurd. I don't know if all that enlightens you much, but I thought of you all night as I read this material. Now I am tired and I didn't write much about it, just the quotes that I underlined in the book. If I see any more anywhere I'll write to you about it.

I really love you more than I can ever say. I look at your pictures a hundred times a day, and am filled with Sabi for the lost paradise, the lost home I once found. I know it will come again. I know it.

Talked to Tom last night and he said he'd written you a letter full of advice et cetera. He's a good fellow, and I like him more every day. He has a hard streak of Yankee independence in him that I find attractive and admirable. He has a good heart, too. And he still thinks you are the best girl he has ever seen. I think he likes me more because he saw that you could love me. I like myself better for that, too.

For now, good-bye. I must go out and find a room, and put my typewriter and books in it, and write to you, and write poems, and entries in my journal, and letters to obscure poets, and read books, and re-establish some order in my chaotic life. I may have a new address soon, but if I do I will send you a special delivery letter telling you about it. My mother and my family repeat that they are with us all the way. They love you because I do, and I hope soon they will get a chance to see you and love you for yourself. They can not really imagine how wonderful you are, even though I have tried to tell them. Everyone loves you, honey, who has eyes to see. You are the most beautiful person I have ever met. I am your husband, your lover, your friend, your brother forever.

All my love,
Ted

March 20, 1962

My darling,

I'm in my new room which is on the sixth floor of a building called Arvia House. The address is 605 West 112th Street, Apt. 628, New York City. It is a small room, but I have my books, and my typewriter, and my solitude. I moved in today. Dick is still living with Eddie, two blocks away. Columbia University is two blocks in the other direction. This is the first time I have lived uptown in NYC, and the change will be interesting. I am near the museums, and the river is a block away and very beautiful. Write to me at this address instead of Joe's.

On the wall in front of me your picture looks down at me and my books. I have just finished re-reading the two letters and the Saint Patrick's Day card I got from you today. Bless Leslie, for sending you flowers. Tell her I love her for being herself, her young self.

Honey, I want to answer all the questions in your letters, and I want to talk to you about the future, and I want to just talk to you, and so I guess I will do all at once. First, about your questions:

I don't know William Burroughs personally, but I have read some of his cut-up poems in *Locus Solus* 11, and also a work of his called *Naked Lunch,* which was very exciting. It was a surrealistic piece of writing filled with horror and hallucination and was very well done. Burroughs is a friend of Jack Kerouac and Allen Ginsberg, and is an older man than they. He was a heroin addict for many years, and perhaps still is. He lived in New Orleans for a while, and also in Tangiers. It is said that Ginsberg convinced him to write. He wrote a book called *Junkie* about his drug addiction, under the pseudonym of William Lee. He also appears as a character named Old Bull Lee in *On the Road,* Kerouac's famous novel. In my opinion he is a good writer, but he has published very little. I think that Harry knows him personally, but I'm not sure.

About Tennessee Williams: I don't want to try to say what I think about him in just a few lines, but I do think he is a very very good playwright, one who knows how to write a play which is exciting both as theater and as ideas. He is preoccupied with evil, as are most twentieth-century writers (many most all writers always). He has limits, and those limits include a certain monotony of theme. He has constructed some marvelous characters, such as Blanche and Stanley in *A Streetcar Named Desire* and Big Daddy in *Cat on a Hot Tin Roof,* and his play *The Glass Menagerie* is one of the most beautiful plays I've ever read. It is full of Sabi, as is much of his work. He seems to me to be a very "American" writer, that is, he is obsessed with things that Americans seem to be obsessed with, such as masculinity, heroism, sex, etc. He is reputed to be homosexual and to take pills such as Dexedrine. He also writes short stories which are much like his plays, and poems which are very musical, very touching, very very lyrical, sometimes very beautiful. I've read nearly all his writings, except for the last two or three plays, but I haven't read anything by him in a long time. Partly because he is not saying much of anything he hasn't said before. Nevertheless I think he is one of the best playwrights writing in America today, a genuine sincere talented artist. Is that what you wanted?

I have only read sections of *Cain's Book* by Alexander Trocchi. It was a big hit here a couple of years ago, and is about drug addiction. It seemed well written to me, but conventional in style. Most of its appeal was its lurid subject matter, but I felt that it was sincerely written, and not written merely to capitalize on sensationalism. A friend of mine runs around with Trocchi, or rather, my friend's brother does, and he says Trocchi is a good fellow, and smart. The book was not one that I considered a great book, but was interesting. Other than that I can't say much about it.

The final literary matter I wanted to talk about was the Grove Press anthology. Do you have it there? Is that where you read "Thank You" and "Fresh Air"? I guess it must be. I thought I'd tell you some of the writers in the book that I liked most. Robert Creeley's short poems seem very interesting to me. He often says very good things in a very good way. Brother Antoninus writes very good poetry, I think. I like Ginsberg's poem called "A Supermarket in California," and his other things too. I like Gregory Corso some of the time, and some of the poems he has in here, like "Poets Hitchhiking on the Highway" I like a lot. I like Barbara Guest a little, and of course Koch and O'Hara and Ashbery very much. I like Gary Snyder's work, too. I like some of Michael McClure's work, but like his books better than selected poems from his books. I think that John Wieners is very good, and sometimes I like Ron Loewinsohn, and Dave Meltzer. Personally, I think I can write better than many poets in the book, but I can't write well enough to satisfy myself yet.

Sandy, I've written nearly two pages without stopping to say I love you. I love you till my heart breaks with love. When you mention anything I think about it endlessly, and hatch giant schemes to send you books on every subject. I am horribly jealous of everyone you talk to, men and women, because I can't talk to you. You are right, of course, I am not an unreal silver knight in the sky, and among my many faults is my insecurity in personal matters such as believing that anyone could really love me. But I believe that we really love each other, and that nothing can change that love. All manner of things could happen if we were separated for a long time. I want you to try to know every second that my love for you does not depend on anything other than the fact that you are you. I want you to be always true to yourself. That is the most important thing you can do for you, and therefore for me. I envy everyone you see, everyone that talks to you. But it is not a malicious envy. I simply love you, and I hate not being with you. I have a thousand dreams a day about you, half of them erotic fantasies or erotic memories, all of them filled through and through with love. Time and distance cannot beat us. I love you more than that.

Honey, I want to try to tell you what I think the actual situation is. In your letters I read your hopes, your speculations about the length of our separation, your ideas on what we can do. Let me try to tell you in a brief sketch what I think the whole picture is.

Some of this of course is guessing. But these guesses are based on facts of one kind or another. This is what I think is happening, and is going to happen: they, meaning your parents, have separated us by placing you under lock in a mental institution. They have placed you in care of a doctor, Doctor Jack Skigen, who, without ever talking to me, is firmly against us being together. Your father is a well-respected doctor in Miami, Skigen is a doctor. Draw your own conclusions. There is a definite conspiracy against us. This, I think, is what they are going to do. Dr. Skigen has told me that he regards you as seriously disturbed, and he feels that you have been that way for a long time, since childhood. He says that our marriage is unimportant in relation to your sickness, and he advises its end. Your parents, of course, want just that. Dr. Skigen is going to recommend that you be confined in some hospital somewhere, for prolonged treatment. Confined. And by prolonged I am sure he (and they) mean to keep you locked up until you are twenty-one, and then later, on the grounds that you are mentally immature and incompetent. They, your parents, in the meantime, are going to get the marriage annulled, and they may even resort to attempting to harass me or even have me jailed if possible. Fortunately, I don't think they can do such a thing to me. I have no secret crimes under which they can imprison me. But they do have direct control over you. After the marriage is annulled, they feel that in time and with treatment you will forget me, or see that I am bad. Perhaps they really believe that you need treatment, I don't know. I am sure they believe you are serious about me, but they think you are a child, and that all children forget their playthings after a while. They think I am your father substitute, et cetera, and they hope that with treatment you will become mature and not need a father substitute, or at least that you will exercise more mature judgment and pick someone who is not obviously a loser like me. Make no mistake honey, they intend to keep us apart, and you locked up somewhere, for a long, long, long time.

As far as legal rights go, you and I have none. We are poor, you are underage, I am not respectable, we didn't know each other long enough, we are of different racial backgrounds, and it is your parents against a relative stranger, and they are backed up by doctors' reports.

Meanwhile, they are not telling either of us anything like the truth. I suspect that you are not going to see any Dr. Caldwell. They are keeping you in the dark about yourself and your future, and are treating you like the child they claim you are. They even advise me to tell you nothing of what they say, and only by lying to Dr. Skigen and saying that I would ask you to cooperate was I able to get him to even think about letting me see you. If he reads these letters he will probably not allow you to get mail from me. He and your parents have *absolute power* over you. They can keep you from getting mail, having visitors, reading the Bible, and being with me, and whatever else they desire. And they have plenty of ideas along that line.

Now, honey, please listen to me carefully, while I repeat what I have said over and over. I know you know this in your heart. I know you know I know it. I am only saying it again because I want to shout it to the skies. THEY ARE ALL WRONG. YOU ARE NOT A BABY. YOU ARE NOT SICK. YOU ARE SENSITIVE AND HONEST! THEY WANT YOU TO BE CALLOUSED AND A LIAR. YOU SEE WITH BOTH EYES! THEY ARE NEARLY BLIND. You must not let them make you think that you have problems that they can solve. We all have problems in how to face our experiences and continue developing. But having those problems is not being sick. They can tell you obvious things about yourself and your inexperience, and twist them so that you may think they can help you face things that are alien to you. But they can't. Everything they are doing and have done proves that your parents and particularly Dr. Skigen are morally and intellectually and spiritually incapable of doing you any good at all until they first release you. There is absolutely no need for you to be confined. Are you homicidal? Are you a sex maniac? Are you in danger? No No No. You face everything better than they do. The Padgetts, Margie, Tom, my teachers at college, Kaim, everyone loves you. These captors of yours are smug frightened people and you must be wary of them every minute. Have no sympathy for them, until you have freedom first. Then we will try to love them. For now you must hate, deceive, escape.

I won't try to advise you how to handle yourself. You are there and I am not and so you know better than I. I know it will be difficult, and sometimes seem hopeless, but I have absolute faith in your wisdom, in your courage, in your ability. You must try to get away as soon and as quietly as possible. How and when will be up to you. Don't worry when the time comes about clothes, money, anything, beyond getting somewhere where you can hide until you can contact me, through Tony, or through Margie, or through anyone, Leslie, anyone. I will wait, and wait, and keep on waiting, and in the meantime do everything I can for us. But it won't be much.

These people, the doctors and your parents, are evil, honey. Evil people are those who do what is evil. For now they are evil because of what they do. When we are not in their power, then we will be charitable, and we will forgive them, we will try to understand them, we will even try to love them. But now we have no time for forgiveness, understanding, nor love. We must hate them, so that we can ruthlessly deceive them. We must know their complete evil, so that we will be prepared to be betrayed at every turn. You must not believe one single word they say. You believed your mother, as she sat in front of us on that Sunday night and asked if you wanted to take her leather coat to New York in the morning, and as a result we were torn out of each other's arms by strangers. You and even I believed in Dr. Skigen as a doctor, a follower of the Hippocratic oath, and in return he advised me to leave you, to "bow out gracefully," because you might never "get well." Those people are sick sick people. They would have it that a Dick Gallup who only wants to read and study and find love, and a Ted and Sandy who want to live and work together, are sick and immature. But it is they who are doing evil. We must give them evil for evil, until we are free.

I wrote a long time ago a poem called "Prayer," addressed to a fierce old prophet-like poet, whose poems were giving me inspiration:

> Old Father, I am young.
> I am afraid. Teach me
> to run, that I may learn
> to fight.
>
> Sing would I, many songs,
> and many candles burn.
> Teach me to fall, that
> I may learn to stand.
>
> Old Warrior,
> guide me now. Help me believe
> the necessary lies.
> Teach me to hate.
>
> I would preserve my Love.

I love you, Sandy, Sandra, my eternal wife.

Your husband forever,
Ted
I Love You.

[Undated]

My darling, I'm not even sure I want to write well or even write at all when you are not with me. I love you so much. But to love, I must live. And to write is to live/to live is to write. I love you.

I'm reading the poetry of John Ashbery, of Vladimir Mayakofsky, of Kenneth Koch, of Frank O'Hara, of Garcia Lorca, of whoever else, including Dick Gallup. Maybe my biographers will use this letter to prove I am a giant plagiarizer of everybody's poems. But my poems will still be standing on their own two or three feet. Tell Leslie I like her anyway. Would you like me to send you my copy of *Steppenwolf* for her? Or send it directly to her? I'd like to, if you want me to. We could always get another, or she could send it back. I'm trying now to get a book for you called *Growing Up Absurd* by Paul Goodman. It's a fine book, about growing up now and in the recent past in America and it tells the truth as a man of letters who is concerned about his country and his kids and his self sees it.

Besides thinking of you in everything I do, I ache for you physically so much I think the top of my head or somewhere else is going to burst open soon. Sublimation, says Sigmund. But he figured that out when he was fifty.

Sigmund Froyd says "Shucks,
if you're out of luck,
don't frown,
write pomes,
and you won't need to do whatever rhymes
with luck and shucks."

I'm getting delirious. Don't eat so much. Don't sleep so much. Get to work. I love you.

Your husband forever,
Ted

March 21, 1962

Dear Sandy,

this will just be a short letter, because I haven't gone to Joe's to get my mail yet. I'll write again later tonight. It's 4:45 in the afternoon here, on the first day of spring. Outside it is bitter cold and raining. In my small warm room I am surrounded by books and you are everywhere, your letters, nineteen of them are on my desk, your pictures all around me, everything makes me see you.

I'm sending some Ibsen plays today, and a new book of poems of Garcia Lorca. Maybe you can do better translations than some in the book. I haven't read all of them yet, but Lorca is really a good poet. He wrote *Poet in New York* while living in Harry's dormitory over at Columbia.

I'm reading Enid Starkie's biography of Arthur Rimbaud, and also a book of Chinese poetry called the *Book of Songs* translated by Arthur Waley. I'm also reading O'Hara, Koch, and Ashbery all the time.

Last night I went to see the movie of the Tennessee Williams play *Summer and Smoke,* to see if there was anything more to tell you about Williams. But as usual Hollywood had killed everything good in the play, and had turned a poetic drama into a pretentious unsubtle horrible bore. Unbelievable. I left halfway through the movie, in pain at the sight of such rot.

On my wall I have pictures of Hans Hoffman, and Zborowski. Do you know who they are? My mustache is nearly grown out now, and I look amazing. I'll send some pictures soon, after I have them taken in the subway. Here are a couple of pictures from my old albums. Also, here's a picture apropos of something or other.†

I love you very much. I hope I find a letter waiting for me at Joe's. More tonight, all my love, Ted.

March 22, 1962

My darling wife,

it's seven in the morning, and I found a letter from you waiting for me at Joe's when I went down there last night. I've been composing a letter to you in my head most of the evening, but I've thrown most of my energy into a night of odd writing. Lauren and I wrote a collaborative short story called "Hide-and-Go-Seek," which is insane, and then Dick and I and Lauren wrote a collaborative poem which was plain bad, and then Lauren and I collaborated on a poem in strict meter and rhyme, and then I wrote a parody of it, and in between all that I read a poem by Kenneth Koch and fifteen poems by Arthur Rimbaud and a hundred pages of the biography of Rimbaud by Enid Starkie, and a poem by Byron, and two poems by Lauren, and the *Village Voice,* and all of *Kulchur* magazine including an article on the Guggenheim Museum, and somehow most of the letter I'd written in my head to you got used up. So I'm not exactly sure what I'm writing. I'm only sure that I love you, I need you, I want you, and I miss you terribly.

Barry sounds like a defensive sort of fellow. Why should he make judgments about me without seeing me or talking to me? I suspect all his thoughts and abilities if he really doesn't think you have what it takes. Even fools can see that you are special. But if he is nice to you sometimes, I give him my permission to totally scorn me if he wishes. He has lots of company, at that.

I wish I were a sad funny old man, who could wander naked into your room, day or night.

Hans Hoffman is an old man, over eighty, who is a painter. He is a geometric abstract expressionist, who is a leading influence on the New York abstract expressionists. He was born in Sweden, and is now an American citizen. He gets greater with age, and is really an inspiring person, and a great painter.

Léopold Zborowski was a Polish poet who was a good friend of Amedeo Modigliani, and Modigliani did a painting of him which looks a lot like me.

There are many books of ours at your parents' house, including *Artists' Theatre*, with plays by Koch (no, not Koch), O'Hara, Ashbery, and others; also Erich Neumann's *The Origins and History of Consciousness*, also *The Greek Anthology*, also a journal of mine with a few entries, and some more books, I am sure. I also left a bottle of Scotch whiskey there, and my gray poet's cord coat is in the closet. I don't want them sent. Unless they do it. I prefer having some of our things, my things and yours, there where they sit in your room, for you and them to see.

Your impressions of the hospital were frightening, and also good. You have talent, honey, you should write often, anything.

I'd like to write a dead serious letter, telling you to make yourself tough-minded toward the doctors there, and everyone. But I am not up to it this morning, and sometimes I just like to talk to you about anything and nothing. But beware, beware of all the official people who seem friendly. No one, and I mean no one, is going to be on your side, no matter what front they put up. Those doctors and your parents are 100% against any kind of combination of you and me. Their decision and plans were made weeks ago. But their tactics are still in formation.

I filled some more pages in the book I am making for you, and it looks very good.[4] It is a black covered sketchbook, with blank white pages. I am filling it with special poems that I would like to read to you, to show you, and with pictures of poets and painters, and paintings, and whatever else I really want to show you. I will

[4] See pages 274–294.

try to finish it as soon as possible. Last night I added two poems by O'Hara, one by René Rilke, a painting of O'Hara, and two pictures of painters with paintings, Franz Kline, and Willem de Kooning. It will take a few more days at least to complete, but I know you will like it.

Dick is reading giant French books, the works of Rabelais in fifteenth-century French, and a book, in French, on the history of the French language. He is also writing a book in his head, about the whole thing that has happened since we met (You and Me).

I am still in my room, living alone, writing, reading, Dick is still at Ed's, as is Ed, and Lauren, too. Ron has moved in with Joe, and he and Pat are having a kind of romance. Anne is also having a romance of sorts, with someone she goes to school with. I haven't seen any of them since Saint Patrick's night, five nights ago, except for Joe, briefly, when I go to get your letters. By them I meant Pat and Ron and Joe. I see Dick and Lauren and Ed and Harry fairly often. In fact, Lauren and Dick both cut big scratches into my arm fencing last night. They too have their scars. But I'm getting better. And so are they. Fencing is a good trick, requiring quickness and agility, of mind and body.

I'm working on a translation from French to English of a long poem called "The Drunken Boat" by Arthur Rimbaud. I'll send you a copy when I finish. I'm also keeping all my collaborations to show you. I haven't seen O'Hara yet, and won't until next week. I don't feel up to it yet. I am still a little weak from breaking down. But my spirit is strong, and my love is stronger than ever.

I wish I could send you roses every day. Or bring them. I must end now, and go to sleep, until noon. I'll write again this afternoon. I love you very much.

Your husband forever,
Ted

March 25, 1962

My darling Sandy,

it's eight thirty Sunday morning, and in a minute or two I'm going to work some more on my translation of "The Drunken Boat." But I wanted to begin this letter to you first, to begin my day by talking to you. I borrowed Eddie's big radio, and I'm listening to some Spanish church music, and it makes me think so much about you. I'm listening to them praise God, and I can only understand their tone, not the words, and maybe it's even better that way.

I'm going to write today to the Miami Legal Aid Society, to find out what is going on. My mother talked to the Legal Aid people in Rhode Island, and they told her to tell me to write to Miami, but they said that we have little if any chance legally, since the doctors seem to be going to claim that you were incompetent when you married me. The dopes.

But I don't want to talk about such things till later today. This morning I want to tell you how much I love you, but no one has words to describe my love, not the greatest poets of all. I want you in my bed this morning so badly I can taste you, smell you, feel your soft warm flesh . . . and so once again I'll throw myself into my work, a poor substitute for you, I've been aching for you so terribly especially the past two weeks, since I've been alone in my quiet room, with time to sit and think and dream. I love you, I love you, I love you.

Here are a couple of pictures.† One was taken last summer, when I was clean-shaven and weighed 162, the lowest since I was sixteen. The other was taken this week, I weigh 175, bearded, sleepless, yearning for you, for love. Have I changed?

I'm going to stop for a few minutes now, before thinking about you drives me crazy. Tom is so happy that you wrote to him. Dick wrote to you yesterday. He is still running around homeless and unsettled in body and mind. He asks forgiveness for his silence, but he knows you know his thoughts are with you. We all love you, Sandy.

[Unsigned]

March 25, 1962

It's afternoon now, almost one o'clock, and I worked on my poem for almost five hours. I'm enclosing what I hope is the final version, in a little booklet I made for you. Lorenz Gude came up to see me, bringing me English muffins, and instructions for the papers I'm writing on labor and management. He's reading the poem, and we're listening to a tremendous weepy version of the "Ave Maria" in Spanish, which is punctuated with the usual refrain of "Pauvre de me" (or some such spelling).

The official title of the paper I must write for fifty dollars is "The Effects of Labor Legislation from the Wagner Act of 1935 up to the Present on Labor and Management Relations." Imagine that!

I finished reading a book called *Art and Outrage* today. It's a correspondence between Alfred Perles and Lawrence Durrell concerning the shameful censorship of Henry Miller's work in America. It also contains comments on the correspondence by Miller himself. Miller is a great man, and invariably I am cheered when I read his books, which are full of indomitable courage and faith and strength. I hope you like *Big Sur and the Oranges of Hieronymus Bosch.*

I know it must be boring there, and the temptation to inertia must be very great. Maybe you can get the doctor to give you a few pills! But seriously, do you think you could interest yourself in some sort of single project? You could translate Lorca's poems, for example; or read Rilke, or make a study of Shaw, or anyone you are interested in. Or poetry in general. I could send books, and whatever else you need, and maybe suggestions, comments, et cetera. I've always found that to sustain myself in any project it was important that I talk about it, write about it, make voluminous notes, even if I discarded them all later. But the discipline of forcing oneself to study *one* subject consistently, for a certain amount of time every day, is great. It gives you a realization both of how much can be accomplished through reason and discipline, and of how much cannot be accomplished that way, but rather must be blundered into. If you wanted to study Rilke, I have all his works, including prose, and I think he is possibly the greatest writer of our time, and one of the saints . . . or Shaw, I have nearly all his plays, much of his prose, my thesis, et cetera. Or poetry in general, I have thousands of poetry. Or anything else, I can get the necessary books quickly. I think it is necessary for your self-preservation that you get tough inside. But I find it hard to explain exactly what I mean. I love you the way you are, and I wouldn't want you to become like Barry may be. I mean a different kind of toughness, the internal toughness of being unconcerned with the approval or disapproval of people who do not understand you and me, and whose approval therefore is a bad sign anyway.

For example, I did my thesis for myself, to learn both about Shaw and about writing, and also to learn about discipline, and research, et cetera. But when I finished it seemed to me that if it was really good the people in high places shouldn't approve of it. They might think it was good, but if they wholeheartedly approved I would feel uneasy about my progress. And that is exactly what happened. The young professor who didn't know me admired my thesis. The older professors who knew me thought it was of sufficient merit to "make" me a "master of arts" but thought it necessary to remind me of rules of grammar, etc. Hell, they didn't even know what I was talking about, just as your mother and father didn't know what Jean Giraudoux was talking about, and just as they and the doctors no longer know what you are talking about.

Reading Rilke, or Lorca, or Shaw, or many others, seriously and with a fairly long-range plan of study, is not a crutch, it will not make you stronger, for you have to have it to begin with, but such a project will be a good reminder that you are strong, and that you are not alone, and that there is much to be done. Not to mention all that reading, for example, Bernard Shaw, will teach you about so many different subjects. What do you think?

Which reminds me, I am enclosing a book I got for you yesterday from among my things at Joe's. Shaw wrote it when he was just a young man, and I really like it. Tell me how you like it when you finish.

I'm going to stop again for a while, I want to work a little on the book I'm making for you, while some ideas are still fresh in my mind. But before I forget, I have a great new work from Joe to hang in my room. It's the collage he made of a poem of mine and a Pollock painting and some other things as a kind of portrait of me. He put a white frame around it, and it looks fine. We now have three paintings and a marvelous drawing by Joe to hang in our first place of our own. I love you so much, I pray we will soon have that place. More later. Meanwhile, here's a rough sketch of my room:†

It's three o'clock now, honey, and I just finished putting two poems into your book, one by Rilke and one by Hart Crane, and a painting by and picture of Hans Hoffman. The poem by Rilke has been running through my head for days, and the one by Hart Crane is one that never fails to thrill me. It's a marvelous Sabi poem, and as I was rereading it, typing it, once again I felt great shivers up and down my back and shoulders. I won't tell you what the poems were, but you'll get them soon, I promise.

Pachanga! says the radio!

Last night Tom and I and Dick went to see a movie made by the British called *The Day the World Caught Fire*. It had gotten a good review in the *Village Voice* (whose critic is good, though opinionated and a little intolerant). It was a very fine movie. The story involved a newspaperman and a girl, the newspaperman divorced and with a small son whom his wife didn't want to let him see. But that part of the plot was incidental. Mainly the story concerned the possible end of life on earth. A simultaneous nuclear test by the Russians and the Americans in two parts of the Arctic was of sufficient force to throw the earth off its axis, changing the climate by changing the polar regions and the equator, and also putting the earth in a path of movement which led it toward the sun. Everything got hot all of a sudden. The movie was in black and white, and there was a brilliant use of various shades of black and white, different kinds of lighting, to indicate the increasing heat on the earth. There were no villians in the picture, except for everybody. Which was what made it awful. Everyone, and I mean everyone, was caught up in pettiness, and everyone, and I mean everyone, was responsible, and I mean RESPONSIBLE for the ultimate crisis and destruction. The newspaperman was bogged down in cleverness, the girl (who was beautiful and reminded me of Margie, her name was Janet Munro) was an unquestioning sort of nice kid who was sure that "the government knows what is best." Everyone was well meaning, and no one really ever wanted to do any harm, but somehow everyone hurt everyone else all the time. There were some beautiful beautiful moments when one person or another came to for a few minutes, and tried humbly and haltingly to be loving and gentle, but of course everyone continually fell back into the old blind insensitivity. The picture played down all sensationalism. The major world powers exploded giant bombs at the end, to try to get the earth off its destructive path, and the results were not shown. But it took near-complete destruction to make everyone concerned and cooperative, and loving. But since we are all faced with complete destruction, namely death sooner or later, we are all going to die, why do we have to wait for war or scientific holocaust to love? The movie made this point marvellously, but I doubt if anyone or very many anyway noticed anything except that the H or I or JKLMNO bombs might mean the end of the world. It's the lack of love, the failure to be responsible, that is destroying us. Et cetera.

I think I have the Jonas Mekas review of the movie here, and if so I'll send it.

Gude is bursting to read me some section in his book (Erich Neumann's *The Origins and History of Consciousness*) so I'll stop a minute.

Introversion and extroversion and all that. Self-development, et cetera. I'll copy a poem here† for you that I wrote just before I left New York to go to New Orleans and Tulsa. It's not a good poem, but it should be interesting to you and I just thought of it while Gude was reading, and I was thinking not of his words but of your troubled face in the picture above me, your warmth and how much I want you and need you and love you.

[Unsigned]

March 26, 1962

Dear Sandy,

two letters from you today! And this is now one of those days
when I'm slightly delirious, and I don't know whether I want to
laugh or cry at the absurdity of everything! Goddamn! What's the
matter with everyone? The doctor! Goddamnit, doesn't he look at
you, talk to you, read your letters? How can he keep you locked up
there? Is he insane? Blind? Stupid? Dishonest? Is the world
upside down? All we want to do is love each other and live
together. What the hell!

These people! Goddamn, I can't believe it! Poe, Baudelaire,
Henry Miller, Tom Wolfe, Whitman, Céline, Arthur Rimbaud! A
drunk, a psychopath, a pornographer, a baby, a homosexual, a criminal, a satanic madman! Lock them all up, they're raving nuts. If we
don't put them behind some kind of bars they might murder us all,
rape the Blessed Virgin, blow up the White House, embarrass
everyone, make a disturbance, or write "Annabel Lee" and *Flowers
of Evil* and *Tropic of Capricorn* and *Look Homeward, Angel* and
Leaves of Grass and *Journey to the End of Night* and *Illuminations*!
Illuminations, hah, that's a good one! Better lock up Socrates, he's
inciting all the kids to quit work, mock great men, be beatniks; and
Jesus, that sonofabitch keeps telling everybody to quit work, too,
and give away all their possessions, and don't worry about it! And
Buddha, that bastard wants everyone to beg! That's o.k., but who
does he expect to feed all those people? I mean, some of us have to
put our shoulder to the wheel, and be responsible, and why should
we feed people who don't work? Why don't Buddha and Jesus and
Socrates get a job? What is he, a beatnik? Beatniks! Goddamn,
they're everywhere! Never work! Take pills! Make fun of America!
Ginsberg! Miller! Whitman! Poe! They should all be put in the
Jackson Memorial Hospital so that the world can be safe.

You know, honey, that's exactly the point. The world is not safe when you and I can be together, and when Dick and Tom and me and Lauren and Dave Bearden can be running loose, allowed to appear happy, vibrant, alive, and yes, right, and even great! Because if we look like that, and if you and me have a good life, and real love, then the world must be messed up. Because we are the minority. And look at the majority. We are different. We see it, they see it. We just want to be left alone. But violence is always the savior of the majority when they are faced with a danger that they may be wrong about how to live. They crucify Jesus, condemn Socrates to death, take Shelley's children away, ban Miller's books, label Ginsberg and Kerouac and thereby dismiss them.

What I'm trying to say, Sandy, is that I don't think it matters too much who your doctor is. I don't think that you are going to find one doctor who believes in me and you. Escape and/or deception are our only hope. I am tortured by a wish to run to you, to Miami, to try to get you out legally, to protest to the courts that you are my wife, we love each other, et cetera et cetera et cetera.

But when they look at me, then what? And I don't just mean my beard either but also when they look into my eyes. And when they ask my profession, then what? And how long we knew each other? And who thinks we should be apart? Only the eminently respectable, respected, prosperous, tolerant, kindly, well-dressed, well-liked, understanding physician and man of culture, that Freudian psychologist, published writer, and anxious tortured father, Dr. Louis Alper. And he is supported by his hardworking, strong-willed, well-liked wife, and that scion of knowledge and master of patronization, Dr. Jack E. Skigen. And just who thinks we should be together? Who is for us? Well, there's Tom Veitch, nineteen-year-old ex-Columbia student, unemployed. And Dick Gallup, ex-student at Tulane, twenty years old, unemployed, bearded (as well as he can do). And there's Margie Kepler, twenty-three years old, single, technician at a hospital in

Houston. And Mrs. Lucille Padgett, wife of a bootlegger in Tulsa, Oklahoma.

And all the rest. And I know you know all that I've just said (!), but I want to say over and over and over, even though I wish I didn't believe it, THERE IS NO ONE THERE THAT IS GOING TO BE FOR US. NO ONE. You will meet people who will be kind, intelligent, love their families, pat dogs, and treat patients kindly. But they are against us. They are against us. They wouldn't be there if they weren't. There are no Freuds at Jackson. There are no Henry Millers in Miami. There are only George Babbitts, who have been to college, read books, and gotten prosperous. These days the Babbitts have culture. But they are still invincibly ignorant. They are troubled occasionally, but not often. They rise up and unite very quickly when trouble shows up from outside "the Right Way to do things."

Get tough, honey. Get tough. Run away from them all, fast. And I'm not talking about running out of the hospital, although I want that, too. I mean run from their outstretched hands, their offers to "talk things over rationally," run away from sympathy with them. For now, they are the enemy. They want to be your friend. They really do. They want to help you. They want to make sure you are well-fed, clothed, and secure from pain and disease and hardship. The only catch is that you have to do it on their terms. If you don't, then it's the lock-up, the padded cell, the prison, the hospital. And their terms are very simple. You must *kill your soul*. You must destroy your spontaneity, your capacity to love, your generosity, your openness, your childishness, your big-eyed wonder at life. You must get your shoulder to the wheel, be responsible, make contributions to mankind, shape up and make money. Your contributions to mankind are measured by your income tax. Louis Alper obviously makes more contributions to mankind than Ted Berrigan. Look at the record. What record? Why the only record available. The income tax report. Berrigan has no money. Can he support a family? Since he has no money the answer is of course no. Why isn't he dead of malnutrition himself? Must be something sinister there. His poor old mother must work her fingers to the bone for him. Or maybe he robs banks. He must be trying to marry for money. Maybe he's homosexual. A writer? How come we never heard of him? Shelley died at thirty, and look at all he did. Berrigan is nearly thirty. How come we never heard of him? If he's a writer, where's his books? (Shelley died unknown except by a few.) Sandy, the deck is stacked, and so to win in this game, since we have to play, we have to have some new rules, or else a gun under the table. One thing at a time for us. First, to get you out. Next, to be together. Third, to keep us away from anyone who wants to try this kind of game again, until we have the power to destroy them if they try to destroy us. When that happens we'll be respectable, since power makes for respectability. When you can kill them they leave you alone, and grudgingly admire you, even if they fear and dislike you. Well, when we get that power, if ever, then we'll hold out our hands to them, and forgive them, and try to love them. Except of course we'll have to keep our eye on them for a while. But for now, we have to get a gun to keep under the table to make sure we have an equalizer for their stacked deck.

I don't think you should try to pretend that you don't think of me. They are very smart people. They have read your letters, most of them, and seen the "power I have over you." (Hah, they haven't seen the power you have over me! Maybe you are the sinister one, and I'm sick.) They know we will try to get together. That is why they are making long-range plans to keep you confined. They know that time does a lot of things to people. They think I will desert you in time. "Get out gracefully," says Dr. Skigen. "She'll get worse before she gets better." "It might be years," he says. Bullshit, I say. He is more obvious to me than I to him. Always remember that they are very smart. Never forget how your parents got you in there in the first place. They are smart, tough, unscrupulous, and dedicated. And also experienced. The only way to beat them is to stab them where they least expect it. To play by different rules than they expect you to.

Honey, all this is just a suggestion, and is out of the dirty lowdown part of me. I know this kind of stuff because my innocence is not like yours. What I have come from, going through things rather than from being beyond them. I've looked at these people carefully, and was very close to them once. The army, and college, and work, are the training schools where one learns to be capable of doing things such as your mother and father did to us. And I didn't ignore them, I watched them, all those years I was in those places. So I know how they play their games, and maybe I know how to beat them. If it was me in your place, this is what I would do. But I don't advise you either to do it, or not to do it. I feel I could do this, and my good feelings and love would still survive. Because of my own "age and experience." But I wouldn't want you to ever do anything against your own feelings. So much for that. Anyway, here is how I would fight them:

What ace do you have up your own sleeve, to counteract theirs? What weapon do you have to play against them? The answer is, that they are your parents, and they love you. They love you. I am sure they do. It is their fear and ignorance that made them do this, and I'm sure they think they are doing it out of love. So, that is where they are vulnerable. You can try to get them to leave themselves open through their genuine love for you. An example of what you could do is this: somehow you might try to get to see them more often. Tell the doctor you want to see your parents, you miss them, etc. Promise not to cause trouble with them. Then, if that works, try to act like your love for them, the sense of family, et cetera, is very important, and you want the whole family to love each other and not let misunderstanding cause a permanent rift. You want to be with me, but you love them, and don't want to upset them either. Et cetera. You must convince them that they are more important to you than I am. And you must do it subtly. Not let them know you think that, rather let them see it, than hear you ever say it. They will consider that a sign of progress. Show them that you fear being sent somewhere away from them, some hospital, that you are convinced that if you do have problems, family love and communion will help them most get solved. In other words, try to get to live at home, and if necessary, undergo analysis in Miami. Or anywhere where you aren't completely confined. Everything you will be working for here is less confinement. If your parents get convinced that you won't run away, they may relax their confinement a little, for an instant, so that you can run. You might have to do things like make false promises never to run, or always to go to your daddy in time of trouble, et cetera.

You see what I am saying, I don't need to try to detail it all. It might not even work at all anyway. And maybe it would be bad for you to try such a thing. But I must tell you about it anyway. I am not sure that to fight evil with evil is a good thing. But I am not sure that to act that way would be evil. For me I don't think it would. But I'm me, you are you.

It's just that I love you so much, I ache for you so much every day, every hour, I want so much to be with you, that I cannot refrain from telling you things I think might work to get us together again. I do know this: in order to achieve something as difficult as us being together is going to be, singular dedication and singlemindedness of purpose are absolutely necessary. As long as you are troubled about the morality of the situation, as long as you have faith that things might work out O.K., or that someone might help us, or that time will take care of it, then nothing will happen. The age of miracles is NOT passed. But there seem to be fewer people around who are willing to make miracles by backing up their giant faith with giant effort. I'm not railing at you, honey.

I'm trying to tell you that without the effort the faith is not enough and what is even more important, without the faith the effort is wasted. I know you love me. If you can set our love above everything until such time as we are together and equilibrium is restored I think that between us we may be able to work the miracle of thwarting your whole world and being together. But the balance of the effort in the beginning is all on your shoulders. I can't come to Miami with a band of merry men on white horses and get you out. The Sheriff of Sherwood Forest[5] has gone modern, and Robin Hood is outdated. But I can keep you out, I think. I can keep us together once we get together. I can get to you wherever you are, as long as it is not behind the bars of Jackson Hospital. But to break modern jails it takes money, and if I had money I could get you out with lawyers, and also if I had money they wouldn't be doing this to us anyway.

Sandy, dear, I love you so much. I didn't start out to write this kind of letter. All my bitterness at your parents and Dr. Skigen and all the other people who won't let us love in peace came bursting out on the clean white paper. If I've talked a lot of nonsense, forget about it. I won't read this over. The important thing in this letter is all the feeling that went into it. I have to hurl the energy it would take to ride a white horse to Miami out onto a white piece of paper. The reason I can read and write so much now is that I am bursting with rage and frustration and jealousy and love and lust and desire and every other feeling from A to Z, because of this impossible world where we cannot make love, cannot eat eggs and bacon, cannot walk around, cannot cry and laugh together, because I am some kind of creature called a "beatnik" (and I can't find a definition of that label anywhere) and because you, if you say you love me, are "disturbed," "immature," and whatever else they label you.

[5] Ted probably meant Nottingham. —Ed.

                              I love you.

I love you.

        I love you.

                  That's what I want this letter
to say.
             I am and mean to stay
          your husband
          forever and ever,
                 all my love,

                           Ted

March 27, 1962

Dear Sandy,

Hello. It's seven thirty at night, and I'm alone, reading books and thinking a lot about you. I'm sorry about Leslie. I like her a lot, and I'd like her to like me, and to feel good about you and me. She's got guts, and brains, too. But she has her own battles to fight. Don't worry too much about what she says about us. She needs to be against certain things right now, and maybe I symbolize some of those things and maybe you do too, and maybe together we symbolize a few more.

In one of the two letters I got today from you you asked me again about the illegality of the court procedures. Honey, we don't have a chance in any court, and if they have you in there illegally, nevertheless we cannot get you out. Those are the facts. They have the law on their side, and if somehow I could prove to someone that you are held illegally, you would not be released, you would be bound under some other provision, or else I would be confined, one way or another. We can't beat these guys under their terms, and the courts are strictly their home field. We positively cannot beat them in the courts. I wish it were different. But it isn't.

Sandy, these people are doing a terrible thing. And by "these people" I mean your parents, and all the doctors who cooperate with them. They are using our separation to break us apart. They plan to simply keep us apart and rely on our natural fears and desires and uncertainties to split us up. Every doubt that enters your mind as to whether or not you are sick, or we are somehow wrong about something, serves to help them. We must stick together, you and me, as if we were surrounded by enemies. For the time being we must believe 100% in each other. Everything you do must be 100% all right with me, and everything I do must be 100% all right with you. We must not think ever that the other is fallible in any way. We must not allow any doubts to creep in. There are people waiting around you with the only purpose of sowing doubt until doubt defeats us. A letter from Leslie for example can do much damage. The fact that you are in the mental ward no doubt influences Leslie's opinions, whether she thinks so or not. That is the kind of thing your parents are doing. To keep you locked up casts a shadow on your action, and your friends write you worrying about you, and you worry about yourself, and another doubt opens a gap between you and me, they think. We must guard against this tactic of theirs through complete belief in our love and complete faith in each other.

Please, please, you must not defend me, not to Leslie, not to your parents, not to doctors. If you want to praise me, to speak of our love, that is wonderful, but you must not defend me. These people are superior logicians and masters of tricky reasoning, and they will stand you on your head with Freudian terminology, intellectual claptrap, and cerebral hogwash if you try to argue with them. You must exhibit your faith, not with defense, but simply with calm decisive belief. You must show these people that their arguments may be brilliant but their points are not made. Leslie is their unwitting tool. To her you must illustrate that you are right, not by disdaining to argue the point, but by showing that you see she simply is unable to understand.

I'm sorry. I don't mean to lecture. But I feel very strongly that these people have no right to attempt to discuss us with you. Let them release you from their prison, and we will talk to anyone. They take away all your rights and then they want to talk things over with you, as one human being to another. I'd like to talk to them for fifteen minutes alone.

And so much for bombast. Honey, I miss you so much. Today I felt very good. I read fifty pages of a book called *The Origins and History of Consciousness* by Erich Neumann, and it was a great experience. And Dick and I were reading together, and being moved by the same book, and it was very good. And my day began with two letters from you, and my love for you filled me up and overwhelmed me with the joy of living.

Lauren and Bill McCullam came in separately a few minutes ago, Bill with a cup of coffee for me, and he and I had a long talk about Neumann's book, and Henry Miller, while Lauren read Arthur Rimbaud. I'll be glad when you meet these two, they are two of the smartest and best people I am acquainted with here, although they are both excessively cerebretonic and sometimes forget about Pepsi-Colas and underarms and their significance in the socio-politico-economical-microcosmic-macrocosmic struc-ture of human existence. (What?) I'm delirious.

I got a letter from Margie yesterday, she says she has written to you, it was a very beautiful letter, and it had a five-dollar bill in it, which she didn't even mention. Tell her, when you write, that I love her and it was one of the happiest things in my life that I could have you and her meet each other, and like each other, and like me, too. Goddamnit, maybe there is some good around here somewhere, there has to be for the world to produce its Margies.

Here's a picture of Arthur Rimbaud when he was sixteen.† My poem is not meant to be considered a translation, and is called an imitation in deference to Rimbaud. The poet often uses other material, and the test of its validity as art is how the poem itself stands up to itself. I mean for you, and any reader, to consider it only as a poem. That it has a frame of reference in Rimbaud's poem may provide some intellectual activity by way of comparison, etc., but mainly it is a poem by Ted Berrigan. I myself do not know more French than you, if as much. The poem in its final version is almost all mine, each image coming to me as a result of the organic development of the poem, not because Rimbaud used them. I did not hesitate to use my own meter rhyme rhythm et cetera.

Honey, I'd like to talk to you a little about the poem, mostly for my own benefit, to get straight a few things in my own mind. I haven't discussed it with anyone yet. So bear with me, if I seem to be talking to myself. I mean the poem to be about an individual, namely me, or whoever, in the journey of life thus far, which is roughly to about twenty or twenty-five years of age. The symbolic structure is that of a vessel sailing in a sea, or many seas which make up one vast sea. The rhythm of the poem is that of sailing on an ocean, with consistent sailing, at different paces. I don't want to try to analyze it stanza by stanza, but I do want to talk about some specific things. I mean to apply a scheme of Bergsonian evolution. That is, life as a creative process, striving for more life, life as a flowing stream endlessly moving on toward higher consciousness, more life, more light. In the first stanza the "I" of the poem says that he has shed all "masters" and is on his own, trusting his own whims. He has no need of disciples either. Once rid of masters and disciples he was free to travel his own ways, free. By this I mean that he has shed himself of all guides except the necessary guide, that is, his will, and of all responsibilities, except the most important one, himself. (This is the process of development which Shaw talks about in *The Q of I* in the section about the evolution of man's consciousness, which ends "Duty is the primal curse from which we must redeem ourselves . . .") The poem goes on to say that once he did this, he got in harmony with the flow of creative evolution and from then on no isle, nothing, knew greater triumph. Being in this harmony he was cleansed of all the stains of mundane activity and thought, of "rotgut wine and puke." The imagery throughout the poem is meant to suggest that the creative forces approved his obeisance to their drives, which of course seemed like aimlessness to people in general. Then the poem describes the storms, marvels, excitement, and despair, and fear of the journey of life. The "I" does not avoid all emotions, he experiences everything, denies nothing, but underlying it all, by means of his acceptance of everything, is a state of blessedness. The flow of the sea of life is its own reward, it excites you when you are dull, warms you when you are cold, lulls you when you are weary, as long as you remain true to life itself. To the "I" his only affinity is with children ("I'd like to show a child these Eldorados") for it is only children and the mad who understand these things. And this voyage encompasses both the male and the female, for one must be womanly as well as masculine to understand and live all the beauty and joy and sorrow and love of life. But there is loneliness involved, too.

He speaks of this. "I, a ship, wound in the hair of covers, / and hurled by hurricanes to a birdless place, / What Monitor or Hanseatic galleon, / would care for salvaging my tattered hulk?" Who would want him now? What commercial ship, what every-day person, would want a man who has experienced so much, and therefore seems battered, and/or dissolute?

But he would not turn back, away from his journey, which is in itself marvelous. It is not that he is going anywhere, like commercial ships. No, it is the actual sailing which is marvelous. He longs for new seas to sail, for the ancient seas of Europe and of magic, the Sargasso sea, Atlantis, anything unexplored, uncharted. Having seen the storms, can he pretend life exists without storms or would he even want life to exist without storms? No, he neither denies nor condemns any of his visions. He notes them all, praises them by his very tone.

But sometimes he feels bad. One cannot always sustain the pitch of intensity of the summits. He dreams of the force to come, the new life, where all shall sail their own ways, free. But it is not that way now. He weeps because of that. He weeps too much, it breaks his heart that he must be alone, the acrid romances which he must be involved in if he is to have any romance at all bloat him with their torpor. But no one is up to his own courage, his own journeying. He despairs and cries out, as Jesus cried that he was forsaken, "O let me burst, and I be lost at sea." But his very words deny their superficial meaning. He means let him be lost from acrid romances, not lost from life. He goes on, joyously. He does not look back and regrets nothing. The only European sea he still remembers, still fondly dreams of, is the sea upon which he set out. Because of his callow youth and ignorance then, he sees now that the sea he set out on was really only a puddle, but it was cold and black, and it took courage to begin. He remembers it with pride and nostalgia. All else is forgotten for it is now he rejoices in, and the future. He sees what men sometimes have thought they've seen. He has the vision of the holiness of life as it is. He ends by singing, "O Waves, since you have cleansed me, since I have become free from the forces of death by allowing myself to be in harmony with the sea of life, I have come awake, I am awake." And he repeats his beginning remarks about masters and crews, but with a new consciousness about his relationship with others. Now, he need no longer compete with others, no longer "brave the waving flags," no longer be conventionally heroic, and now, also, he no longer needs to hate those poor people imprisoned in their lives. He is free. Once, for his own development, to assure that he stayed free, he needed to hate crews, and masters. Now he is beyond good and evil. He is bathed in the waves of eternal creative energy, and he surges as freely as a child's mind, on his own ways, free, and at the same time on the way of eternal creations and life.

This poem represents to me a manifesto against my own need to hate those people whom I must not be like. Through my love for you, which in itself required a giant period of self-development by me, I feel I have reached a stage where I do not have to hate the Barrys and the Hoffmans and maybe even the Lennys, so that I won't be like them, I feel that I have been smiling on the sea of creation for a sufficient time, with sufficient consciousness, that I have killed in myself these elements which made me like Hoffman at his worst and Barry at his worst and Lenny at his worst. I need no longer be afraid of succumbing to intellectual emptiness, or cynicism based on fear, or collegiate poeticism. Once I had to hate people who were like that, because if I did not hate them I might succumb to being like them. Now I rejoice for them that perhaps the way they are is a stage in their development, especially the young poets for even if they are only poets for the self-glory of being a poet, nevertheless they have come a long way. Maybe they will surpass me, and teach me something.

Wow! I'm not sure what I just said, but it was a lot in quantity if not in quality.

My darling, the wordiness of my letters is all meant to add up to three words, which cannot express themselves anyway. I love you. I could say those words to you so much better with my mouth, my hands, my eyes, my flesh and warmth, if only we were together. But now I must say them with my words, words about friends and poems and courts and self-development and letters and books and love. Forgive my inadequacies, my bumbling proud arrogance and boyish stupidity. Before you I am naked, I am humble, I am my true self. "A jackass with the heart of a lion" said Saroyan with much truth. And if I am not always up to my best self even with you, it is because I am still trying to grow, still a baby. Have patience with me, my wife, have faith in me and in us, love me, and I will grow strong for you. I shall be forever your husband.

All my love,
Ted

March 28, 1962

My darling Sandy,

this week in *Time* magazine, in the column called "Milestones,"
following announcements of the marriage of Linda Christian and
Edmund Purdom, and the divorce of Coya Knutson (the ex-
congresswoman), there was this announcement,

> DIED. C. (for Charles) Wright Mills, 46, angriest of
> the U.S.'s younger sociologists, a burly, motorcycle-
> riding Columbia University professor from Texas,
> who aroused wide-spread ire among the U.S. middle
> class with his jeremiads about them and the upper-
> class. Mills contended that "there are more men of
> knowledge in the service of men of power than men
> of power in the service of men of knowledge." Died
> of a heart attack in NY.

Goddamn! Honey, I don't know if Wright Mills was a great man
or not. But he was a painfully honest man who was terribly
distressed about America, the country he loved. His books, like
The Power Elite, were scholarly, well-written, detailed accounts of
the diseases which are eating up America. Mills pointed out with
undeniable accuracy just who runs America (the rich, the generals,
the power elite), and just what the results are (decay). In his book
The Causes of World War III, he wasted little time talking about
Russians or Chinese, and showed exactly what we, as Americans,
were and are doing to make World War III inevitable. And finally,
in his book *Listen, Yankee*, he told the truth about Cuba and the
Cuban rebels. Kenneth Tynan, the eminent British critic and man
of letters, who served as drama critic for the *New York Times* for a
year on an exchange basis, said about *Listen, Yankee:*

C. Wright Mills has written the indispensable book
on the Cuban revolution, an inside look—urgently
needed—at a unique historical test case.

Among Mills's points in the book are that the Cuban revolution has been misrepresented by ignorance and lies; that the
Cuban resentment against the u.s. is based on real grievances; that
America is in danger because its own ignorance and arrogance are
causing it to lose all respect by Latin America.

Sandy, I thought *Listen, Yankee* to be one of the most important books I have ever read. It further awakened me to my own
ignorance, which is partly due to the lack of honest information
available to us in America concerning what happens in the world.
The newspapers and magazines are complete liars, and also complete boobs. I'm enclosing the book for you to look at when you
get a chance. And for Mills, dead at forty-six, I can only offer him
these words to you.

Here's a poem from a book I got yesterday. It was one of the first
poems I ever fell in love with. I wrote an imitation of it when I
was twenty-two that I've since lost. It's by Robert Herrick, who
used to hang around with all them Mermaid Tavern beatniks like
Chris Marlowe and Ben Johnson and Will Shakespeare and those
other bums.

THE ARGUMENT OF HIS BOOK

I sing of Brooks, of Blossoms, Birds, and Bowers:
Of April, May, of June, and July-Flowers.
I sing of May-poles, Hock-carts, Wassails, Wakes,
I write of Youth, of Love, and have accesse
By these, to sing of cleanly Wantonnesse
I sing of dewes, of raines, and piece by piece

Of Balme, of Oyle, of Spice, and Amber-Greece.
I sing of Times trans-shifting; and I write
How roses first came red, and lilies white.
I write of groves, of twilights, and I sing
The court of Mab, and of the Fairie King.
I write of Hell; I sing (and ever shall)
Of Heaven, and hope to have it after all.

Robert Herrick

"Small-voiced, perfect-singing Herrick," wrote Tom Wolfe. Do you like Herrick?

Honey, Mr. Beam sounds interesting. He seems to have spirit and a sense of humor, too. But his changes in your poem are terrible. And your poem is wonderful. It is natural, a little stiff, which only adds to its reality and presence. It is very natural and good. Let him change them (your poems) all he wants, if it makes him feel good, and if it makes a bond between you, but send me the original copies first. I love your writings. They are you, and I feel thrilled when I read them in the same way that I am thrilled when I see you. I love you more all the time, if that is possible. Last night I lay in my bed, tortured once again by the problem of what to do. I want to run to Miami, and raise hell, and at least have both of us locked up, instead of me out and you in. But there is a faint possibility that we may get together soon, as long as one of us is out. And I can do no good there. But it tortures me to sit here, to write to you about my freedom, when you are there. Honey, don't be resigned. Don't give up. You need to be actively unresigned, or inertia will beat you down. I worry terribly when you write that there is nothing to do but eat and sleep. They are trying to make you soft, and vulnerable. Today I am going to write to your parents, not because I think it will do any good, but because I want to remind them that their solution cannot work. I want to tell them that they must not think that if they wait long enough everything will be all right. I'm spinning in circles trying to know what to do. I can't write, my poems are not there. My translation was the only kind of thing I could do. I'm tied up in knots and desperately in need of you. I love you very much.

I have more to write, but I want to write your parents right now, so I'll write to you later, of how I sat in on Kenneth Koch's lecture on Wallace Stevens yesterday, and what NY is like today, and how much I love you.

Your Husband forever,
Ted

March 31, 1962

Dearest Sandy,

it's noon Saturday and Easter vacation has started at Columbia. Harry and Eddie and all the rest have gone to their assorted homes, and only Dick and Tom are left around. Ron is still here, but still in the hospital. Now that everyone is gone, things are much quieter.

As I told you, I sat in on Kenneth Koch's class last week. Dick and Tom did, too. Koch lectured on Wallace Stevens, and it was the best lecture I have ever seen or heard on a poet. He read selections from "Le Monocle de Mon Oncle," and from "The Comedian as the Letter C," and also a few shorter poems, and he read with such verve and enthusiasm that the lines just leaped off the page. He also read from *The Tempest* to show that Stevens writes language very much like Shakespeare. He talked about Stevens's devices, and he said that it is the surface that really makes a poet interesting. Because if you cut deeply into poets you find sayings, but on the surface is the way they say them. Koch is very graceful, almost effeminate, and he reminded me of Nijinsky. The whole performance was like a ballet, and was glittering and sparkling all the way through. At one point he read twenty lines or so, and then said not to ask him what it meant, but didn't it SOUND great. At the end of the class when he was passing back papers to people, and everyone was running around to get their papers, and the room seemed to be filled with chaos, Koch paused in the middle of calling names and said, "What excitement!" It was great. When you come to New York, we will sit in on classes by Koch, and also by Robert Lowell, who teaches at the New School for Social Research.

I just got up, and I'm having some brownies and a Pepsi for breakfast. Yesterday I worked some more on your book, putting in poems by Herrick, and Andrew Marvell, and William Carlos Williams, and Archibald MacLeish, and some paintings and portraits. But it is a bigger book than I thought. It will take a little while longer to fill it. Also, in a day or two I'll have some money, and I'm going to enclose five or more dollars, so that you will begin to have a little money in case you can use it. I wish I could send a hundred, but it will have to be a little at a time.

I still am not writing much, but I am getting a lot of reading done, and the book I am reading now is one of the greatest books I've ever read. It gives order to much of the thinking I've done in the past couple of years. To me a great book is one that does just that: gives order to your thinking. This book is Erich Neumann's *The Origins and History of Consciousness*. It is a study of self-development on both a microcosmic and macrocosmic level. That is, it treats self-development from the standpoint of mythology, covering the development of the individual with reference to the various creation myths, etc. It is the story of the various stages of development in the development from unconsciousness to ego consciousness. I guess that is pretty vague, but the book is great. It will be good for you to read sometime.

It's later now, nearly six, and I haven't gotten much accomplished today. But I did get one thing settled. I got evicted from my room. It seems that I have too many visitors at odd hours of the night and day. It's too bad, I like this little room, and I dislike getting disrupted and having to move again. It seems that anyone who sleeps days and stays up nights and has visitors is bad. There were no complaints from the other tenants. All Dick and I or Lauren and I or Tom and I did in my room at night was read books. But the owners just thought that something was wrong. They don't like it when things don't fit their patterns of thought. They could give me no reason for not having visitors except that "it isn't right." And I didn't press them much. I'm getting used to it. But

I hope I can find a place where I can relax. Meanwhile, another tiresome change of address. I'll get mail here until Tuesday. So you better write to me at Eddie Kaim's until further notice. Dick is staying there, and I'll get my mail from him. The address is c/o Edward Kaim, 320 West 106th Street, Apt. #4. I'll send you my new address as soon as I have one.

I went to see a movie called *Last Year at Marienbad*. It's the new movie by Alain Resnais, who made *Hiroshima Mon Amour*. It's a collaboration with the French writer Alain Robbe-Grillet, and it is one of the greatest things I have ever seen. Do you know anything about it? It is the story of a man and woman at a rich resort. The usual partying, dancing, shooting, card-playing, and concerts are going on. The woman is there with her husband. The other man makes her acquaintance, and tells her, a little bit at a time, each time they meet, that they know each other. They met last year at Marienbad, or maybe it was Friedrichsbad, or somewhere else. She denies it. He tells her exactly what they did, what she said, what he said, what they were wearing. She continually denies it. He tells her that they made love. That they deceived her husband. That she asked him to go away for a while, a year. That now he is back. She denies, and denies, and denies. The movie shows the two of them. It shows the scenes he describes, as he describes them. It shows the vague flickers of memory in her. It shows her husband doing this and that. It shows some things that might have happened, things that did happen, things that maybe didn't happen. She seems to remember some of it all, but denies it. He insists, not that it really did happen, but that she gave herself freely, it was not forced. She denies and denies. Finally, she goes off with him, leaving her husband, after giving her husband a final chance to *see* her. He does not see her. The movie is presented in such a way as to make it all seem unreal and real at the same time. The characters sometimes move as if they were in a slow-motion ritual dance. Sometimes they are completely symbolic, other times completely flesh and blood. There is no story nor plot as such. Time is almost nonexistent in a chronological sense. There is only day and night, darkness and light. Throughout the movie there is the recurrence of a game, played with a number of matches laid out on the table, and two people alternate picking up any number of matches they wish, from one row at a time. Whoever picks up the last one loses. People watching the game, played mostly by the woman's husband, who always wins, keep saying that whoever moves first loses. But it isn't true. There is a trick of knowledge to it. Whoever knows wins. The husband always wins the game. But everything isn't a game. His wife remembers last year at Marienbad, or maybe it was Friedrichsbad, and she leaves him. When she first meets the man, she asks his name, and he says it doesn't matter.

The movie is masterful. It concerns life and death, and the chance for new life. If only people would remember when they were alive, they would always renew their lives. But they don't remember. There is always something between them and life: walls, games, responsibilities. They don't remember.

I remember when you were Chris Murphy, and I remember you when you were in high school and you had a crush on me. I remember when I was Lenny. I remember when you were Pat, and Anne. I remember when we first made love. When we were alive. We are alive. I want to be with you, because we are alive together. We are not concerned with who moves first, or who doesn't, because we aren't concerned with games. We were together last year at Marienbad, and shall be together again. We are together now. I love you so very very much.

Yesterday I looked at pictures of you as you were in 1960, and in 1959, and in 1958. You were so beautiful, even as you are now. In 1959 you looked more like you did at Tulane than you did in 1960. You were so cute when you were a sophomore in high school. Just a baby. In 1958 I was in college. A big bad college boy, running around, reading a few books, trying to make the love scene, the sad scene, the mad scene, the poet scene. We try so hard. Honey, I worry about you all the time, every hour, every day. You've never been kicked around like this before. You are so trusting, so good, I am afraid that these people are going to get to you, because you expect only goodness from everyone. I love your innocence and your sweetness. But the innocence that comes from experience is often vulnerable. I know you've got the stuff, that they can't break you. But I can't help being terribly afraid much of the time. Nothing as good as you ever happened to me before. I never came together before as I do with you. I am afraid. Fight for us, honey. Fight. The only way I can fight for us is with words. To you, to your parents, to the doctors. And they are liable to do as much harm as good. Help me, Sandy. I need you. I need your strength to supplement mine, as I want mine to supplement yours. Let's beat this game. Let's prove that love must win. I love you and need you so much. I've never told anyone before that I needed them.

Good-night for now and all my love forever,

                                        your husband,
                                        Ted

April 1, 1962

My darling Sandy,

it's April Fool's Day, it's raining out, Bach's *Brandenburg Concertos*
are being played over the radio, and I'm sitting here in my room
with two April fools, Tom and Dick. Tom is reading my secret journals, looking for material to prove to himself that he is better than
me, and Dick is reading a French article on poetry. Tom just gave
me a picture he had taken in Chicago, to send to you.

It's 2:45. All day every day in everything I do I find myself
mentally writing a letter to you. By the time the end of the
evening comes I have so much to tell you that I forget half of it.
But I'll tell you all of what happened today, or a lot of it, anyway.

I woke up at ten, after reading late last night until about three
thirty. When I got up I decided I was hungry, so I dressed,
brushed my teeth, washed my face and hands, and gathered up all
the money I had, which was four cents in the form of two empty
Pepsi bottles. I figured out that I couldn't eat much on that, so I
took my book with me and went out and cashed the bottles and
went down Broadway the six blocks to Dick's place (Ed Kaim's).
I woke Dick up, and made coffee, and ate a raisin roll which
someone had left there. We drank the coffee, and I read some of
my book while Dick came to life, and played the Gregorian chant
record that was on the phonograph. We decided we were still
hungry so we gathered up a bunch of bottles, thirty-one cents
worth, and went to the store where we bought a ten-cent coffee
cake and two Pepsis. On the way back we decided that that wasn't
enough, so we flipped a coin to see who would go find some more
food. I lost. Dick went back to Ed's, and I wandered down to
Tom's which was four blocks farther down Broadway. He was
asleep, but the door was open, so I went in, knocked on his
bedroom door, told him to wake up, and went into the kitchen. I

looked in the icebox, and saw some canned pears, so I immediately ate half of them. Then I looked in the freezer, and saw three cans of frozen orange juice, so I took one. Then I looked in the cupboard, and saw two cans of ravioli, so I took one. I also took four pieces of bread and put them in my pocket. Then I went back to Tom and asked him if he wanted to come over for breakfast. He asked me what we were having, and I said ravioli. He laughed, and said that's what he was having, too. He said he'd be over later. So, I went back to Dick's, and we flipped again to see who would cook, and I lost, so I cooked the ravioli, and we ate ravioli and bread and drank Pepsi and had coffee cake for dessert. Then he played the guitar, and I read the last sixty pages of my book. I finished volume one of *The Origins and History of Consciousness*. Ron showed up about that time, and while he looked around for food, I rearranged the room a little so I could move in for a week until Ed came back. Then Dick and I decided to go and see Gude, and look around the bookstore at Columbia, and he wanted to try to get some cigarettes. Gude wasn't home, but Dana was there, and he gave Dick some cigarettes, and gave us fifteen cents, with which we bought a Pepsi and came to my room to drink. Dick is going to carry some of my stuff down to Ed's while I write to you, and read a little and take a shower. While we were drinking the Pepsi Tom showed up and wanted to look in my journals, because he's making a list of every book he ever read and he thought I might have listed some books which he has forgotten. So, that's what he's doing now. Also, we decided to go to the movies tonight, so we discussed where we could get some money. We decided that Padgett and Edelblute (Tom's roommate) might have some money. From time to time Tom makes obscure comments on what I've written in my journal. He also showed me a picture of his secret love, named Sandy Frey, which he once kept wrapped up in paper and didn't look at for a year (the picture, not Sandy Frey).

Also, I thought a lot during the day, about writing to you, about girls passing by in the street, about H. L. Mencken, about telling you about the book I'm reading, about Dana's writings which he showed us while we were in his room, about moving out of here, about not getting a letter from you yesterday, and about the Marx Brothers in modern poetry.

What do you think about all that?

I'm going to take a shower now, and read a few pages, and kick Dick and Tom out, and try to figure out why my typewriter keeps making mistakes, and then write some more to you.

I haven't done any of that yet, but Dick and Tom left, and I read a few pages of Mencken, and thought of quoting something from them to you, but instead I want to show you this poem, which I keep meaning to show you but keep forgetting.

BALLAD OF THE GOODLY FERE   (fere = mate)
Simon Zelotes speaketh it somewhile after the Crucifixion

Ha' we lost the goodliest fere o' all
For the priests and the gallows tree?
Aye lover he was of brawny men,
O' ships and the open sea.

When they came wi' a host to take Our Man
His smile was good to see,
"First let these go!" quo' our Goodly Fere
"Or I'll see ye damned," says he.

Aye he sent us out through the crossed high spears
And the scorn of his laugh rang free,
"Why took ye not me when I walked about
Alone in the town?" says he.

Oh we drunk his "Hale" in the good red wine
When we last made company,
No capon priest was the Goodly Fere
But a man o' men was he.

I ha' seen him drive a hundred men
Wi' a bundle o' cords swung free,
That they took the high and holy house
For their pawn and treasury.

They'll no' get him a' in a book, I think,
Though they write it cunningly;
No mouse of the scrolls was the Goodly Fere
But aye loved the open sea.

If they think they ha' snared our Goodly Fere
They are fools to the last degree.
"I'll go to the feast," quo' our Goodly Fere,
"Though I go to the gallows tree."

"Ye ha' seen me heal the lame and blind,
And wake the dead," says he,
"Ye shall see one thing to master all:
'Tis how a brave man dies on the tree."

A son of God was the Goodly Fere
That bade us his brothers be.
I ha' seen him cow a thousand men.
I have seen him upon the tree.

He cried no cry when they drave the nails
And the blood gushed hot and free.
The hounds of the crimson sky gave tongue
But never a cry cried he.

I ha' seen him cow a thousand men
On the hills o' Galilee.
They whined as he walked out calm between,
Wi' his eyes like the grey of the sea.

Like the sea that brooks no voyaging
With the winds unleashed and free,
Like the sea that he cowed at Genseret
Wi' twey words spoke suddenly.

A master of men was the Goodly Fere,
A mate of the wind and sea.
If they think they ha' slain our Goodly Fere
They are fools eternally.

I ha' seen him eat o' the honey-comb
Sin' they nailed him to the tree.

Ezra Pound

That's one of the first poems I liked by Ezra Pound. I think
his use of the Scotch dialect must have been influenced by
Robert Browning, and maybe Lawrence, as well as Robert
Burns. But it seems very effective to me, and the tone is similar
to "Scots Wha Hae Wi' Wallace Bled." Do you like it? Do you
like Ezra Pound? I'd like to send you some books of poetry, to
browse around in when you feel like it. Shall I? I have a lot of
anthologies. Then you could quote some poems to me too. Tell
me which poems of Lorca you like best. Someone told me
yesterday they thought Lorca was very conceited. What do you
think about that?

I wrote to your parents yesterday. I told them I didn't think a letter
would make any difference, but that I felt like writing it anyway. I

begged them to let us live our life together. I told them that you know how to tie your own shoes, tell time, carry on a conversation, read, write, and come in out of the rain, and that I did too, and what more could we start with. I told them we wanted no money, no anything, just a chance. I tried to tell them how much I love you, how much we love each other, how no annulment would end our marriage. I tried to tell them that they were only making any kind of happiness for you, for me, and for them impossible. I told them that we all knew that you could be released anytime they gave the word. Honey, I am sure it didn't make any difference, and maybe only made things worse, but I wanted to do something, and I wanted to show them, and partly you, too, that I am trying with the only weapons at my command to bring us together.

This book which I am reading is a study of the development of human consciousness from unconsciousness to high consciousness. It is a Jungian study but goes further than Jung. It deals with the mythology of all peoples of all times, and correlates the stories of mythology with the development of human consciousness. Basically, as far as I've read, Erich Neumann considers the development of consciousness as a creative evolutionary process. He talks about it on two levels at once, the level of the archetype and the personal level. That is, the abstract and the concrete. On the personal level, we are, to begin with, nearly completely unconscious. We are completely dependent upon our parents, our instincts, et cetera. Later we become aware of our differentness. Differentness from everything. We are we, everything else is else. From that moment on our development is a matter which we must attempt to take in hand, or else we are doomed to a lower life, and incomplete life. This I am telling you is so incomplete, and superficial, but it ties in with all that we have talked about, about selfishness, et cetera. The person who becomes aware that he is, that he is different from everything else, and everyone discovers it sooner or later, is then faced with the problem of how to live. The answer is to be more conscious, to search the darkness and the dust for more life, more light. Light is always a symbol of consciousness. The major way that this is accomplished is through the casting off of all masters, until one can stand on one's own two feet. The obvious masters that must be cast off first are the parents. Often we need other masters or goals to help us cast off early ones. Everything is relative. It is not the parents we must break from, it is our dependence upon them. Gradually, by combining the will, the instincts, with the mind, and reason, we become reasonably self-sufficient. But we are not "saved," we are only ready to go on further by ourselves. At this point we must reunite with some of the very things we have discarded in the past. But we do so from a new point, not the old. What we reunite with is the unconscious, we mate our will, our desires, with our consciousness, our reasoning self, and try to be even more creative. That is, we try to again be innocent, but from the vantage point of having seen and known good and evil. We may reunite with masters, but from the point of knowing what the dangers are. I would like to go on and on, but I'm getting further away from specifics and I don't want to do that. It seemed to me as I read that there were many things in this book about us. About me, about you. You are the person who can make me, help me. Because you are yourself, not for any magical reason. Because you are so good and innocent, and beautiful. And I am good for you, I think, I hope, I'm sure. But the old order wants itself to continue, and your parents as representative of the old order of things are fighting very hard to keep you under their dominance. You must throw off their dominance. But you must be careful not to think that it is them you are repudiating. You are demanding your natural rights, you are not taking anything from them. If it hurts them, that is bad, but it is worse that you will be hurt. When they see that you continue to be good they will feel all right. But right now they are calling all their weapons into play to keep you under their dominance. They feel that you cannot take care of yourself. They think you are a part of them, and that if you separate from them you cannot possibly avoid harm because you will be incomplete. They refuse to allow you to have self-consciousness. They deny your individuality. The first step you took away from the family without guidance from them, they jumped on you with both feet. It is up to you to assert and assert and assert that they cannot have you that way. But I don't know if they will ever give in. Will they? They are convinced with all their hearts, it seems, that you cannot make it on your own. I know they are wrong, and you do too, but they have much support for themselves. The mass is always against the coming to life of the young, because the mass is always the old order, and the young are the heralds of a new order which must overthrow the old order in order to have a place. What is happening to us, honey, is something that happens all the time to all children in all ages when they try to be adults. And sooner or later we always win. But our situation is more vivid, more dramatic. And while it is true that they cannot get you back into the unconscious, nevertheless they may be able to maintain the status quo and keep us apart. The least bit of sympathy on your part, of weakness, will strengthen them even more. You must learn to "believe the necessary lies." You must "learn to hate," that you "may preserve your love." If you are to love your parents later, love anyone later, you must love yourself now so much that for yourself you will do anything necessary to avoid being killed, to avoid being swallowed up and kept from your natural right to grow. I weep for all you must go through. I am not you, and my advice, often bad for myself, is liable to be contradictory, confusing, wrong, whatever. But I love you very much. I want you to be, to grow. I don't want a pupil, or a slave, I want a lover, a wife, to walk by my side, and hold my hand, and lead me where she can see better than I. And I don't want to be a father, I want to be a lover, a husband. With you I am a husband, with me you are a woman, a wife. Every day every minute I want you, I need you, I love you.

Your husband forever,
Ted

April 2, 1962

Dear Sandy,

Ravi Shankar is an Indian musician. He plays the sitar, which is a stringed instrument, and it produces some very strange exotic sounds. Shankar played the background music for *The Apu Trilogy* movies *(Pather Panchali*, etc.). I underlined his name because I was surprised that Miller mentioned him. Miller seems to have read or known or heard all the somewhat esoteric figures that I've liked, such as Shankar, and Korzybski, among others.

Big Sur is a very good book. It is not as "wild" in one sense, but it is Henry Miller all the way through. I want very much for you to read *Tropic of Capricorn,* and *Tropic of Cancer,* but I'd rather have you read them when we are together, and when I can re-read them and we can talk about them. They are the most stimulating books I have read in a long time. Miller is very alive, and he is a slap in the face to every convention of our time. He is perhaps one of the few true legendary heroes of our time, a figure to rank with Perseus, and Odysseus, particularly the latter. Miller is the hero of new consciousness, the explorer of new concepts of ethics, morality, honor, and dignity. He is a good man.

I haven't seen Joe in almost two weeks, and Anne in over a week, but I am glad they wrote to you. Joe is surprising looking to people who don't know him. And you are right, his hair is beautiful. I'll enclose a picture of Anne that I have in my scrapbooks, if I can find it, in case she didn't send one. As for bursting into success, it just isn't going to happen. Frank O'Hara, whom I consider the best poet in America, is thirty-seven now, and is just beginning to be known. *Meditations in an Emergency* was a failure commercially. Koch has published one book, which also was a commercial failure. Publishing houses like Grove Press support their ventures into poetry by publishing such books as *Cain's Book.*

They lose money on all poets except such people as Cummings or Eliot, who are established. And when a poet does become popular it is usually because his work is superficial. Poets, once the few know they are good, make their money through lectures, through teaching appointments, by writing reviews, and through writing other kinds of books, such as Robert Graves does, or by editing anthologies.

Honey, I sent "Words of Love," and "Poems for Biographers," and "Poem in the Traditional Manner" to *Locus Solus* in Paris, and gave them your return address if they wanted to get in touch with me. I wanted you to know first if I got published. It won't be for a little while, and if you are gone, the mail will be forwarded somewhere. Is that all right?

I'm going to stop for a while. It's nine in the morning and I just got up and went and got your letter and a Pepsi for breakfast. I like to start off my day reading your letters, and writing to you. For a little while I'm going to drink breakfast and read Neumann. I'll be back in a few minutes.

Hello. It's much later now, almost seven o'clock at night, and I'm all moved over to Eddie's. Dick and Tom helped me move my stuff. We loaded everything into a baby carriage which we borrowed, and made it in two trips. Now I have a little corner to work in here, and the first thing I'm doing in it is writing to you.

I have a lot of small art books for you, all pictures, and I'm going to send them tomorrow. I want to talk about them to you, but I have to look at them again before I can.

I also have a small book by Henry Miller called *To Paint Is to Love Again*. It's just an essay, with some reproductions of some of his watercolors in it, and a few pages of writing. I like it, and maybe you will, too.

Are you well? I know that's an odd question, but I mean how do you feel besides bored? How much do you weigh? Tell me how you think you look, how you feel.

What do your parents say about Mimi? I wonder what she thinks about us, about me. I wonder what they tell your older sister, and what she thinks. Does she write to you? Do you write to her?

My mother says your letters are lovely, and that you call her Mother Berrigan. She wrote to your mother for the second time three weeks ago, asking her to let us be together, but she received no answer. I guess your parents think I have my mother fooled, and that she doesn't realize what a bad fellow I am. My mother doesn't fool easily. My mother also said she hadn't sent you a picture of herself, so I'll put one in. I'd put one in of my father, too, but I only have one, it's not very good, and I want to show it to you rather than send it. He was a man that could not be captured in a photograph.

I'll also draw a picture of Ed's place so you can see my new room. It's much bigger than the other place, which I'm not sure is so good, and it has a lot of things in it which have nothing to do with me, but it's home for a while anyway.

I thought of you very often today, and especially when I took your picture down from the wall to move. One of these days when I move we will move together, to our own place, where everything in it is you and me. Then we will break in the bed, the floor, and the closets by making love everywhere. And we will just lie still and look at everything and each other for a very long time. I love you very much. Good-night.

Your husband forever,
Ted

Here're pictures of Anne and my mother (2) and me, Kathy, and my mother.† I love you.

April 4, 1962

My darling Sandy,

it's ten in the morning, cold out in spring. I just woke up, ate a
hamburger, drank a Pepsi, read your two letters, and then read
Dick's new poem which he wrote last night while I was asleep. ·
Here it is:

LOVE SONNET

To the single and embodied Muse

Your hair
Moves slightly, and your hand in mine
Rains through my mind in torrents,
Melting the snowdrifts with wine.
How the smell of such becoming skin
The delighting pressure of such thighs
The taste of such delicate mouth
Draw my flesh to where you lie!

As flesh is made to touch, my love,
And minds, too, must touch to be complete,
Then welcome tonight my hands upon your skin:
The night's chilly winds will then depart,
And as the sun's light will be your kin,
So will I ever take your song to heart.

Dick Gallup
New York City
April 4th, 1962

I really think it is very good, especially the first four lines, which are truly poetry. Do you like it? It is the third or fourth poem Dick has written since we got to NY, and easily the best.

But I started to write to tell you how beautiful your letters are, how they make me sad and happy at the same time, how alive you are, how your beauty and life shine through your words, your handwriting, your expressions. I love you very much.

Sandy, I hope you keep a list of all you're reading. It's fascinating, and enlightening too to be able to look back later and see what books you were reading during a certain period of time, and it may be especially interesting to see what you read while you were locked up. I'd like to see it, anyway.

I think Wright Mills's book on Cuba is essentially correct. It was written three years ago roughly, but I think we are still wrong, we meaning America. Anyway, the book is good, don't you think? He is a good writer as well as a good arguer.

Here are the art books I told you about. Henri Rousseau is a fascinating man. His paintings have a weird fascination. They achieve a three-dimensional effect, and at the same time they embody absolute stillness and a sense of impending motion. Even where there is action in the painting there is still a kind of quiet and unearthly stillness. You may have seen his *Sleeping Gypsy* in the Modern Museum. It is a great painting. The lion's tail is marvelous.

Raoul Dufy has always been a favorite of mine. His color is so fresh, so alive, so airy. He uses a dominant color often in a painting, and shapes the painting to the color. His greens, his blues, his reds, always make me feel light and happy and healthy and like skipping rope. There is a Dufy in Providence at the School of Design Museum that is very good, and the greatest Dufy I have ever seen is at the Museum of Modern Art.

Maurice de Vlaminck is a man I know very little about, but there is tremendous strength in his paintings. I first discovered him when Joe and I used to go around to all the galleries in New

York and look at paintings. His skies are tremendous. They make me feel the wind before the storm blowing on my face. Purple skies or blue, and then the rains. His still life in here seems good to me, too. He is a wild man who has tremendous control, and in fact his control is what he uses to make wild paintings. I am beginning to like him a lot.

Do you like Chagall? He is Jewish, and very popular right now, because he recently finished a world-famous series of twelve stained glass windows for a Jewish temple in Israel. The windows were exhibited at the Modern Museum before they were installed, and I saw them. They were bright, and strong, and a lot like some of the paintings in here. He is one of the few painters now who paints the human figure effectively and not banally. His earlier paintings I think are better than his more recent ones, but I like him. I tried to get all books of painters I liked. Chagall I think influences Henry Miller's watercolors. Miller always was attracted to Jews as influences and bed partners. Incidentally, one of the greatest minds of nineteenth- and twentieth-century painting was Jewish, Camille Pissarro, the real inventor of pointillism, without which modern painting might be very different. Henri Rousseau is Jewish, too. The goddamn Jews are everywhere, as usual. Scratch a genius, find a secret Jew. That's why I married you. I want you to tell me all the Jewish secrets, so I can be a genius.

Joan Miró is truly a hero. I think he is one of the great painters of our time. It's hard to tell from these reproductions, because they are so small, and his paintings are so big. But he is a great mind, a great wit, a great painter. I have seen his most recent works, painted last year and this year, and they are even better than his early works; like Rembrandt and Hans Hoffman, he gets better with age. He is a mystic, a human man with a human mind and a human eye, and his eye is on the sun. I almost didn't get this book, because it's hard to see Miró in little books.

You probably know as much about Goya as I do. But in here

there is a good self-portrait of him when he was in his fifties or sixties. Hotheaded Goya. I like him. His *Horrors of War* is something else indeed, and beyond words.

And here are Modigliani's nudes. They make me hungry for you. Don't you think the doctor would let you come out and come to my bed just for a little while, like twenty-seven thousand hours?

Dick's just going out to eat, and Brahms's *First* is just finishing. And I am loving you. It's very fine to wake up in the morning, read your letter, and write to you. It makes me sad that you aren't here, but it makes me feel honored that I am privileged to write to you, to get letters from you. You are the most beautiful thing in my life, now and ever.

I just put Haydn's "Twinkle Twinkle" symphony on the phonograph, and some baroque trumpet music by Henry Purcell. Music to write letters by. My letters from you today came to my old address, maybe tomorrow they will come here. Last night Dick and I made lists of ten or eleven men, literary men, whom we thought influenced our lives, and still influence them. We made the lists independently, and then compared them. Here they are:

DICK	ME
François Villon	Albert Camus
Thomas Wolfe	Percy Shelley
Albert Camus	Lord Byron
Walt Whitman	René Rilke
Percy Shelley	Ralph Emerson
André Gide	Bernard Shaw
René Rilke	Ezra Pound
Paul Goodman	Thomas Wolfe
Arthur Rimbaud	Alfred Whitehead
John Milton	Friedrich Nietzsche
	Arthur Rimbaud
	John Milton

Of course, when we finished we thought of a lot more, but it is interesting that we had six people in common right off hand. Maybe that's another reason why we get along.

I'm reading Wallace Stevens's poems again, and he is such a great writer. He uses language in a way that very few writers can, and he illustrates that English is as beautiful a language as any poetic language. Here is the opening stanza to his poem called "Sunday Morning":

> Complacencies of the peignoir, and late
> Coffee and oranges in a sunny chair,
> And the green freedom of a cockatoo
> Upon a rug mingle to dissipate
> The holy hush of ancient sacrifice.
> She dreams a little, and she feels the dark
> Encroachment of that old catastrophe,
> As a calm darkens water lights.
> The pungent oranges and bright, green wings
> Seem things in some procession of the dead,
> Widening across the wide water, without sound.
> The day is like wide water, without sound,
> Stilled for the passing of her dreaming feet
> Over the seas, to silent Palestine,
> Dominion of the blood and sepulchre.

And here are the opening lines of a poem called "Like Decorations in a Nigger Cemetery":

> In the far South the sun of Autumn is passing
> Like Walt Whitman walking along a ruddy shore.
> He is singing and chanting the things that are part of him,
> The worlds that were and will be, death and day.
> Nothing is final, he chants. No man shall see the end.
> His beard is of fire and his staff is a leaping flame.

And here is this: "Frogs Eat Butterflies. Snakes Eat Frogs. Hogs Eat Snakes. Men Eat Hogs":

> It is true that the rivers went nosing like swine,
> Tugging at banks, until they seemed
> Bland belly-sounds in somnolent troughs,
>
> That the air was heavy with the breath of these swine,
> The breath of turgid summer, and
> Heavy with the thunder's rattapallax,
>
> That the man who erected this cabin, planted
> This field, and tended it awhile,
> Knew not the quirks of imagery,
>
> That the hours of his indolent, arid days,
> Grotesque with this nosing in banks,
> This somnolence and rattapallax,
>
> Seemed to suckle themselves on his arid being,
> As the swine-like rivers suckled themselves
> While they went seaward to the sea-mouths.

There are times when Stevens is my favorite poet in the whole world. Only Shakespeare, and a rare few others, can write the English language like Stevens does. The purity and loveliness of language is one of the few things that is not for sale these days.

I feel like quoting a hundred other poems. I am in love with you, and I am in love with poetry, and I want my loves to love each other, but poetry is a fickle woman at first, and offers nothing until she is loved. Ah, but then, everything, delights unimaginable.

It grieves me that the doctor treats you the way he does. Perhaps I shall meet Dr. Skigen someday and we will talk all this over. I wonder.

Sandy, what's happening? We must not become resigned. I need you. I love you.

All my love

your husband
forever,

Ted

April 5, 1962

Dear Sandy,

hello. It's eleven in the morning, I've been up for two hours, ate some eggs, and read a novellette by William Styron called *The Long March*. It was very, very good, and almost made me cry for its picture of human spirit and humor. I'd like you to read it sometime. William Styron is one of the best prose writers now writing. His other two books, *Lie Down in Darkness* and *Set This House on Fire*, were as good as most books I've read. Styron reminds me of Dostoevsky in a way, but he is very American. I think you will like him. I tried to find *The Torrents of Spring* for you, but couldn't. I'm sorry.

Last night, and yesterday afternoon, I suddenly could write again, and wrote three poems, one of which I've already sent, "On the White Paper." I don't really know how good they are, but I suspect that "Poem" is good, and I feel good about the others, not ashamed of them as I have been of most of my attempts lately. Two of the three were directly written to you, and so my renewal of spirit is directly due to you. If ever any beauty I did see which I desired and got, 'twas but a dream of thee.

Here is my poem, called "Poem," which is written in a kind of James-Joyce-John-Ashbery-stream-of-consciousness style. It is full of literary allusions, but it is not necessary to know them to understand the poem. You will simply know more if you do understand them. I don't want to say more about it, except that I have paid a lot of attention to the musical phrasing of the poem, and have used punctuation oddly.

[Remainder of letter missing.]

April 5, 1962

My darling Sandy,

I don't know where to begin this letter. Are we losing? Are they coming between us? Honey, I love you so very very much. I want to answer all your questions very carefully. I want to tell you everything, give you everything you ever want to ask of me.

But forgive me, I must talk a little first.

Sandy, they're beating us. They're getting us down. All this about the annulment, and the detective reports, is something we knew from the first. I told you that this is exactly what they would do. Their plan is to separate us, to annul the marriage, and to use your sympathies and your natural feelings for your parents to drive doubts between us like a wedge until finally we are apart for good.

I beg you, I beg you again, don't defend me. Not to them, not to doctors, not to other patients, not even to yourself. Remember how it was when we were together, remember how I look and seem to you. Remember the love we have for each other. Have faith in your judgment, your feelings, yourself, in me. If you try to argue with their ideas about me, their supposed "facts," you cannot win. Their logic is superior to yours, and mine, their age and experience and their determination are something you cannot cope with by fighting them according to their rules. *They know how to handle you.* In only five weeks they have gotten you to write a line to me which reads

"I am not sure I will believe either of you," meaning them or me. What will they accomplish in another five weeks? or ten? or fifty?

Honey, I haven't heard one word from your parents. I have received no legal notice from anyone. What right do they have to decide whether it is all right for you and me to be married? We must not allow them to even question us except as equals. We cannot act like all they want is what is best for you, when they have you locked up. It seems that all they want is what *they say* is best for you.

Sandy, don't forget that Sunday night in Miami. Don't forget your mother asking if you wanted to use her leather coat in New York, your mother and father handing you over to strangers. Don't forget.

But I don't want to lecture at you anymore. My insides are torn apart by all this. I'm afraid, honey, I'm afraid. I haven't been put in situations before that I couldn't fight my way out of. Now there are two that have to fight. I wish I could fight for both of us, but I can't.

"Tell me everything, even the bad things," you write me. I wish I knew what to tell you. I don't know what kind of things they are telling you. I can't think of anything important about me that you don't know. It must be evident to you from what they say about my master's degree that they are slanting everything to appear the way they want it to. You were there. You heard what Professor Winchester, the young fellow who was on the committee, said about my thesis. You met Doctor Johnson, my advisor. You were there when I came back from the test. You saw the letter. Of course I wasn't awarded an M.A. To receive a degree one must make application for it, and pay fees. But I was passed by the thesis committee, I completed all the courses, and I was told by the committee that "you are now a Master of Arts." Then, *after first asking you if you minded*, I wrote that letter. What do they mean by cover up?

What else is there to tell? I am obviously not, and never was homosexual. I am not addicted to anything, no drugs, no barbiturates, no alcohol, no tobacco. I have tried various stimulants such as Benzedrine, Dexedrine, Desoxyn, Desbutol, Ritalin, Dexamyl, all members of the amphetamine family of stimulants. All I can say to you is that I knew and know what I am doing. I have also tried at various times peyote, mescaline, LSD 25, and marijuana, all of which affect the nervous system and give hallucinations, space/time transformations, et cetera. These things are not dangerous when taken in small amounts. Aldous Huxley has written many things about their use and the benefits to be derived from them. So have many other writers and medical men, from Havelock Ellis to Carl Jung. If you want to know about them I will send you a book called *Drugs and the Mind* by Dr. Robert S. De Ropp, a copy of which I saw in your father's house.

For over two years now, off and on, I have used stimulants such as Dexedrine, in doses of five mgs. These pills are used by students everywhere, especially in medical school. Many artists use them. They do nothing for you except make you awake the way sleeping pills make you sleep. I never hear people screaming about the use of tranquilizers or sleeping pills. Are stimulants something else again? I have talked to psychologists and doctors about this, and read widely about them, and all agree that these pills are not harmful when not used to excess, they can do some good for fatigue, and the effect depends upon the individual. The most I have ever taken is fifteen mgs a day for a period of time. It is a recognized fact that it requires some six hundred mgs a day for addiction. The pills set up no need in the system. I have gone without them for months at a time. I will gladly stop using them if it makes you uneasy, but it disturbs me a little that you are against me using them on the say so of Mr. Bean, and of your father, who wants us apart and is liable to say anything.

How did I seem to you when you were with me? Did my brain or heart seem about to fail? You couldn't keep up with me walking in the streets. As Ed Kaim said, I go to bed full of energy and spirits and wake up that way, too. I use pills rarely, and I think wisely. There is good precedent for their use in the history of artists, and no reason against their use in medical science as far as I can see. Your father may say there is, but your father also said some things on the certificate to commit you which were of equally doubtful veracity, to say the least.

Honey, I just want you to judge for yourself. All you want me to do is everything they want a young man to do, namely, be upstanding, honest, forthright, and the respectful all-American type. I want to be honest, but it was our forthrightness and honesty which enabled them to sneak up on us in the dead of night and drag you away and put me through hell. All the things you ask may be necessary for us. If so, all I want to do then is do them. To me the most important thing is us. For you, and for us, I will do nearly anything. But I want it to be because we really feel that we are doing what is best. It must not be because someone is imposing external standards on us, and proving to us that we cannot be happy unless we conform to those standards. You married me, Sandy. You love me. I ask you to believe in me, to believe in the feelings that make you love me. Let you and me decide what is best for you and me. Hell, I don't have to steal books, or food, or anything else. I have done both of those things, still do on occasion, but they are not necessary nor is anything *necessary* that you are worried about, that they are protesting about. It is not the *things* they don't like, it is me. This country is rotten from top to bottom, the system of government, the economic structure, the whole thing is rotten. It is crumbling so fast we can hardly see it falling. The old-timers are holding on for their lives. And they are trying to stamp out whoever is against their way. That is nearly always the way it is with youth and age, but in America the historical and the natural are meeting. The country is falling apart. The American dream, which is what your parents want for you, precludes you marrying me. And so they wipe our marriage off the books.

What I am saying is that whatever you ask of me I will happily do. But please ask me from your heart, when you are unsure let's work things out between us, please let's not let anyone come and tell us the way it must be or else.

And what else could they have told you? That I'm a moocher, that I live on handouts from girls and my mother, that I'm a bum. Honey, when I got out of the army I drove a truck for three months, sold phonographs for three or four months, taught school for a year, all while I was going to school. My GI Bill paid some of my expenses, I worked to pay the rest. I did this for over two years. Then I decided I was a writer, a poet, or nothing, and so I quit work and did the best I could. Pat gave me money sometimes when we were going together in Tulsa, let me use her car, but she didn't support me by any means. My mother also sent me money from time to time. Part of her dream was that I should go to college, and often when I wanted to quit I didn't because of her dream. When I came to New York I had little money, I lived in Joe's apartment, which was a store, and paid small rent. I filled out my income by selling my guitar and most of my books, once I even sold a pint of blood to buy typing paper, and I worked ten and more hours a day on my thesis. Ron used to pay my way to the movies on weekends. I helped him with his schoolwork, but not because he took me to the movies. In the summer of that year Pat came to New York, and so did Dick, to live with me. Pat and I had broken up over religion, over direction, over many things, but she thought she still loved me, and maybe I thought we had a chance. She came with a hundred dollars and stayed three months. We used her hundred dollars, and then Dick and I supported her and ourselves the rest of the summer. We worked at hard labor for a few days. Once I cleaned a Jewish lady's house for her on a Friday for seventy-five cents an hour of backbreaking work waxing floors, cleaning the stove, etc. I sold blood every eight weeks. I sold nearly all the rest of my books. I wrote three papers for Columbia students for which I was paid. And so we made out. At the end of the summer, when Dick and I had lost twenty-five pounds each (and Pat was in better health than ever) Dick and Pat went back to Tulsa.

Ron and I had decided earlier to room together this semester. He came back to school and we were going to get a place. Then Pat came back, and wanted to work here and live with me again. I didn't want her to work. I preferred to live the way we had in the summer and I had a chance for a rent-free apartment. But she didn't feel respectable unless she worked, and she wanted to live better than in the summer. When she returned I had been off pills for over a month. She and I and Ron took a place together and they paid the rent. I soon found I had no solitude, and took to staying up nights to write and read alone. But I couldn't sleep days because Ron was there. So I started pills again. Pat and I weren't working out because she was always tired at night from working (as I'd known she would be) and had no enthusiasm for other interests, and you know me. After a while I knew I had to get out. Dick had suggested to me that I come to New Orleans and stay with him for a while. Also Joe wanted me to move in with him so we could work on some things together. Meanwhile Anne had come to NY, and I liked her, and all things added up. I moved out of Pat's to Joe's but I didn't want to leave NY because I was writing well. But Anne and I were very strongly attracted to each other and as soon as I was away from Pat we began to make love. Both of us knew it would not add up to marriage, because we had different ways to go. She was working too hard to grow into a musician, and I into a man and poet, and we could not work together. But it didn't matter, we wanted each other. I thought it wasn't a good situation, and so when Tom showed up wanting to leave NY I decided to get out, take my thesis test, stay away a while, and then start fresh away from Pat and maybe Anne too, with Joe, when I came back. Joe and I were working on some very good things. So, I left NY, and . . . . . .

I'm not exactly sure where they fit Margie into it all. She is my dear and good friend whom I love very much. We had a brief painful romance when we were both young and inexperienced and we were the first for each other. Last summer while Pat and Dick were gone she came to visit me in New York and we had a good visit. She had vacation money, and paid for things when we went places. I spent an entire week taking her to the park, to museums, to the movies, the Empire State Building, on the ferryboat, to a play, it was one of the nicest and finest things that had happened to me. She stayed at my place, we didn't even sleep together.

But Sandy, you know all of that. What is there that I haven't told you? There are thousands of details I want to fill in for you when we are together, as we get to know each other better. I have picture albums to show you, my journals, everything I am and was is part of you now. I don't understand. What are they saying? What can it be that is disturbing you this way? You know me. You looked at me, touched me, we slept together, made love, you looked at me while I was sleeping, and I watched you sleep sometimes. We rode on the bus together, and walked in the park, and took a blood test, and slept in the bed with Margie, and you met Dick, and Tom, and talked to Joe and Tony on the phone, and met David Bearden, and the Padgetts, and saw me half drunk on wine, and high on pills, and naked, and nervous, and touchy, and wide awake, and sleepy, and you love me, you married me . . .

What have detective reports and your parents got to do with all that? They don't know me. They know what they want to know. Of course their investigations proved exactly what they wanted them to. They don't even know you. But they know enough about you to hurt you, to hurt me.

I told you they would annul our legal marriage. I told you that a lawyer could not help us. I told you that Dr. Skigen was not getting you another doctor. I told you that the detectives would prove me to be bad. I told you what their tactics would be. I'm not omniscient, not clairvoyant. I simply see them from outside their scheme of things. If it was not that I am so terribly in love with you, so terribly involved, so painfully vulnerable, so afraid for you, for us, their whole plan would be laughable. But you haven't had this kind of thing happen before. To have faith is to be beyond logic and before logic, Sandy. They will prove beyond a shadow of a doubt that black is white, I am bad, you are sick. They will prove to you that I am not the Ted Berrigan you saw and married just as easily as they have proved that you are sick.

> Sandy, I love you.
> I am and always will be your husband
> your lover
> I am not what they say I am
> You are not sick.

I will do whatever you say. Shall I come to Miami right now, and try to see you? Shall I go to work somewhere right now? Tell me what you think, what you want. If you want me to tell you what else I think, I will. All I want is for you to love me.

> All my love,
> Ted

April 6, 1962

My darling Sandy,

your letter today was so good, and I had been waiting all night for it, waiting for the first letter from you written after the initial shock. And it came, and said all that I knew it would, I love you so much.

And I see that my mind was three days ahead of myself this month and I put the wrong dates on some letters.

You said Eddie and Lauren might come to see you. Did they? Have you heard from them at all? Eddie called while I was out today and said he needed some money, so Dick and I sent him twenty dollars which we made by helping a student write a paper on American Aims. Hah! But at least we were able to help Ed and Lauren and Harry. Now we've paid Eddie back all he sent to us, and lent him some ourselves. In this give-and-take business it is not all take, honey, and even I give sometimes.

But I'm not serious. I know you know that. I wish I had millions of dollars and could be a patron to all young poets and artists, and plain bums, too.

Today I'm reading a book called *American Capitalism,* and another called *Labor Legislation.* This time I will send you a copy of my paper, for whatever it is worth. And that reminds me. Don't worry about not thinking much about the books you are reading. Only a small part of the good that books will do you has to do with thinking about them on a conscious level. Most of the effects of the things you read will work on you below the level of consciousness, will come to the surface later. At that time you will find yourself correlating books read in the past with ones you are reading then. John Livingston Lowes, a professor at Harvard in the twenties and thirties, wrote a book called *The Road to Xanadu* in which he illustrated what I have just said by showing what books Coleridge read and how they influenced "The Rime of the Ancient Mariner" partly without Coleridge's even realizing it. I have seen many examples of this myself in my own reading and writing. Simply read all you feel like, and more, and it will all be good.

I hope your parents will let us correspond when you get home, if they really do let you go home. But if they don't, we will work out something. I will talk to you more about this when I hear from you about the letter I sent yesterday.

This isn't much of a letter, I'm afraid. I am in very good spirits because of your letter today, and I am also thinking about the paper I'm working on. But I had a long dream about you last night in which we ran away together from your parents, down the Keys in a car, worried but happy to be together, and it was a nice dream, but when I woke up it was only a pillow that I had in my arms, and I felt lost.

I've turned again to imitation/translations, in order to be writing, to be working, and last night I made a poem from one of Rilke's, just for you.

LOVE SONG
   to Sandy

How shall I withold myself
that you may not touch me?

How shall I travel beyond you,
face a world alone?

I need a strange and quiet place
to build myself in silence,

Where, alone in darkness,
I would not ache for you.

But all that touches you
strikes at me.

And we are drawn together
as a bow

draws one sound
striking separate strings.

Upon what sacred instrument are we?
And what musician plays our melody?

Oh,
strange song!

Ted Berrigan
after René Rilke

Tomorrow I shall send you some books of poetry. At your
parents' house is *Locus Solus,* and also the *Little Treasury of Modern
Poetry.* I shall send the poems of Rilke, and Mayakofsky, and
Conrad Aiken, and Robert Lowell, and *The Oxford Anthology of
English Poetry.*

My darling, I know we will be together again. I know we
cannot fail. Our love is too strong for all the world to kill it. You
are my soul. The only way my soul could ever die would be if I lost
you. And that can never be.

Good-night, I love you
very much. Your husband forever,
Ted

April 8, 1962

My darling,

two beautiful letters from you today. They make me feel bad about my letter yesterday. I want only to write to you of love. But today's mail also brought further confirmation of my thoughts about what is happening to us. More about that in a minute.

I am forever grateful to Leslie for going to you, for bringing you her self, her interest, her goodness (which is real, even if she doesn't think so). It made me feel very good to hear you talk about her, and her visit, and how you felt. It made me feel that you are not entirely alone in Miami. I thank her very much, and I repeat what I told her once, that she is good, she is going to have it tough, but she's good.

About what she asked about writing, and hurt. Shall I quote Henry Miller? To write is to love again. Or William Saroyan? Art will not help, but if it seems like a good idea to look at things carefully, for that is what art is, looking at things carefully, then do so. And it's better than nothing, too.

I write because I feel like it. It makes me feel—no not "good" or "bad" but—alive. It makes me feel as I feel when I see the sun in the morning, or hit a home run, or something. It does not take away pain nor give pain. W. H. Auden says "Poetry makes nothing happen. It survives, a way of happening, a mouth, / it survives in the valley of its saying, where executives would never want to tamper / it flows south from ranches of isolation and the busy griefs / Raw towns that we believe and die in."

I like to talk. I write to talk, to you, to whomever my poem is addressed to, to anyone who wants to listen, mostly I suppose, to myself. Nothing changes from this, except that I grow. And there are so many et ceteras to add here.

Sandy, you asked about a letter your father mentioned. It is a letter I wrote to Anne from Tulsa. Before I left New York Anne and I were close. You know that. I was her first lover. We both knew we would not marry. It didn't matter. When you and I arrived in Tulsa I found a letter from Anne waiting for me at the Padgetts. It had five dollars in it, in case I was broke. She wrote me that she missed me, that she felt love for me, that she would be glad when I came back. She didn't know yet that I had found you. I wrote to her immediately. I told her of you, of our marriage. I told her I loved her. That my love for you did not change that. That I didn't love you more than I loved her, but that my love for you was different. I told her that you were complete. That you were not searching, you didn't need to search as she and I did, because you are a child of God, born whole, without blemish. I told her that I had thought I could never marry, but I had not anticipated you. I told her that you and I would be happy, because I had no need to fight you, no need to compete with you. I told her that perhaps she and I had more "sympathy" in certain ways, because we had to fight the same kind of battles, but that that very sympathy was what made it impossible for us to ever be married. I told her that she and I came from opposite sides of the tracks, too. Meaning that I could not fit her dreams, because I was trying to fit my own. I wanted her to know that I loved her, and that I was married to you, whom I also loved. I wanted her to know that I didn't marry you because I loved you better than her, but because I loved you differently. I ended by telling her that I wanted to bring you to her, and say "Sandy, this is Anne, whom I love very much," and that I knew you and she would love each other.

Anne was very upset when all this happened, and she sent the letter back to me, after reading it, to your parents' house, with a note saying she could no longer believe me. But when we met again, she was as understanding as I knew she would be. I see her very rarely now, she has a boyfriend but she believes in me, in me and you, and in herself. I'm sure the letter sounded to your father as if I married you because it would make life easy for me. Well, my dear, my beautiful wife, that is why I married you, but it doesn't mean whatever his poor tortured mind thinks it means.

But didn't you already know most of that? I wrote the letter in Ron's room in Tulsa, while you were there. We have no secrets.

My poem (poems) shows that I am troubled! My darling, may I always be troubled, until everyone loves his neighbor, his god, and above all his self. It's a bad world these days, and maybe it always was, and it troubles me, but there is a major difference between troubled and crippled.

And I am troubled that a doctor, a man who studies mental processes and disorders, could ask such a question as am I a beatnik. A *beatnik?* Will someone in the world please tell me what a beatnik is? But never mind. No, I am not a beatnik. I am not anything that can be labelled. Pin me down and you find me gone. Human begins cannot be labelled, and especially with words that are nowhere defined, such as *beatnik.*

I can only be general about the use of "white rhinoceros" but white is the color of innocence, of purity, et cetera, while a rhinoceros is a big clumsy bumbling awkward and maybe even ugly animal, so the combination of the two provides a good almost paradoxical image for men, for human beings. An example of this kind of usage is a line such as ". . . hugging / and kissing / and fucking like little children / in bed / this afternoon." Hugging and kissing are almost childlike and innocent words when used together, especially hugging. It makes me think of teddy bears and things. Then *fucking,* which is a "vulgar" word, with obscene connotations (Fuck you, etc.), but used after hugging and kissing, and with "like little children" it makes the whole scene ever more innocent which is the desired effect. So a word like *fucking* need not be rigidly thought of as obscene. What do you think?

Honey, this isn't a light letter. I have things to show you, but your letters were so good that I want to talk to you a while first, as if you were off on vacation or something, and everything was fine. Because in one sense everything is fine: I love you and that makes it a good world for me even after all.

So here's something you may sink your critical teeth into if you feel like it. I enjoyed doing it very much, and right now I like it. It is not an attempt to write Garcia Lorca's poem in American. It is an attempt to write a poem like Lorca's, in American, using whatever of his that fits, in the voice of Ted Berrigan. With credit to Lorca for whatever taken. What is most important is that it is an attempt to write in Lorca's tone of voice with me as the speaker. The poem is meant to stand by itself without reference to Lorca's poem. Wherever the literal meaning differs from Lorca's, I know it, it is deliberate. Etc. Etc. Etc.

THE LAMENT

I am closing my window.
I don't want to hear the weeping.
But from out of the shadowy darkness
nothing may be heard but the weeping.

I hear no angels singing
and no dogs crying.
The sound of violins
may never find me.

For the weeping is a terrible animal
and the weeping is a terrible angel
and the weeping is a terrible sound

Tears silence the wind

Nothing is heard but the weeping.

after Garcia Lorca /7 Apr 62.

As a final note, I think in my final version I am going to leave out all the punctuation. To imply no beginning, no end, just weeping. Or something.

Honest, I love you more every day. But not really, I could not love you more than I did at once. There is no more love than that.

Ted

April 8, 1962

My dear, I love you so very much. It is your very principles which in part make me love you. But

Wake up! Get tough, Sandy. This isn't "Mary Worth." There ain't gonna be no happy ending unless we *take* it. The other side thinks God is on their side. Unless we think God is on our side, and realize that that takes precedence over everything else, then we are lost.

Honey, days, months, are passing. We are going through experiences the other is away from. We are changing. Time is on their side. If they keep you a long time I'll be someone else from the picture in your heart. They know all that.

All of that is a part of what I think. Don't be deceived by the tone. I would never in the whole world issue orders to you. I'm trying to tell you how I see that situation, from a distance, from the age of twenty-seven, from many bitter experiences with people like your parents. Back them into a corner and they fight with any weapon handy, and damned hard.

I don't think it will help you or us one bit for you to cooperate with anyone there in any way except as a means of escaping as soon as possible.

I think that it is dishonest or unperceptive to think that there is any chance that your parents will not try as hard as they can to keep us apart for all the days of their and our lives.

I think that to be concerned with such things as the philosophical question of honor and honesty in your situation is analogous to considering whether or not it is fair play to hit someone who is cutting your throat below the belt. There is no question of honesty involved on your part. All that, all possibility of honor and honesty between us and them was wiped out one Sunday night in Miami.

Run, Sandy. Come to me, or let me come to you. Be my wife. No one, no one, will help us, except those who love us. Us. Those who love us. Like Tom, and Margie, and Joe, and Dick.

These people aren't playing games. There is no rule book. It's run or we both shall be wasted. And that would be a terrible tragedy.

I love you. I've talked to you tonight almost as if you were here with me. The way I could only talk to you, whom I love, my wife. With honesty. With ruthless honesty. I love you.

> All my love forever,
> your husband,
> Ted

April 8, 1962

Dear Sandy,

this will just be a note. It is Sunday night in New York, cold and damp. Ed and Harry and Lauren arrive here tonight or tomorrow, and I must move. So, I'm in the middle of moving, and at the same time, I'm sick. It's just a cold, just an annoyance, but enough to rob me of energy and will to work.

By Tuesday I will be moved again, this time to a more permanent place, I hope, away from everyone except Dick. I'll send the address, meantime you can keep writing me here.

I made a translation/imitation today of Lorca's poem called "Casida del llanto." I'll send it later, after I move. Right now I'm tired, don't feel well, and about to try to sleep ten or twelve hours to gather strength to move. I wish you could be here to rub my back, hold my hand, baby me a little.

I'm sorry to write so little. I'll write tomorrow in between moving, and a long letter Tuesday. I love you very much.

All my love,
Ted

April 9, 1962

Dear Sandy,

it's so odd writing letters. I write to you about something, and then the next day I get a letter about something else, and I write to you about that, and then the next day I get a letter about what I had said the first day, and time becomes confused and mysterious. But anyway, even after and in the midst of annulment letters, I'd like to talk to you about poetry.

The poem I sent called "After a Long Silence": this is part of what I was trying to do:

When one is a child, one is relatively unconscious. That is, one is aware of everything as whole, unified, harmonious. That's an oversimplification of course, but true as far as it goes. For example there was harmony between you and your parents before you met me, even though there may have been disturbances sometimes. However, as one grows older, has more experience, consciousness develops. Awareness of self as real and individual. The harmony of youth depended largely on the fact that the child has no real identity except as a member of the family. But with the advent of consciousness, one then realizes the existence of the family, and also the self. Since part of the family is what becomes conscious, the result for the new ego is schizophrenia. The part of you or me that is part of the family exists side by side with the part of us which is completely individual, and the two parts do not always exist in harmony. Is this good or bad?
or:

> Is it so catastrophic
> that I grow more schizophrenic every day?

That is what I am talking about in my poem. Me in this situation, as me personally, and me as a representative human being. Well,

> Once I knew how to sleep. Now I dream
> Dragons
> and I punch them with weightless arms.

Once I was one, harmonious, bathed in the peace of lack of individuality. Then I had no bad dreams, because dreams are reflective of unconscious elements which disturb, and then I was (relatively) undisturbed. Now I have bad dreams in which I fight dragons, ineffectually.

Ineffectually because as my schizophrenic self my loyalty and power are divided and I am not as strong as I would be unified. So perhaps it is bad to grow more schizophrenic. BUT perhaps the development of individuality is inevitable, and perhaps to become aware of dragons and the need to kill them, is to begin to grow, a natural, and therefore good process. Then what?

> A cool green wind is blowing
> in a painting by Raoul Dufy!
> Wind, how can you be in a painting?

Although schizophrenic, and possessed by bad dreams, that is, "troubled," I still am able to be stimulated, to feel good things, to enjoy, to question. And what I enjoy, my enjoyment, is also schizophrenic. I see a painting. It is green. But it is also cool and has wind in it. How can a painting have animation and feeling in it? My enjoyment is not unconscious, it is both sensual and analytic, giving rise to questions which I cannot answer right now, dragons which I must cope with. Because they are there. So, not everything that seems to be the result of my schizophrenia is negative. There is enjoyment, even "happiness" though not a quiet kind, but a troubled kind. However

> I do not want to be touched
> when you are not with me.

meaning first of all of course, you, Sandy, to whom the poem is addressed. I don't want to enjoy anything while I am deprived of you and you are deprived of me. But on another level, I don't want to be touched by enjoyment while I am schizophrenic. I want to be undivided, whole. I don't want to be "sick" to enjoy art. So

> Poised like Nijinsky
> or
> believing in poems   (notice the change)
> I am still
> facing the sea

that is, I am caught between desire for wholeness, harmony with my unconscious, on one hand, which will mean a lack of awareness of the dragons, the things I don't know, like how wind can be in paintings for example, and on the other hand the fact that to conquer the dragons of my own ignorance and problems of development I must not try to be more in harmony with myself, but rather more schizophrenic. That is, I must be aware of my unconscious and my conscious at the same time. I must enjoy a painting, and wonder how (and try to learn how) a painting can seem to have a cool green wind in it. But, to be schizophrenic is to be sick. Quote, unquote.

And why Nijinsky? Because I am caught between motions, still, caught between the dance of life, and the sea of the unconscious. Even though "believ(ing) in poems I am still facing the sea."

What about the unconscious then? Is it bad? Is it dangerous? Is it death? Will an attempt at harmony mean death for me, because once schizophrenia, is it too late to try to regress? Well, I am still facing the sea

> darkness of sea

the unconscious is a mystery. It is potential death because it desires to kill consciousness, end schizophrenia, unite. And since consciousness is awareness of individuality, how can I be sure that union with the unconscious will not mean death to my individuality?

> the sea which is cool and green

but the unconscious is also the source of life. For in the beginning there is only unconsciousness. Consciousness rises out of it. And the sea of unconsciousness is also cool, refreshing, because it is rest from dragon fighting. To be conscious is to know problems, to be troubled. But this is mostly negative (How can a painting have wind in it?). And to be conscious is to be awake. But for strength one must be positive sometimes, too. And one needs rest, healthy harmonious sleep.

> the sea which is dark, cool, and green

the sea is dark, and a mystery, but it holds the possibility of more life, of a renewal of consciousness, a renewal of strength. There is a possibility of death, but also a possibility of *more life, more light.* (Light is always a symbol of consciousness). Whenever the choice is between more consciousness at the risk of death, and maintenance of the status quo, which is surely death because if we do not go forward we go backward, we cannot remain poised for long, then the answer seems obvious. BUT

> I do not want to be touched
> when you are not with me

you see, I know the way to unite with my dark side, my unconscious. It is to throw myself into the things that are making me schizophrenic. To question how a wind can be in a painting, and question and question and question, until I find out. Then it will no longer be a problem, a dragon. When I see a painting that has a wind in it I will not be puzzled, I will know how it is there, and will be in harmony when I see the painting. It will be even more enjoyable because my analytical procedure will not be in the way. The way to good is through evil. We can't know good unless we know evil, if there is any evil. We cannot be truly harmonious until we know what it is to be schizophrenic. If we do not know, then the danger of schizophrenia will be ever-present, a dragon waiting to pounce. But having faced the dragon, even though afraid, one is no longer afraid of dragons.

But I am not sure I want to grow when you are not with me. To write is to love again. Yes, there is the influence of Miller there. To write is to love again. For me, to write is to be alive, to have love, to feel good. And I am not sure I want to do that without you here. I feel that you and I are now one, and I am not sure I can write, can grow, when you are not here. That is why there has been a "long silence." However, in spite of my hesitancy I know

. . . to love / I must live.

I do not want to be touched, to feel good when I see Raoul Dufy's painting, or when I write, when you are not with me. Because I love you so very much. But the paradox is that I must stay alive in order to continue loving you. And to stay alive I must be touched. I must write. And to write is to love again. So my decision has already been made, before I even thought about it. The fact of my writing this poem shows that. I must try to gain harmony, to unite my warring selves, by plunging into the sea that although dark (for to be a poet is a dark thing in America) is cool (renewing) and green (the color of growing things).

Like Nijinsky
I plunge into poetry

And there is the final irony. Because it isn't as easy as it just sounded. Maybe the end will be death. Nijinsky was the greatest male dancer of all. A supreme artist, admired by artists of every profession, and his art did not save him. He died in an asylum, mad.

But I'm not Nijinsky. I plunge into poetry, as Nijinsky plunged into the dance. With all the effort and faith and dedication possible. As singlemindedly as possible. And with eyes open. Not as Nijinsky, but having seen Nijinsky, like Nijinsky. I don't want art to *save* me.

I want to be alive. To look at things carefully. To write is to love again.

I want to be touched. I still do not want to be touched when you are not with me. But I will write. I will plunge into poetry. I will be touched. Because I cannot help it. It is natural. It is good. It will keep me alive and growing and I *want* to be alive

now

to love you

Honey, there's so much more to say, and yet if the poem doesn't say it, no other words can. Poetry is saying the most in the least words or something like that. I didn't say a word about the stanza arrangement, the why of it; or the use of certain words like *Raoul Dufy* for the painter because I like the sound of his name as well as his paintings; or the element of fugue form in the section which begins "darkness of sea," a device you will notice in a poem by Delmore Schwartz in your book, when I finish it; or why I used the / in that line (I'm not sure why, but it seemed to be the best piece of punctuation available). But I want to tell you about the poem a little, anyway.

And later I'll tell you about my poem called "Poem," which is the style I am working toward, the kind of poetry I want to write, except it is only a first attempt.

But now for news, I'm moved again. This time, I hope, to stay in one place for a while. Eddie and Harry and Carol arrived Monday evening about nine. Dick and I stayed at Tom's last night, then moved today into a room for the two of us on 113th Street, Room 307, I don't remember the street number, but will put it on the envelope. It's W. 113th Street. The rent is only $13.50 a week for the two of us, and I've made arrangements with the fellow

---

And now for the rest of this letter. Sandy, perhaps you have a copy of this already. But I don't think they would have shown it to you. So, here's a copy of something I received in the mail today, along with two letters from you, and our bridal gifts from the world.

COPY

IN THE CIRCUIT COURT OF THE ELEVENTH
JUDICIAL COURT OF FLORIDA, IN AND
FOR DADE COUNTY, FLORIDA

IN CHANCERY   NO. 620-3662

LOUIS ALPER, as father   :
natural guardian, and
next friend of Sandra Kay
Alper, a/k/a Sandra Kay   :
Berrigan, a minor,

                         :

        Plaintiff,

v.　　:

EDMUND JOSEPH BERRIGAN,　　COMPLAINT FOR ANNULMENT

:　　OF MARRIAGE　　.

Defendant.　:

Plaintiff, LOUIS ALPER, is the father, natural guardian, and next friend of Sandra Kay Alper, a/k/a Sandra Kay Berrigan, a minor, sues defendant, EDMUND JOSEPH BERRIGAN, JR., and says that:

1. Plaintiff, LOUIS ALPER, is the father, natural guardian, and next friend of Sandra Kay Alper, a/k/a Sandra Kay Berrigan, a minor, born on August 24, 1942. Louis Alper has been a bona-fide resident of the state of Florida continually from July 1, 1956.

2. Defendant, EDMUND JOSEPH BERRIGAN, is a 27-year-old resident of the state of New York. Diligent search and inquiry have been made by the plaintiff to discover the name and residence of defendant, and they are set forth as particularly as they are known to the plaintiff as follows:

EDMUND JOSEPH BERRIGAN
605 West 112th Street, Room 628
New York, New York

Plaintiff knows of his own knowledge that defendant is not now in the military service of the United States and has not been ordered to report for military service at any known time in the future.

3. On February 13, 1962, defendant and Sandra Kay Alper went through a purported civil marriage in Houston, Texas, after a 6-day "courtship." The purported marriage occurred without the knowledge or the consent of the parents of Sandra Kay Alper. The

parties lived together for 12 days thereafter as purported husband and wife.

4. Sandra Kay Alper is not pregnant as a result of the purported marriage.

5. On February 13, 1962, the date when the marriage ceremony was performed, prior thereto and to the date hereof, Sandra Kay Alper suffered from a major mental illness so acute that on the date of the marriage she was deprived of reason and incapable of exercising rational judgment, and was in such a mental condition that she had no understanding or comprehension of the nature, the effect, and the consequences of the marriage ceremony and contract of marriage, and was mentally incompetent and therefore incapable to consent to or to contract marriage.

6. In her mental state Sandra Kay Alper was easy prey to the suggestions of others. Defendant took advantage of her tractable condition and proceeded to have the marriage ceremony performed.

7. On February 26, 1962, on application of Dorothy Alper, mother of Sandra Kay Alper and the wife of the plaintiff, dated February 25, 1962, and the order of the Honorable Frank B. Dowling, County Judge, Dade County, Florida, dated February 25, 1962, pursuant to Florida State Law sect. 394.21(3), Sandra Kay Alper was taken into custody and transported by the Public Safety Department of Dade County, Florida, to The Institute, Jackson Memorial Hospital, Miami, Florida, where, on February 27th, 1962, she became a voluntary patient pursuant to F.S.A. sect. 394.20.

8. The purported marriage ceremony between defendant and Sandra Kay Alper was and is illegal, null and void, and of no legal effect, and should be annulled.

WHEREFORE, plaintiff, LOUIS ALPER, as father, natural guardian, and next friend of Sandra Kay Alper, a/k/a Sandra Kay Berrigan, a minor, prays that the marriage between defendant, EDMUND JOSEPH BERRIGAN, and Sandra Kay Alper, be declared null and void, and that plaintiff have such other, different, and further relief as may be deemed just and equitable, including the cost of this action.

Dated at Miami, Dade County, Florida, this April 4, 1962.
(Signed) <u>Louis Alper</u> .
LOUIS ALPER

Sandy, darling, this is no less, no more, than we expected. We knew that they would annul the marriage. But there are some surprises in this, too. They are annulling the marriage only on the grounds of your "illness." What this might seem to mean is that their detectives did not unearth any information with which they could annul the marriage on grounds that I'm a bad guy. They are claiming that we should not be married because you are not fit to be married, not mature, not healthy. But we both know that that is not it at all. They object because they don't want you to be married to me.

I mention this, because it might help balance the things your father says about me. I have no doubt that his detectives found things about me that he didn't like, but it seems that they found nothing against me that would be grounds for annulling a marriage.

Another thing, and although I'm sure this is only a formality, they have neatly taken care that I will be in very hot water if I lose the suit (and of course we will). Your father is suing for annulment and costs. If I lose, I must pay the court costs and his cost for lawyers, etc. Naturally, I won't be able to pay. So, if I try to remain in Florida to be near you, he will have me arrested for contempt of a court order unless I pay the costs, which will be plenty.

Smart man your dad.

Sandy, there isn't much to say about this. I am instructed to file a reply by May seventh, which means the case will be heard shortly after that. Otherwise they will annul the marriage by default.

We have been all through this already. With the testimony of the doctors, including Doctor Skigen (who advised me that you would be sick for years, that I should "bow out gracefully"), there is no chance in the world that we can prevent them from annulling the marriage. Your father's reputation, your age, your "illness," the length of our "courtship," and our religion differences are factors which we cannot overcome by telling them the truth, that we love each other, and will they please let us live. On May seventh or thereafter our marriage will be legally nonexistent, and the state of Florida will hand me the bill for the whole business.

Honey, what shall I answer to them? What do you think? I'll tell you my thoughts, please don't feel that I am doing anything other than talking this over with you. Even if my tone is that of a man shouting from the rooftops. What I want is whatever *we* want.

I think that before attempting to file an answer we need to be 100% aware that we have no chance, that to fight them in court on their terms would only be wasting time. That the marriage is definitely going to be annulled.

Since that is true, then I feel we should simply tell them the truth:

1. That we love each other.

2. That we are husband and wife.

3. That out marriage is something sacred, having nothing to do with courts, and that no one under heaven can dissolve it, no matter what legal documents they produce.

4. That we are married till death do us part.

5. That we do not recognize the right of your parents or anyone else to attempt to dissolve our marriage, we know that this is something that cannot humanly be done.

6. That the statements and charges about your mental condition are complete nonsense, we were married with our eyes wide open, with no coercion but that of love, and that what they sneeringly refer to as our "6-day courtship" was not even that, for we consider ourselves married as of the day we first looked into each other's hearts and found love, the first day we met.

7. That you are being held against your will, apart from your husband, without cause, and therefore

8. under such conditions we feel that we cannot with honor take any further notice of these proceedings.

That's roughly what I would say if I were speaking for myself. Tell me what you think, what you think we should do. We have time to talk before we need to answer. If you want I will come to Miami, petition the court, or the Legal Aid Society, for a lawyer to take our case, gather character references for both of us, etc., etc., and try to contest their claim. I feel sure that it would be useless, but nevertheless I would fight it with all my energy if we decide that that is the best course.

But what I believe is what I wrote above.

———————————

I'm sorry that my letters must be full of things like that. I want only to write of love, laughter, and my need for you. The rain here, cold and chilling, the strain of the situation, everything, have pulled me completely out of my cold.

Also, as a strange note to end this letter, Harry went to see Carol Clifford in Florida. He didn't go for lack of money. But he went. They haven't returned yet, we expect them any minute, but Lois, Ed's girl, who flew back, called and said the three of them would be here soon. Ed. Harry. and Carol. Wow.

Sandy, for now good-night. Tom just came in, I'm going to go eat, and mail this special delivery. The drawing by Leslie and the stamp make me feel closer to you. I send Leslie my love, my sympathy, my affection, and (through you) *Steppenwolf.* Also for you, some more books. I am your husband forever and ever. All my love,

Ted

April 11, 1962

My darling Sandy,

I'm sitting in my new room, Dick is reading *Ulysses* by James Joyce, and I have just finished a poem to you. Both Dick and I still have colds, and I'm full of antibiotics which Harry's girlfriend gave me.

I'm waiting to hear from you in answer to the letter I sent with the copy of the annulment suit papers. So, I haven't too much to say, except that I love you, which is what my poem tries to say.

I'll send a couple of books with this letter. I don't have any of O'Neill's works, but I'll see if Tom does. I read all O'Neill's plays four or five years ago, and some biographies of him. He was a strange, fascinating man. There is a dark color to his plays, most of them, and that is what is most exciting about them. He is a very dramatic writer, in a theatrical sense, and his plays are even better seen than read. I'll send something of his as soon as possible. My favorites of his are *The Great God Brown* and *The Iceman Cometh*, but I liked most of his plays.

This poem is very similar to the poem called "Poem." In the poem called "Poem" I tried to weave a web of imagery, thoughts, lines of poetry, color, and haze, about a central theme. Instead of saying roses are red, violets are blue, therefore it's spring, I tried to say something like Roses are red, violets are blue, there is an old woman who lives in a shoe. Only with the sense of my poem more obvious, but not logically obvious. As dreams are obvious but not logical sometimes. Maybe that is vague, but what I want is for the meaning of the poem to come to the reader as he reads, through flashes of recognition, rather than the way meaning comes in algebra textbooks. I wanted my poem to be read as poetry, not prose.

Saxifrage is a flower that grows up through rocks. *A Book of Torture* is the name of a book of poetry. So is *Paradise Lost*. "No truth except in things" is a line from a poem by William Carlos Williams[6] in which he says "Saxifrage is my flower, that splits the rocks." So: Poetry and a flower that splits the rocks, that grows in spite of "torture," have some connection. *Paradise Lost* refers to the good old days when everyone loved everyone and there was no torture (did those days exist?) and the feeling about it seems to have been brought on by someone strumming on a guitar. But this feeling must be real, there is no truth except in real things. Like rocks, to be split. And feeling, with which to split them. And a whole lot of other stuff.

But now a change of tack. Two people, obviously. Perhaps a man and girl. "What are you thinking?" the kind of question girls ask. He's thinking of poetry. Of being great. Of philosophy. Of record jackets which bring on Sabi, of lines from Allen Ginsberg which at the same time refer to eternal things. And, almost as an afterthought, of the game of mating which they are playing. "Of fucking, I suppose." Why I suppose? Because they are so far apart in their thought. She is thinking about "Do you like Chinese food?" but he doesn't answer. Triggered by his previous thoughts, his mind runs over lines of poetry, about waking up, about saintliness, about God and thinking of someone as that someone descends the stairs, of humor in poems and the oddness of HE, of fire . . . etc. But she blissfully continues her train of thought, alien to his, and without noticing his preoccupation:

"I often think of sweet and sour (I left out the final word here)."

She stops. But he and the poem go on, his thoughts, just plain thoughts, maybe my thoughts, of disorder and haze, of distance, of space, and deserts, of the withering weather of the climate in this particular place . . . . of a book of torture . . . of how poetry

[6] Actually it is "No ideas but in things." —Ed.

can live, it can grow, a life can be good, but it must split the rocks. Like saxifrage it must grow in spite of the rocks of insensitivity, cruelty because of ignorance, mindlessness, habit, et cetera.

> A book of torture
> or to split the rocks

I hope that all means something. In [this] poem I am sending you I am trying to say that I love you as I love my lost childhood, as I love *Paradise Lost*, with innocence, with strength, as I love my lost saints, my lost childhood heroes, like the Texas Rangers . . . and that things are bad now, but even though they may not get better soon I shall love you all my life, as my love, and as you are a member of the communion of saints. And a whole lot more, too. The title refers to my highest level which is when I think of you, love you. The poem is partly a collage, based on "How Do I Love Thee?" by Elizabeth Browning, and "Lycidas" by John Milton, with echoes of Ted Berrigan, Frank O'Hara, and Zane Grey thrown in, but when taken all together it is all me for you.

> I love you very much. Good-night for now
> and all my love,
> your husband forever,
> Ted

April 14, 1962

My darling Sandy,

two letters from you yesterday, and three today, and I am ashamed of how little I've written in the past three days. But my mother has always said that there is one thing the Berrigan men have little sense about, and that is their own vulnerability to such things as colds.

I've been miserably sick for three or four days. I lost my voice completely, couldn't sleep because of a sore throat, and all the rest of that kind of nonsense. So Harry's girlfriend Annette filled me full of antibiotics, and at last I seem to be recovering. I'm sorry for my silence.

Your letters are so good. I know I haven't answered all your questions. Some we need to talk about in person, and words on paper can only be misleading. About some others:

I can always read your writing, except in the case of whatever George's religion and/or religious book is. I don't think I know of it, or I'd recognize the name, but I can't decipher what you have written. What is the name you've written?

And about using George to help you; you need to decide that yourself. You should know better than anyone whether or not you will hurt him. Also, how reliable he is. Whatever you decide will be right, I'm sure. All I care about is that you don't overtrust the people such as doctors and hospital staff. They are something quite different from patients, and will betray you very quickly.

I'm sending some money in this letter, fifteen dollars. It's my pay for writing a paper comparing an anthropological report on a village in Peru with a travel journal of 1867 about South America. Leslie to the contrary, it isn't illegal to write papers for people, but the people themselves might get expelled if they are caught. However, that has nothing to do with me. I am learning a lot, and getting paid at the same time for writing. Who am I to judge them? I wouldn't have people write papers for me, but that's no standard for everyone. I don't respect these people very much, but if they want to pay me to write papers for them, well, to write is good for me, and they would pay someone else if I didn't do it. I feel like Andrew Undershaft in *Major Barbara* about the whole thing.

Some other cities you could go to are Atlanta, which is about a thirty-five-dollar bus trip, or Savannah, but both of these will probably be watched. If you had enough money, and maybe you will have by then, you could go to somewhere much farther, like [blacked-out word], or [blacked-out word]. The main thing is to get out of Florida, and call Tony. He will contact me right away, and I will call you back, even at a pay phone. Then we can talk, and make plans for you. Until you are out of Florida everything is speculation. Starting with this letter I'll send you money often. I have some coming in every week, and Dick is sending some, too.

Honey, your parents are very smart. The only way they could have photostated some of my letters was to have read them while you and I were out. They will not hesitate to read these letters too if they get the chance. And they'll get a chance if they want to. Perhaps you should send all my letters back before you go home. I'd rather have you send them to me than destroy them, wouldn't you? When I write to you at home if they allow it, and if they really let you go home, I won't mention plans.

I'm so glad they let you go out, and downtown. These pictures are unbelievable! You look so great, in such a funny way. I can picture you sitting in the machine posing this way and that. I'm so happy to be married to you.

Sandy, I hope they really do let you go home. It will be so good for you, and you are looking forward to it so much. But don't forget 1) they regard you as mentally incompetant, and are liable to tell you anything, as one tells a child things to make him feel better, and 2) with the annulment suit coming up in May, how will it look to the court if you are home, running around free, when you are charged with a serious mental deficiency, in which state you can be taken advantage of? 3) there is something suspicious indeed about all the doctors that come to see you and then don't take your case.

Don't worry about my mother. After bringing up two boys like Rick and me she has a very hard head on her shoulders. She says that she doesn't understand how they can do such a thing, but what she means is that she doesn't see how anyone can just say that I am bad, and my choice of wife is "sick." She understands very well how people can do these things. My mother lives very much in the world, with both eyes open, and both fists swinging if necessary. She is a good kid, and she likes you very much.

My darling it *is* hard for me to wait, just as it is for you. And I do get frantic at times. But the fact that I sound frantic doesn't mean that what I say isn't true. I love you very very much. I am afraid for you, because I fear it is not in you to harden your heart, even superficially. And the people we're up against will take advantage of every softness to strike at us, as they already have. I'm not going to say anymore in these letters about this kind of thing, nor am I going to preach. I have been neglecting to write what is always uppermost in my mind and heart, that I love you and need you and want us to be together. But let me end my lectures with this: you mention carefully each time you talk about me that you are aware I have weaknesses too. I want us both to be aware of these weaknesses in each other so that we can love and help each other. But it is our strengths that are the basis of our love, and we must keep in mind never to let someone criticize us unless they are *doing* better. No man who locks you up has any idea in the world whether or not you or I have good points or weaknesses. They have no right to speak and their actions have made everything they say a lie and an error, even if they seem to be speaking the truth. It is not what is said, but who says it, that is important.

Margie writes her love to you, and her sorrow about the whole situation, which she says she finds impossible to believe. Meanwhile, the private detectives have descended upon Tulsa, Oklahoma, to question the general populace concerning what kind of people are Ted Berrigan, Tom Veitch, Joe Brainard, et cetera. My spies (the Padgetts) report to me this information. It seems peculiar and almost funny that your parents are having you studied by psychiatrists, and me by private detectives. I guess I'm just a criminal, not sick, while you obviously are honest but sick. Well, what they find out should make interesting reading for my biographers someday. I hope the detective agency keeps a copy of the report on me on file. It will save my biographers a lot of trouble. I'd like to read it myself. I thought of sending your parents a list of names of people they could have the detectives talk to about me. I could divide it into three lists, those who will say good things, those who will say derogatory things, and those who are indifferent. It seems a shame that your parents are spending all this money. They could have used it in Europe, or at least given it to us. I'd be glad to tell them anything they want to know about me, and that would be a lot more than they will find out from detective agencies. Well, anyway. . . .

I'm really glad you are getting some reading done. Shaw is a great man, isn't he? Read *Heartbreak House,* if you get a chance. How did you like Caesar's speech to the sphinx at the opening of *Caesar and Cleopatra?* Caesar is the first complete hero in Shaw's work, and the tragedy is that he does almost no good, because the world pays no attention to him. Even Cleopatra understands him only partly. But she may be the next Caesar, if she continues to grow. I'll send a copy of my thesis after you finish *Candida* and *Major Barbara* and *HH* if you want to read it then. Maybe you can read it here by then.

Joe has gone out, and Dick is reading in the other room, and it seems that this is one of the few times I've been alone since I've been back in New York. Alone, my thoughts are filled with you, with your freshness and beauty, and my love. Sandy, it's desolate here without you. A poet wrote somewhere "Music I heard with you was more than music, and bread I broke with you was more than bread . . . now that you are gone, all that once was beautiful is dead." I couldn't say better how I feel.

Here are a couple of pictures of me,† to show how I've looked at different times. The youngest one is my high school picture. Do you recognize me? I was seventeen years old, tall, thin, intense, a kind of literary South Providence wiseguy, cocky, but very very lonely and afraid underneath it all. I thought I knew a lot, I knew I was a genius, but I didn't think it meant much, I wanted to be John Wayne instead.

The army picture is me at nineteen. I thought I was John Wayne then.

The third one is last March in New York, when I was living in a store and writing my thesis. I had a great thick mustache and I thought I was Bernard Shaw. Here's a picture of Shaw as a young man, to show you what I mean.

I'll try to draw a picture† of what Joe and I are doing. We are working on thirteen flag collages. Two are totally finished, others partly finished. The first is a flag with writing all over it. (See drawing.) The writing is a fantasy about a boy and his dream, which involves sex, lady poets, the fifty states, the Statue of Liberty, boats, and self-development. The second flag has a poem written on it called "(Remember) Poem for Annie Rooney." It is pretty drab, compared to the first, but the drabness is intentional, and (I think) good. (See drawing.)

While I was drawing (!) in flags and pasting pictures, Joe drew this picture† for you, of me writing to you, sitting in the sun by the window.

I'm afraid the flags don't look much like what we are doing, but they're something, anyway.

Your bunny (Sleazus) is sitting on my desk, looking at me quizzically, as if to ask, "What's happening, man?" He's leaning on a giant plant Joe gave me.

Everything reminds me of you. The sunlight, Joe, the flower and the plant, the whole room, the whole city, everything.

I'm going to stop now, and go to the library, to Columbia, to see Tom, and then come back and write and read. I'll write again tomorrow, or tonight, or in a few minutes if I feel that I want to. I feel like writing to you at all odd times of the day. You ARE more than part of my last poem. It is written to say that now that I've seen you, I am invincible.

I love you very much.

> All my love, forever
> your husband
> Ted

April 16, 1962

My darling Sandy,

it's almost midnight Sunday night, more than twenty-four hours since we talked, and the first time I've had to myself since then. I had to finish writing a paper on anthropology in return for the money I've sent, which took all night, and then, since I hadn't slept in forty hours, I fell into a coma and slept ten hours. And here I am.

My lovely beautiful Sandy, hearing your voice was so unbelievably wonderful, so thrilling, I can hardly remember what we said, but I remember every inflection in your voice, and every image of you that came to me as I heard you laughing and crying and talking. Hearing you was better than all these letters, all the words in the world.

I love you so much. We will be together again, I'm more sure than ever. No matter where they send you, I'll come there. Perhaps even the farther away from your parents and Florida, the better. My darling, you do whatever you think, and I'll be there come hell, high water, or the complete force of Pinkerton's detectives.

I called at quarter to ten, and had to wait until one minute to ten to get you. I was afraid they wouldn't let you talk. And then it was so great, so good.

Don't worry about me, my physical condition, anything like that; I can take care of myself, and I have many friends here who won't let me die of pneumonia without filling me full of hundreds of antibiotics first.

Honey, we have to talk again before long. I'll afford it, don't worry. Write and tell me when I can call you again, and you won't have to wait for hours this time. I can call anytime of the day or night. Unfortunately there is no phone where I can be reached directly, but if you call Ed Kaim's, person-to-person to me, Ed will come and find me. He has an unlisted number which can't be gotten through Information. It is UNIVERSITY 6-3859. Maybe I could call you Easter Sunday from Providence. I think I will go home for a couple of days, to reassure my mother that I am still alive and kicking. Write to me right away and tell me if I can call you then, or if you can call me, and what time. The telephone number there is STUART (ST) 1-3606.

I'm going to send this with a couple of books. The book I am working on for you is still growing, but stopped while I was sick. It is really good, though.

Honey, in your last letter you said you didn't drink, smoke, curse, use drugs, bite your nails, eat too much, steal, murder, or commit adultery . . . et cetera . . . you forgot to mention that you were kind to animals and children, respected motherhood and the flag, and worked hard all your life. Believe me, all those things have little to do with how "good" you or anyone is, and how "sane" you or anyone is. To paraphrase Dostoevski, *Fathers and Teachers*, I ponder, what is murder? What is stealing? For that matter, what is good or bad?

Jimmy Hoffa doesn't drink, smoke, loves his family, works very hard, and contrary to public opinion, doesn't steal. He doesn't take drugs, probably doesn't bite his nails, although he might resort to a stray murder now and then. How many people did Einstein murder by suggesting to Roosevelt that we develop an atomic bomb? Or is that murder? Did the U.S. steal from Cuba for two hundred years? Did Americans steal Texas from Mexico, and murder Mexicans when they tried to get it back? Or was that something else? Does your dad steal by taking fees from sick people? Is he murdering us slowly? Did you steal from him when you took his money for everything all your life, and then ran off with me? Is coffee a drug? Is Pepsi-Cola? Is codeine? Is penicillin a drug? Is it wrong to use drugs which have a harmful effect on the system? Like marijuana? Is it all right for doctors to tell people that marijuana leads to other drugs, when it doesn't? (Even the AMA says so.) Is it selfish to try to be happy? Why should you be happy if it makes your parents sad? Why should they avoid being sad only by making you unhappy? What is the answer to all of this? Could it be that the list you made has no relevance to how the world would be if things were different? Byron, Shelley, Keats, all smoked, drank, used drugs (probably bit their nails). Walt Whitman drank, smoked, was bisexual or perhaps only homosexual. Aldous Huxley used drugs. John F. Kennedy takes amphetamine pills (Dexedrine) by doctors' orders to alleviate an adrenalin deficiency. (He gets high, too, of course.) Is he bad, or crazy? Better not answer that. Hitler didn't drink, smoked rarely, didn't bite his nails (chewed rugs instead), didn't steal, and never personally murdered anyone. Took baths, too.

I'm not sure what the point is, except that I'm a good man. I don't drink much, although I can and have drunk plenty. I don't smoke but tried it a couple of times for various reasons. I don't curse really, but I like words which have color, and hate sterile language. Shakespeare's plays are full of "cursing." I've tried lots of drugs, and hope to try lots of others. I'm not addicted to anything except maybe Pepsi, but I think the drug experience is really a good thing in every way. I've been known to steal, if stealing means to do such things as take books and or food without paying. As for committing adultery, the Catholic Church says, and rightly, I think, that wanting to, thinking about it, entertaining the idea at all, is the same or maybe worse than doing it. In that case I'm afraid I'm guilty about eleventeen hundred and thirteen times a week. But it's God's fault, not mine. I didn't ask for a penis, he gave me one (hah! he can't have it back, either). And as for being clean, which like all crazy people you mentioned twice, *clean* is an unbelievable word. You've been reading Horatio Alger books again, or maybe the *Reader's Digest*.

It strikes me that all those words are just words, to be talking to you. What I want to say is that I love you oh so very much, want you very much. Sandy, my love, my wife, wherever you are, I'll be there. Whither thou goest, I will go. No one will come in between. Good-night, and I love you.

Your husband forever,
Ted

April 16, 1962

Dear Sandy,

you know, it suddenly occurs to me that we've never talked too much about what these people say is wrong with you. Have they told you exactly in what way you are "sick"? What is it that they say is wrong with you? When I talked to Doctor Skigen he was very evasive, and used terms such as "general nervous breakdown," which are meaningless. I've not suggesting that you ask them, because they'll only tell you what they want to anyway. And they'll be able to be very convincing, too. That's their business.

But let me talk a little about Carl Jung and his ideas about human development, in relation to what these people might be claiming about you.

Jung (and Erich Neumann) say that in the first, childhood stages of development, a person has an essential unity of self. The child is spontaneous, creative, free, in touch with nature, and also with himself. This is a kind of innocence, similar to the garden of Eden perhaps. Then there is a stage where the development of *self*-consciousness begins. Previously the child thought of nature and himself as all part of the same thing. Now he begins to feel that he is "different." He becomes aware of himself. He gains ego consciousness. This is natural. But it sets up a conflict. The child becomes "a split personality, or schizophrenic." He is partly conscious, partly unconscious. The emphasis is upon his ego consciousness, and his unconscious is de-emphasized. An example of this is in sex. The natural biological structure is bisexual. But the culture demands emphasis upon femininity in women, masculinity in men. This is what is conscious. But the other side is not stamped out. It simply becomes unconscious.

This separation of the self is inevitable. It happens always, to everyone. So, the problem is to regain unity with the unconscious, in such a way as to also take advantage of all the good of consciousness. To do this is to be "genius." Also, "well-balanced." Actually, it is to regain the lost innocence, in a new way, a better way, because it includes knowledge of all things unknown before. It is analagous to "gaining heaven," or becoming a "saint." It is innocence and good in the face of evil, rather than in ignorance of it. Thus the biblical emphasis on the fact that Jesus was tempted by Satan, but won out. The winning out was vitally important, because it showed that he could be good even under severe test.

How to accomplish this reunion with the unconscious? Well, the paradox is that the only way to do it is to develop the conscious as much as possible, until one can become conscious of the unconscious. It is like being so selfish that you suddenly become selfless. It is like doing every selfish thing you have an impulse to do, and thereby seeing that there is no value in those impulses, and becoming selfless because you really want to. Rather than doing it because you have been taught that it is a good idea, and then someday your unconscious impulses sneak up on you and you do selfish things without knowing it, rationalizing them into what you call unselfish things. "The way to heaven is through hell" wrote Blake. Jesus, before he went back to heaven, died and went into hell. Odysseus had to go down into the underworld to find out how to get home again. Etc.

And there is always the danger that you will get involved in the underworld, and never come up again. But if you don't face the danger, then you can't make it. And trying to stay in the original state of innocence is a psychophysiological impossibility, and can result only in sickness and maladjustment.

Well, honey, that's all a little vague. But I think the doctors feel that you never became sufficiently self-conscious, and that your goodness and innocence are a delusion, that although they may be "true" now, nevertheless you are not equipped to face the world, you are retarded, and you are bound to suffer serious sickness unless you become sufficiently adapted to reality, and develop accordingly. They feel that your desire for everyone to be happy is childish, everyone can't be happy, and you have to learn to choose whenever necessary the path which provides the most happiness, the best happiness, for the most people, for yourself.

Well, I think they are right. But don't get excited. All that is elementary, and you and I have talked about it before, in different terms. It has little to do with being "sick." I told your father once that I was trying to get back to the way you are. What these doctors don't seem to be able to see, what they aren't ever going to be able to see, is that you are not maladjusted or sick. You do have a lot to learn about the world, but it is only lack of experience that has kept you from knowing it, not sickness, or mental retardation. And most of all, what they don't see, is that when you come upon a new situation in which you are inexperienced, you don't crack up, you utilize your wonderful, sincere, creative, and good instincts, and adapt accordingly. They can't and won't believe that this is possible. They simply can't believe, for example, that you could be competent to raise a family. They won't see the noses in front of their faces.

But they have reasons. And that's where everything I have been saying about the world and us applies. The one thing which reveals you to be "sick," which illustrates that you are still a child, still falsely innocent, still prey to evil because of being mentally retarded, *is that you married me.* Because society, of which your father and the doctors are important members, measures stability in terms of ability to function under the ethics and mores and code of the West of that society. And you, in your innocence and incompetence, they see, the first time you were taken from home and exposed to the evils of the world, fell victim immediately (after only a year and a half) to a man, a boy, who violates all the canons of society, and who therefore is obviously sick himself. Thus, you are not to be trusted outside until you can reason for yourself, see for yourself, and keep away from such evils.

What does all this mean in cold hard facts? It means this, whether they deny it or not: *That the proof of your illness is your protestation of love for me. And that the proof of your cure will be that you see the light, realize that your "love" for me was the result of your childishness and lack of sight, and realize that you don't love me and that I am sick.*

Honey, do you see what that means? It means that as long as you continue to protest your love for me, they are going to keep you under treatment. Even if that is for fifty years. It means that they are not going to let you go home, unless they are completely confident that you will not try to run away, and see me, or any other sick person. It means that all you really believe in are the very things which are keeping you in there. It probably means that they definitely are going to send you to an institution of some sort. And it definitely means that unless I change completely into the image of your dad or Dr. Skigen, that they are never going to let us alone, ever.

But what about me? Am I sick? Well, they believe that I left the stage of innocence that you are in, and became ego conscious, but that I didn't go any further. They believe that through instability, insufficient guidance, or insufficient insight, I got hung up on ego consciousness, to the point that I am completely egocentric, that I am schizophrenic and don't take half of myself, my unconscious, into consideration, that I am selfish, dangerous above all to someone like you, whom I would use for my own benefit, and then carelessly toss away.

A good part of why they think this is because there is a social pattern of development in any given society which members of that society consider parallel to the individual development. In other words, members of a society believe that if you are well-adjusted and properly developed it will be evident in your social behavior. If you are antisocial, obviously you are unbalanced and improperly developed. This is simply a vicious circle which is based on the erroneous idea that society remains the same from year to year. But society changes, and it is always the young who feel the need for change, and the old who uphold the old patterns.

New societal patterns don't form easily. They meet stiff resistance all the way. Consequently, as Shaw pointed out in *The Quintessence of Ibsenism,* it requires a hero to live by and make real the new patterns, when they are new. And sometimes the result of attempting to establish new patterns makes the hero seem like all he wants to do is destroy the old. But you can't build new buildings until all the brick of the old is swept away. When sexual morality is stupid, it requires a Henry Miller to reveal it, and Henry Miller is called a dirty old man by scions of society, simply because he likes to fuck, and writes about it. Don't we all, and couldn't we enjoy it more if we didn't have to be so schizophrenic about it, having to act like it's something either nasty, or even worse, sacred, instead of something natural and fun. Feelings of love are sacred, but fucking is fucking, dogs, cats, eels, and we do it, it ain't sacred it's just nice. *But to the world Henry Miller is sick.*

What did I just say? This: I don't want to be a "success," make a lot of money, fulfill the fake American dream. So, I'm sick. I want to write, it doesn't pay, but I know better than to believe that you can work some of the time, write some of the time. So, I don't work. I'm sick. This means I have no money. So, I steal food. I'm sick. I steal books. I'm sick. I like to experience feelings which I have never had before, because I think that experience is enlightening and good. I trust my competence to decide if such experiments are harmful, even if my judgment agrees with popular opinion (especially if someone such as Aldous Huxley agrees with me). So, I'm sick. I don't want to steal. I want to work hard writing and reading, and developing, and be married, and have children, but these patterns of the society I live in say I can't do that, because they deny that writing is worth payment until you are dead or universally accepted. I don't agree. I refuse to accept their directions on how to live. I not only steal, but I think it's all right, when I think about it. Usually I don't think about it, I just go steal a hamburger and eat and steal a book and go home and read it. So, I'm sick. Living like this causes me to be poor, so I wear odd clothes (which I prefer) unlike the type worn to work every day by the respectable (although they are somewhat like the type worn by the workers). This proves I'm sick. I don't particularly like haircuts. I'm sick. (I think I look better in long hair.) I like my beard, most people don't have beards. So, I'm sick. And worst of all, from their point of view, I don't feel sheepish about the whole business, instead I am proud of my work, proud of my ability, angry at society because I don't have enough money to go to the movies, angry because they say that if I want to go to movies I ought to work (What the hell do they think I do all day?), and as a consequence of the resistance I meet on every side I am pushy, defensive, aggressive, disdainful, and a smart aleck without proper humility. So, I'm sick.

But am I?
I say no.

And are you?

I say no. I say that you are more healthy, more honest, more beautiful, and more good, than all of them, and me, too. But the presence of them makes the presence of me necessary so that you won't change into them, which you will if they have anything to say about it.

I love you, Sandy, and I love the idea of you and me. I don't think we can win, I don't think we can make them let us alone. But I think we can get together anyway, and show them a united front. We can't ignore them. We can't. They won't let us. But if I go down, it'll be fighting. And if we go down, they'll be worse losers than us. My darling, always I am touching your hand, your hair, your heart, always I love you very much.

Your husband forever,
Ted

[Undated]

My dearest, my darling,

never a morning like this before! Rain is pouring into the Hudson River outside my window, music on the radio, Dick translating poems from the Greek anthology behind me, I've written two poems tonight, and I am drunk with poetry! I have drunk the heady wine of Mayakofsky, of Rilke, of Lorca, and of Walt Whitman all night! So if I am delirious, forgive me.

Sandy, my love, my wife, you think too much. Such men are dangerous.

This is not prose we are living. It's poetry. We love. That's rare, Sandy. There is no time for love in 1962. But we love. And that's what poetry is: Love.

> Honey, no doctor can *help* you
>> unless you need help
>> unless you are sick
>> unless you wanted help
>> unless you help him help you

IF they get you another doctor
IF they let you go home
IF they give you any kind of freedom at all
>> after locking you up
>> chasing your husband out of town
>> being totally dishonest with you

then you have a choice between being dishonest and biding your time till you can escape, or cooperating fully with the doctor, that is, being honest 100%.

IF the doctor is any good at all, which is unlikely
        you are wasting his time if you keep anything from him.

If you are wasting his time
        why not be honest with yourself by being totally dishonest?

You can't straddle the fence in this business.
Your parents have set the terms for you:

                                live their way
                                or not at all.

They don't say, "Let's work this out."
They do say, "Do what we tell you or else."

And that's the way it is. Do what they tell you or else.
That's us, honey: the "or else."

    You can't be a happiness girl here, and make everybody happy.
You are going to make someone unhappy here. If you try to play
it so no one is hurt, then I'll be hurt by our separation, so will you,
and your parents will be lulled until the next time we try to get
together, which will make it worse for them then. You can't win
them over. You can't. You can't. You can't.
    This is not preaching. This is the facts.

You are free of every obligation to honesty with anyone there.
You are a prisoner. You have no rights. They bind you with your
code of honor, and use it themselves only when convenient. You
have no idea what is really happening there. You are a prisoner
locked up in a room in a mental ward, told whatever they deign
to tell you.
    Your parents have two goals:

    1. To keep us apart.
    2. To make you forget me.

They have attained one. They are working on the other. We don't want to play the game that way. *They are wrong.* The only sure way to change the state of affairs is to regain the ground which they have won. We must be together. I cannot come to Miami. We can't win there. You must get away. To anywhere. We have nothing nothing absolutely nothing to say to them until we say it out from under their prison walls.

Sandy, don't you see? They've got you writing me letters telling me my faults, your faults, our weaknesses, in short, why some of what they do is right. You need to forget everything for the time being except that we are husband and wife, and someone is keeping us apart.

If you run away they will chase you. Maybe they will chase you and me forever. Is that worse than the way things are now? THEY AREN'T GOING TO PERMIT US TO BE TOGETHER IN TIME. What is the good of acquiescing to their demands for three, four, five months? Will they like me better then? Even if I shave, go to work, etc.? No. they'll claim it's a plot to fool them. If we must run to be together, let's run. Run when you can to where you can. Contact me through Tony, or Margie, and I'll come. And we'll run. And we'll fight if necessary. And if they catch one of us or both and lock us up again, then we'll run again as soon as we can.

I don't think there is any other way. Time is going to make things worse. You should run as soon as you get a chance. Take the first plane out of Florida going in any direction. From there take a bus, or train, to some city where you can hide. Any big city, and medium-size city. Anywhere. Call Margie in Houston, have her telegraph Tony at Johns Manville. He will get me, I'll get in immediate touch with you, we'll run to Canada, to Mexico, to the coast, to some-where. If you need money, and you will, I'll send it next week, or tomorrow if necessary. Run Run Run as soon as you get a chance.

The best place to run from is home, of course. To do this they must think you won't. And you must do it all at once, not slowly.

Take the car to go to the store, drive to the airport, take a plane immediately. You must be as ruthless as they. Perhaps they will relent a little when they see you, we, are serious. As long as they think they can control you, control you is what they will do.

As they have proved that you are sick.

Sandy, I love you.

I am and always will be your husband
your lover
I am not what they say I am
You are not sick.

I will do whatever you say. Shall I come to Miami right now, and try to see you? Shall I go to work somewhere right now? Tell me what you think, what you want. If you want me to tell you what else I think, I will. All I want is for you to love me.

All my love,
Ted

April 18, 1962

Dear Sandy,

my darling, don't ever worry about nagging. It isn't nagging to tell me what's on your mind. I want you to tell me, I want to be able to tell you. To be able to talk to each other is to love honestly and openly. I love you very much, and I would feel terrible if you didn't cry out to me when you need me. If there is something you need from me, please, just ask, if I am not wise enough to perceive it in advance. I wish I could do everything without being asked.

Honey, about Leslie, and lawyers. I knew you could be released on a habeas corpus writ. I checked very closely into everything that the law could do for us. Please don't think I am idling away my time here waiting for you to do something, meanwhile casually reading books and writing poems. I torture myself every day with thoughts of running to Florida, of what to do, what to do.

First, about the law: After you are released on a writ, then what? There is an annulment suit pending, charging that you are mentally ill and unfit to be married. Do you think we could be together? You might get pregnant! Also, you are underage, and therefore subject to your parents until such time as it is proven you are competent to be married. Your parents would get an injunction keeping us apart, and have you placed under their care at home. And they'd keep you there. So, what would be accomplished by such a writ would be that you would get out of the hospital, and confined elsewhere, where we would be unable to have any communication at all. Your parents would either not allow you to receive mail, or else read it all. Honey, in the eyes of every single person remotely connected with this case, with the exception of a few of my friends and my mother, we are dead wrong. Even Leslie half thinks so. *You can't get out and we can't get together any way except illegally, and subject to persecution. That's the facts.* As long as you hope for justification in the eyes of others, as well as freedom, you are going to get kicked around. *All the respectable doctors say you are sick.* You must realize that. And when they say so, the world believes. No matter that everyone from Beethoven to Allen Ginsberg who had an individual idea has been called sick first, and adored later. The world still believes the nonsense. That's the way it is.

And about Leslie, and her father, lawyers, and the rest: honey, don't you see? Leslie is an inexperienced kid, and her father believes basically the same as your father does. He wants to help Sandra Alper, because he knows you and doesn't think there is anything wrong with you, but about the situation as a whole he thinks exactly as your father does. Sandy, darling, what kind of thinking are you doing? Back up a couple of steps from these people, and take a look at what they are saying. I don't even live in the Village. I live uptown, two blocks from Columbia U. I don't live in a cold-water flat. I live in a room, have a kitchen with hot and cold water, a bathroom, with families next door, in a normal New York apartment house in a typical New York area.

I've never associated with or even known anybody who was or is addicted to any narcotics. I don't know a single prostitute. He's been reading *Life* magazine too much. Sandy, damnit, my friends here are Ed Kaim and Harry Diakoff and Bill McCullam and Ron Padgett, students at Columbia University, and guys like Dick and Tom. Are they dope addicts? You know better than that. Honey, there is not the remotest possibility in the entire world that anything of the nature that these people mention could ever happen to you, to us. I'm a serious writer, writing poetry. You can't take narcotics and write, too. What the hell.

As for Leslie, I like her, she's a good kid, mostly with her eyes open, but all she has to base her ideas on are what she knows from her experience as an eighteen-year-old child of her parents who is very inexperienced. She is as much influenced by conventional ideas as anyone. She wants you to be happy, and to help you, but she is as open to influence by what people say about us as anyone is, and she is influenced by it.

Sandy, there are scads of people down there who insist on telling you about me. But of all of them, the only one who knows me is you. And you fell in love with me, ran off with me, and married me, and brought me home to your family openly and honorably. Don't let these people make you think that they know more about me than you. They are wrong. They are wrong. They are wrong.

My darling, you're tearing my heart out. I know how difficult it is for you there. But it's all up to you. I told you before we went there that this might happen. And it did. And now, there is no chance, no chance, that everything is going to work out all right. It's us against everyone, and they've got all the aces. All we can do now is hold tight to each other, and try to keep them away from us. The odds are a million to one that we will be hounded for the rest of our days. From now on the days when it seemed to you that everything was really pretty nice in the world are over. You are going to have to fight for every good thing, and every time you relax a little, someone is going to smack you down. But believe me, even with all that, we can have a very very good life together, a real life with real love. But as long as you wait for the world to recognize that we are right, you are going to be in the same position you are now.

Honey, I'm not sick. I'm not a criminal. We are not wrong. You are not sick. I do love you. We can make a good life together and if it doesn't look like we will be able to give our kids a swimming pool in the yard, well, we won't lock them up when they marry the man or woman they love, either.

Sandy, you thought I was a pretty good man, or you wouldn't have married me.

Now, about a job: darling, we talked all this over just before and after we were married. I was going to get a job, which would pay enough to support us and send you to school, remember? We were going to both do whatever necessary to have a good life.

We told your parents that, remember? Nor did we ask them for money, nor did we ask them to put you through school, although we'd have accepted if they'd offered to. Remember?

But they didn't give us a chance.

Remember?

Now, I'm not working. And you are asking me, begging me, crying, that I get a job. My dear, my wife, I wish you never had to cry to me, I wish I could give you everything before it reached that. But what's happening here? What are you asking me? You asked me to get a job and send money, for us. And I think it's a good idea. Enclosed is some money, too. Did you get the other money?

But then there was a chance you would (will) be sent somewhere where I will follow. And soon. Which means I could only get a job for a week or two or four until I left here. Since I'm getting money, I thought I'd wait until I go where you are, and get a job there. Also, there was a chance I would come to Florida. Also, I don't want to get a job. But I definitely would forget my wants when it comes to us. That's part of what love and marriage are.

But honey, I'm afraid you have seized upon the fact that I don't have a respectable job as part of the key to our problem. As if things would somehow be different if I had a job, or if I get one.

Sandy, I work very hard as it is, and get no pay. Which means, I'm not respectable. *But* in the eyes of your parents, and Leslie, and doctors, will it be any different if I get a job? Sandy, Sandy, you keep talking about things like me getting a job, and us waiting a long time, like until you are twenty-one, as if somehow everything will be all right if we just wait and trust in something or other. *It ain't like that, honey.* If they can keep you till you're twenty-one, they can keep you till you're fifty-one. And they will. And they are smart. You can't convince them with time that you have repudiated me, unless you have. They are too smart. And I can't convince them that I have "turned respectable," unless I do. And by turning respectable they don't mean not stealing books, taking pills, etc. They mean *thinking* like they do. And I can't do that. Remember Saint Joan? After she admitted she was wrong, since it seemed that if she was right she wouldn't be in the trouble she was in, they didn't free her, they condemned her to life imprisonment. Honey, we have to choose the fire. If you don't believe that, I don't know what to say. . . .

But as for a silly thing like getting a job, Sandy, my darling, I'll do anything to make you feel better. I wanted to tell you that I feel that things will not get any better, that only if you run can we be together. But if you know I think that, darling, if you want me to get a job, send me a special delivery letter or a telegram right away and all you have to say is yes, you do, and I'll go to an agency and get a job that same day or as fast as they will get me one.

Sandy, I know your body and brain are getting beaten on. I am terribly afraid every day. But as much as I love you, and as much as I want it to be me under the pressure there instead of you, the cold dispassionate truth always stares us in the face: All those that are going to make it will. All those that aren't, won't.

They'll cut you down, and cut you down, and cut you down, until your head is reeling worse than it ever has before. They'll have you wondering whether black is white, whether you are really Sandy Berrigan, whether you are standing on your feet or on your head. Once in a while they'll give you a little slack, and then just when you are smiling, they'll jerk you off your feet so hard you won't know what happened. They will resort to any kind of trick, honest or dishonest, to do you and us in.

And things will still get worse, and never get better, as long as you are there.

Get on your feet, honey. Put up your dukes. You need to think more thoughts like "Dr. Skigen is a lily-white son-of-a-bitch" and fewer thoughts like maybe the next doctor will be better. You better start learning to hate. It's time for fewer warm tears and more cold fury.

Sandy, what drew me to you so much, as much as anything, was that you can stand on your own two feet. I know that in this kind of stress, it is terrible to feel alone. But in truth, in any kind of stress we are always alone. We always have to stand up by ourselves. I love you and part of that love is because I don't have to prop you up. When they knock you to your knees, I know it is not because you are weak, but because they are too many. But the getting up is always something you have to do yourself. When there are too many the rules of fighting are different than when it is one on one. If you can lower the odds by hitting below the belt you do so. And when that doesn't work, you run. Odysseus told Diomedes when the tide was obviously against the Greeks that day, that there was a time to fight and a time to run. Honey, the day is going against us. They've split our forces, and are cutting us down. It's time to run. Otherwise, it's Little Big Horn, and our last stand. They'll beat us sure as life. I want you to play it the way you see it. For you that's the only right way. But it seems to me that unless we run, we'll lose.

All my love, your husband forever,
Ted

April 19, 1962

My darling,

it's very lonely here today. For the first time since we've been separated, two days have passed without a letter from you. And now I miss you so much I could cry. Sandy, it seems that I am always writing to you about our troubles, about doctors, and parents and lawyers; what I want to talk to you about is not those things at all, but love, the love I feel for you, the good things we've had, how beautiful it has all been in spite of everything.

Maybe you are home now, for Passover. I'm afraid I don't know very much about Passover, or any of the Jewish holidays; you'll have to teach me. Isn't Passover the memorial day for the flight from Egypt? I seem to recall that a rabbi explained it to me once a long time ago when I used to light the synagogue lights on Friday for twenty-five cents at the synagogue down the street in Providence. The flight from Egypt! Do you know that Moses is regarded as the greatest of the prophets, for he was the only one who saw God face to face, in daylight? Light is a symbol of consciousness, and Moses represents the highest human consciousness up until Jesus. I'd like to know about Passover, but I want to learn from you, and not from books.

This week is a very important week in my own religious heritage. Holy Week. Last Sunday is the feast day (remembrance day) of the Sunday that Jesus went to Jerusalem, where he was welcomed by the crowds in the city, who laid palms under the feet of his mule, and held a ticker-tape parade for him down their Broadway. Unbelievable! Jesus passed much of the week preaching here and there, and the city was in a holiday mood. But there was an undercurrent of tension, because the Romans were occupying the city, and the Zealots, the Jewish underground, seethed with hatred of the Romans. They didn't think much of Jesus either, because Jesus preached love, and they preached hatred and force. In fact, it seems after all that nobody liked Jesus except a rare few. When he preached he captivated the crowds with the force of his personality and the magic of his words, but afterwards the people tried to forget him. He asked too much of them!

Today, called Holy Thursday in the Catholic Church, is the day when Catholics visit a number of different churches through-out whatever city they live in, to pray awhile in each, in memory of the events of the ancient Holy Week. The visits symbolize both the preaching of Jesus in those times, and his command to the apostles to preach and teach all over the world. Tomorrow is called Good Friday (I guess you know that) and although the chronology is not exactly accurate, noon tomorrow is the symbolic date that Jesus was hung up on the cross. It is called Good because although Jesus died on this day, his death represented the birth of new consciousness, a new religion of love. At three o'clock tomorrow, the time of Jesus' death, the season of Lent ends, all the altars are uncovered (all through Lent the altars are covered with cloth of purple, the color of suffering), and the church is filled with lilies and other flowers, to symbolize the joy at the resurrec-tion of Jesus.

All of this never meant too much to me when I was a Roman Catholic. I was too close to the woods to see the trees. But now, from a distance, it all seems to possess a simplicity and a beauty that is touching, and seems good. Psychologically the story of Jesus is one of the most revealing, most accurate mythical repre-sentations of the evolution and development of consciousness in men. And poetically it is one of the most aesthetic and attractive stories in the history of literature. Only in organized religion has this story had bad results. More people have been killed in the name of Jesus than any other cause. Unbelievable!

But it has its consistency. More people have been made neurotic in the name of Freud, more been made fascist in the name of Marx, more become tyrants under the banner of democracy, etc. Jesus was a very great man, but he was certainly not a Christian (nor a "Jew" either, although he was Jewish). Nor was Freud a Freudian, nor Marx a Marxist. The worst affliction visited upon great men is and always has been disciples, followers.

Honey, I've always loved Easter. Maybe it's because of the Easter Bunny! My parents used to hide candy eggs (we liked candy, not eggs) all over the house, when Rick and I were little, and we used to spend all day looking for them. And there was always a basket with chocolate Easter bunnies and things in it by each of our beds, a colorful basket, full of green grassy paper and bright ribbons. And Easter was the time of year when we got new shoes, and a new shirt, and new suits, and we would get all dressed up and go to church, and then go to the corner where everyone would inspect everyone else's new clothes. How I wish we were together now! We could go downtown on Sunday and see everyone in their new clothes, and dress up ourselves, walk in the park, hold hands. I've never longed for anyone the way I do for you, never felt about anyone the way I feel about you.

Every day I think about the days we were together. The park in New Orleans, and waiting at the bus stop with Dick and Tom, and Dick singing "Payday" . . . "I'm a poor boy, I'm a poor boy . . . and a long way from home . . . You're gonna miss me . . . gonna miss me . . . when I'm gone . . . gonna miss me . . . oh lord . . . when I'm gone."

John Pupene was terribly jealous in the park that day, and later at the table when we were going to run away. All those people had been watching you and thinking about you, lazily, hesitantly, and now you were all but gone. And then you were gone, and then Dick, too, was gone, and New Orleans turned bitter, and only Morrison was there to say, "You're goddamn right we'll miss you, Dick," but Hoffman and Pupene and the others could only write letters to Dick's folks saying where's your son who owes us money for phone calls, et cetera and all the petty rest. I wonder what Karen is doing?

What a crazy taxi ride to the bus, and such a sweet lovely bus trip, I was so awestruck, felt so humble that you were half asleep, your head on my lap, so trusting, and I resolved to do anything in the world to live up to that . . . but I couldn't keep you when they came and took you. All I could do was watch, and try to be calm, so that you wouldn't cry too much. It was unreal somehow . . . and didn't get real until the detective threatened me, and my adrenalin came rushing up, and I told him I would beat his head in, and he backed off a little, talking tough to soothe his pride.

But Houston was so good. The man who wanted to help us find flowers, and even the unctuous judge . . . and Margie's unbelievable landlady . . .

and Margie's radio, and you, so beautiful, crying for me, big tears flowing down your cheeks as you read my letter of anguish, written eighteen months before to Margie, crying that I needed love. I never dreamed I would find anyone like you. I'm so happy, Sandy. I'm almost crying now. It is good. We are good. We had something, and I pray we have it again.

If only they could have seen us walking with Margie in Houston at night, or in her apartment in the afternoon . . . don't they know you pawned your watch for us, and I sold my blood for us? If only they could have seen you cooking in Tulsa, or ironing, or carrying my thesis across the campus . . . or typing poetry in the kitchen.

But they did see us in Miami. They saw us babblingly happy together. They saw you come and stand by my side in tears. They heard me tell them not to disturb my wife, heard me ask that they allow us dignity. Sandy, how could anyone who saw us together want to tear us apart? Tony Walters said that when he saw me with you in Tulsa it was the first time he had seen me happy since the middle of the school year at Madalene, in 1959. And Dave

Bearden, wrapped up so intensely in his own unhappiness, nevertheless rejoiced as he immediately saw that we were good together.

Now Lorenz Gude tells me last night that I'm different from when I left here. That I seem unhappy almost all the time. And I read in Dick's journals that "there is a tragic unhappiness underlying everything Ted does these days. He seems unwilling to do anything that he really wants to do, without Sandy." And it's true. Without you I want only to mourn.

Honey, I'm so sorry that all my letters are impatient, and pedantic, and full of lectures and whatever. I want only to write to you of love. Nearly all my thoughts of you are only semi-conscious, I'm afraid to think of you too hard, for fear I'll break down. I force myself to rage, to rant, to read and write, to hold myself together. About this situation I feel only the blackest pessimism. I have absolute faith in you, in us. But I know that the others have all the power, the power to destroy perhaps. And I'm afraid.

I'm writing papers for $20 a week for the next five weeks. So, we have time to work, and a place too. I'm writing a paper on ethnic music of the primitive Eskimos as well as on labor legislation. The two papers don't take up too much time, so I am able to work on my own work. Dick and I are both doing translations, he is writing a story, and I'm working on poetry and poems, as always, as well as reading many things. The room is in a place where there are four or five rooms on the floor, with a community kitchen, icebox, stove, etc., so we cook our own meals.

I'll send books of poetry and *Steppenwolf* tomorrow. We aren't quite all moved yet.

Torrents of Spring is by Ivan Turgenev.

The article you sent about books and the school board is a fairly accurate picture of what America is like in many places. In

Tulsa two years ago a woman teacher was castigated verbally by the school board for telling her twelfth-grade students to read *Catcher in the Rye*. In a way it was funny because I had given it to my eighth-grade students to read the year before. Tony Walters was a ninth grader in the high school where the incident happened, and his class discussed the incident. Tony shocked everyone by telling them he'd read the book the year before, and by writing a paper saying that it was a fine book. The principal confiscated his paper and read it, but without comment. Tony's teacher had scheduled a classroom debate on the book, between Tony and the rest of the class (none of whom had read it), but the principal cancelled the debate. The upshot of the whole controversy, of course, was that *Catcher in the Rye* became a giant bestseller at Edison High School, and everyone from the janitor to the worst student read it. Secretly, of course. What a farce. But the teacher resigned in disgust when she was made to change her suggested reading list for students, and later the library collection of books in the high school library was pruned of such books as *Catcher*, and *Look Homeward, Angel*, by the school authorities. Edison is the biggest and newest high school in Tulsa, a city of some 400,000 people. Wow. Also, as a teacher I was once told never to bring another book by John Steinbeck into the school (although there was a story by Steinbeck in the school eighth-grade reader)! What a world.

I'm still beset by cold pains. This cold is just enough to throw me slightly off stride, and is very annoying. And that reminds me, what do you mean by "gentlemanly" and that "plain language will do"? Hah! I'm a poet, and plain language is something I've never heard of! And I'm not gentlemanly, honey, just rhetorical. When I say I beg you, I am trying to put in words the feeling I would put into whatever I am asking just by presence and gesture and the look on my face if we were together. I don't really beg you. I know we don't have to beg of each other. But it's hard to change tone of voice with black ink on white paper. And anyway, young lady, don't be sarcastic with your elders. (Your horoscope says that you as a Virgo and I as a Scorpio are eminently well matched and perfectly suited to each other. Isn't that good? Even the heavens agree with us. Too bad Conrad Moricand isn't your father.)

Sandy, I'm so filled with love for you that it seems almost trite to say I love you. It seems almost silly to try to say anything about what you mean to me in three words, or three thousand. Words are my business, my game, my hobby. But what I am with you, for you, what you are to me, is before and beyond all words. Carol Clifford asked to see the pictures you sent me, and I almost cried when I showed them to her. Not for any reason except a *Paradise Lost* kind of feeling. I miss you so much, feel you so much a part of me, that I never even dream of you. You are so real that when I dream I am not myself dreaming of you, but both of us dreaming about something else. I pray you will be free soon.

All of my love forever,
your husband,
Ted

April 20, 1962

Dearest Sandy,

today is such a good day. It's cold, but the sun is shining, the city is crystal clear. And I have a letter from you. For the first time last week two days went by without a letter from you. I knew that it was probably because you went home for Passover, but still, I felt bad, worried without knowing what I was worried about.

It must have been a strained period while you were at home. But at least you were out in the air. I would like to have the clothes there, kind of, but I think I'd rather have them be there. You keep the books, too.

My dear, I'm so sorry about Rita, and the way she feels, the things she said. And Mimi and her silence, too. You know, somewhere inside her Mimi knows it isn't like they say, or like they will say when they get around to talking to her. The guy who talked to her about dreams, took her downtown for a ride, upon whose lap she sat all the way back from our drive, Mimi knows he was pretty good, and he wouldn't hurt her sister. She knows it. Even if she isn't sure she does. She knows it.

But Rita. Well, you said that your parents wouldn't be like they were. You knew they wouldn't do these things. Rita feels that way, too. She knows that if they feel the way they do, there must be something wrong, they must have some grounds for it. Sandy darling, believe me, if Rita is anything like you, she will like me. When she meets me, when we talk a little, when she sees me with you and sees how much I love you, how tender I feel toward you, when she sees how I talk to her kids, how they talk to me, she'll know it's all right. It might take a while to allay her fears, but she'll be on our side. Even your parents will see that it's all right, if they'll only give us a chance.

But they won't.

I found the steal books poem and some others in Dick's stuff that came from Miami. I'm glad you have all those things, the Chianti bottle, the books, the clothes. I keep turning up, one way or another. And with love. In books, and bottles and poems, and black poet's shirts. Nothing pernicious about those things anyway? Why don't your people open their eyes?

Sandy, you are Chris. And those poems are for you. And yet they're still for Chris, who was a beautiful beautiful girl. Honey, I never thought Chris would waver . . . even if she was fourteen. But in six months, her parents changed her. Not completely of course, but enough to end Chris and Ted. But you are the sum of all the people I've ever loved, and much more besides.

(Now Dick is playing the guitar . . . "It was early in October . . . I hitched my team in order to roll . . . Timaro . . . Timaro . . . Timarideeeo . . ." and we're all here, Dick and you and me and Tom, all being horrible beatniks, surrounded by books and giant piles of narcotics to give away to school kids so we can corrupt their mow-rals . . . well I'll be goddamned!)

Honey, I'll write more this afternoon. I have to go eat lunch and read books. Don't worry about me and shoes and clothes and food and all that sort of stuff. Do I look hungry or underdressed? I can take care of myself, and I can take care of you, and if we have ten kids I can take care of them too, because after all I am a damned good man, which has something to do with why you married me. I love you very much.

Also. I sent our answer to the court, and a copy to my daddy-in-law.

All my love,
your husband forever, Ted

April 23, 1962

Dear Sandy,

I've just returned from sending you a telegram. I'm so sorry about not calling, but I didn't go home, didn't get your letter about calling, didn't know whether to call or not, didn't have a place to call from, and worst of all, was sick.

I'll tell you all about most of it tonight anyway, but please don't worry about me. I can't seem to shake off this cold, and it keeps going away, almost, and then coming back for a few days, and then doing the same thing all over again. Today and the last two days have been terrible, I'm all congested, my head aches, and I'm giantly annoyed. But it isn't really serious. I just need you to come and make me go to bed for about three days and eat hot soup and all that sickly stuff.

Right now, as usual, I'm working on papers, and listening to Dick play the guitar. I just stopped a minute to read him a poem by Tennessee Williams called "Heavenly Grass" . . . do you know it?

> My feet took a walk on heavenly grass
> all day while the sky shone clear as glass.
> My feet took a walk on heavenly grass
> all night while the lonesome stars rolled past.
> Then my feet come down to walk on earth
> and my mother cried when she give me birth.
> Now my feet walk far and my feet walk fast
> But they still got an itch for heavenly grass
> But they still got an itch for heavenly grass.

I'm glad you're reading about Zen. I'll try to send you a book called *The Supreme Doctrine,* which is very good. I have read about Zen, and talked about it, with Lauren, and Dave . . . and we really

were interested in it very much when we were all in Tulsa
. . . . (Lauren, in answer to a question I just remembered, is not a
poet, or a painter, but rather a scholar, a scientist, a metaphysician,
a priest maybe) . . . but after all, there isn't much to say about Zen
. . . . . except facts, which are in books. As Louis Armstrong said
when asked what jazz was, "Man, if you don't know, I can't tell you
. . . (or maybe) man, if you gotta ask, you'll never know." That is,
once you get interested, and look for yourself, then you'll either
know or won't and no one can tell you.

But a few words anyway. What you said, and I said about not
drinking, smoking etc. . . . . Zen says (except Zen doesn't say
anything) that to think that such things as doing or not doing
something have anything to do with anything is really funny.
What is good is what we do. If we get drunk, that's good. If we
don't drink, that's good. If we're no good, that's o.k., too. (What's
"no good" mean?) To "know" Zen is to forget such things as Zen.
Like, to be so selfish that you forget to be selfish.

I'll make up a Zen parable for you, since everything else I've
said sounds a little delirious, maybe this will cinch my delirium.

Spontaneous Zen Parable

Dick Gallup went to the Zen master and said,
"Master, speak about taking pills." The master
said,"Gallup, you got any pills?" Gallup said, "Yeah."
Then the master said, "Pills are a good thing."

Sandy Berrigan went to the master and said,
"Master, speak about taking pills." The master said,
"What's your kick, baby?" Sandy said, "I just don't
think pills are right!" Then the master said, "You are
very wise. Pills are no good."

Tom Veitch, observing these two incidents, said to
the master, "Goddamn, master, that's contradictory!!"

The master replied, "Goddamn, I'm hungry, let's go get some hash and eggs."

Signed,
"The Snake."

Zen parables can't exactly be explained, only commented on. But to comment on my own parable, since I'm the master in it, I think I meant something like this: the master was asked to say something about pills. Being a master he knew that he was expected to condemn or condone them. So, when he saw that Gallup had pills, therefore was for them, he said they were good. When he saw that Sandy was against them, he said they were bad. But Veitch didn't ask him any questions, so he didn't say anything. Veitch did make a comment about logical contradictions, but that's silly anyway, and what kind of answer can one give to it? What the master did say was what he was thinking. He was hungry.

The idea, thought, motto, joke, whatever else you want to label it, that I base my life upon, is a pure Zen doctrine, although I never read it anywhere associated with Zen. It's "all those who are going to make it will, all those who aren't, won't."

Zen says nothing, gives no answers, makes you responsible. But it doesn't *say* that. Words are words. What do they have to do with Zen? Zen is poetry. Zen is living. Poetry is living. To live is to be religious. Living is dynamic, religion is static. So, religions are not Zen, although they might be. And Zen is DEFINITELY NOT a religion. It is living. Henry Miller is the essential Zen kind of man, so is Dick Gallup. Your father and mother and Dr. Skigen have forgotten about Zen. I mean forgotten too, because Zen is something you are, not something you learn. Which explains why you feel like a "Zen Buddhist" when you read a good thing about Zen.

The best writers I know about Zen are Daisetz Suzuki, and R. H. Blyth, and Alan Watts has some good things, too.

Now, back to architecture, and waiting to talk to you. Here's a poem† by a little boy, that is really good. I love you and miss you especially when I read things like this and wish I could look up and say "Sandy, look at this . . ."

your husband forever,
Ted

April 26, 1962

Dear Sandy,

hello. Lots of letters from you these three days, and I haven't written since Tuesday. But I had another day in bed, with the same cold. The weather keeps changing, and so do I, from bad to worse. I'm sorry for the silence. Today I'm almost healthy, and wildly reading books on Joseph Michael Gandy, British visionary architect of the nineteenth century.

Shall I tell you a Berrigan parable to go with the Zen parable? o.k., since you say o.k., I will.

Some fellows go to school, to college. Their dads pay their way, give them lots of money, as long as they make decent grades (like c or over). They like college social life, they hate studies. But if they don't study they get no money from Daddy. So they hire me to write them papers which will make b or better. They get much money from Daddy, give some to me. They do what they want, and get money, I do what I want (study subjects and write) and get money. We're both happy. Also Daddy is happy because they get good grades. Later, they graduate, work for Daddy, and inherit all his money. All in all everybody is happy. Except you.

End of parable.

What does it mean?

Well, it's a rotten system. I suggest that their dads disinherit them, adopt me, because I like to write papers. But that won't work, because their dads don't care about the papers, they only care about the grades and the diplomas. Something is all messed up there. Honey, I can't change this world. But I can make myself be in shape by developing my own talents, so that if the system ever changes, I'll be here, a writer who can write, ready to offer good writing.

I can't explain, I guess. I'm saying that these kids are not wrong for hiring someone to write their papers. They don't want to write papers. Why should their livelihood depend on something they don't want to do? It's the system that's wrong. And I'm not wrong for writing them. I'm a writer, and I write. If Peter don't pay, Paul does. Have you read *Major Barbara*? All the above is not too clear, I realize. But I think you are putting emphasis on the wrong place. Why should these kids have to write if they don't want to? So they can have money to play. But why should they have to go to school to get money? If someone took away all their parents' money, the situation would be different. Or if they got the money without having to please their parents. Then they could work, or dissipate, and it would be their own business. But as it is, it is their parents who are to blame, and ultimately it is capitalism that is to blame, and it is the "American Way" that is to blame. But if I don't write their papers the only sufferers are me and them. The system goes on. Well, I'll write their papers. It helps me. If it hurts them, that's their business. The abstract principle of honor, which would have me refuse to have anything to do with this situation, is a principle which leads down a blind alley. We live in the world, and we can't keep our hands off the dirt of the world. So, we must use the dirt to grow things in, good things, out of the seeds of ourselves. All those who are going to make it will. All those that aren't, won't.

Well, I see I made another speech. I'm sorry. My words of love seem always to be changed into a lecture, a tirade, a speech by the energy which drives me. My dearest, it is only to you that I can rage and rage. A great man, Alfred Whitehead, said that to be intelligent we need to look at things from a different angle than the ordinary way they are looked at. When we get so used to seeing the world the way we do, then we see it the way we think it is instead of the way it is. Remember the madwoman of Chaillot? She was crazy and so am I and so are you.

Yes, I remember I gave the anthology to Leslie. I forgot for just a moment. And too bad about Karen and Doris, but not too bad. There's Joe. And Tom. And Leslie. Carol Clifford says that she saw *The Madwoman of Chaillot* the same week we did. And she says she had her first drink at your house. And she says if you are sick, she is, too.

Honey, I went to hear Kenneth Koch today, to his lecture on the poetry of William Carlos Williams. He's great (both of them). I'll show you some notes I made:

the last sun Theodore Roethke   John Weiners
                                                          The Hotel Wentley Poems

Queen Anne's Lace
Wms "always" places us in media res
use of colors
Rimbaud
Eluard
Breton   The Marx Brothers & The Mullen
Apollinaire
Saint-Pol Roux
Max Jacob   Edward Lear
Robert Desnos

Whitman and the ing words

    You are a skyscraper
    you are a sailboat veering in the wind
    you are blocks piled high with letters on them
    you are butterflies and bumblebees
    or else
            nothing
    or air.
                "Tone of voice"

THE TROUBLE WITH MODERN POETRY IS NOT THAT IT IS OBSCURE BUT THAT IT IS NOT OBSCURE.

None of those things were said by Koch. They were all things I jotted down casually out of my head (not a pun). It was a good lecture. I wish you were there.

It's almost two hours since I began this letter, I got involved in some rewriting while typing "The Drunken Boat." But maybe it's finished. I'm not sure yet.

Honey, I miss you and dream of you so much. I have such dreams for us, for you, for myself. I've never been able to release the natural affection I possess except with you. I want always to be tender, to be loving, and yet so often I am the way I was that night in Tulsa, when you saw me raging for really no apparent reason. I've buried my desire to love and be loved very deep, buried it a long time ago, and it was a long long time re-emerging. Now that I am at last fully able to love, I love you so much, and my dreams for life center on us, on you. I want us to be alone, to be together, where I can read and write, and we can walk together, and talk, and where you can help me be gentle, I need to learn again to be gentle and kind for I have had to teach myself to be harsh and unkind with myself. Through you I can be loving even in the face of things such as what is happening to us now, if only I have your love. Every day, every hour, something happens, I go to a movie, read a book, walk down a street, or see a sky or a tree, and I realize how much better things would be if we were together, how beautiful things were when we were together. And I think of how much I missed, even when we were together. I believe with all my heart that people have to make it on their own, but I also believe that once a person has founded his fortitude and strength on foundations which are not false, then he can be helped immeasurably by the right other person. "I trust my sanity, and I am proud" but I have had a glimpse of heaven with you, and I pray all the gods that we be together again soon. I am simply trying to say that I love you. And what is hard for me, I am trying to tell you how much I need you. Please, for my sake, be strong.

I hope you like the two poems.† I'll also include a copy of "Biographers," and "Traditional Manner," but on second thought I think I'll send them this afternoon, so you won't read the new ones and the old ones at the same time.

Joe showed me your letter, and also the new postcards he has for you. I got some of my small art books back from him, and I'll send them with this letter. Giotto is almost as geometrical as some of the modern geometric abstractionists, perhaps even more geometrical. (Hoffman is a modern geometric abstract painter, as are Braque, Picasso sometimes, Gris, and then Motherwell and de Kooning.)

I'm waiting for Dick now, and we are going out to eat breakfast. I think of all the breakfasts you made for me, and goddamn, why must this be happening to us? But I suppose I know why. Anyway, my arm is a mass of scratches from fencing, my mustache is growing, my hair too. But Ron Padgett has other problems. He went to the hospital yesterday, and doctors fear he may have a hole in his lung.

My writing has not been good lately, and I'm not sure that this poem is at all good. But right now it seems good by comparison, and I've started writing once again, which makes me feel better. I'd only written one poem since March fourth before two days ago, and now I've done two more and a giant imitation/translation. And that's my proudest accomplishment. I've done an imitation/translation which is in part a translation of "The Drunken Boat" by Arthur Rimbaud. By imitation I mean that I have not attempted to be directly literal, rather I have tried to write as if I were Rimbaud. The feeling and theme are what I have worked for, and I have not hesitated to make changes, use words not in the French, etc. The result I like very much. Lauren says it is the best version of "The Drunken Boat" he has ever read, which swells my pride much, since I respect his judgment considerably. I'm still working on it a little, but I enclose a copy anyway, because I am proud of the effort, and so of course want first to send it to you, since I can't read it to you yet. It's fairly long, and I want to make a carbon for myself so it'll be the next page.

You asked about King Pleasure, and about Seymour Krim. King Pleasure sings the theme song on the *Symphony Sid* show here, which is an all-night jazz show, midnight to 5 a.m. It's very famous, and its disc jockey, Sid Bernstein, is a great announcer. I think I've mentioned it before. King Pleasure is a jazz singer of the same type as Joe Williams (do you know him?) and Jimmy Rushing (do you know him?). He is a kind of blues shouter, with a very masculine voice, very happy, vibrant voice. He sings Count Basie/Duke Ellington kind of music with lyrics like "Baby, you're so beautiful, but you've got to die one day, / Baby, you're so beautiful, but you've got to die one day, / All I want's a little lovin' before you pass away!" (Which makes me think of Andrew Marvell's poem "To His Coy Mistress" in which he writes, "The grave's a fine and private place, but none I think do there embrace.") I like King Pleasure, I don't hear his records too much. He's primarily a nightclub man, I think.

Seymour Krim had a popularity vogue here a few months ago, when he published a book of autobiographical personal essays giving his views on sportswriting, literary criticism, sex, Harlem, dress, personal essays, etc. His book was called *Views of a Near Sighted Cannonneer* (a quote from Whitman). I read his book. He has a certain talent for writing itself, but his mind is not very extraordinary, consequently his views are conventional, although they might seem radical or "painfully honest" to some. He writes in a way that shows he is conscious of Norman Mailer (especially Mailer's *Advertisements for Myself*), Henry Miller, D. H. Lawrence, and some of the "beat" prophets. He is mildly interesting, more as a reflection of a young Jewish intellectual who wanted to make it on the literary New York scene and found it phony, than as a genuine literary talent. He's now about 35-40, a Village "personality" who writes reviews for the *Village Voice*, has published a book, etc. His fame is horizontal, and for me he is a good man not to be like, but I enjoyed parts of his books of essays, and might like him.

Barry seems to know the Village figures. Tell him I know Ginsberg, Dorothy Day, LeRoi Jones, and maybe he'll like me then. I don't mean to sound snide. But I hate to have people label me and thereby dismiss me. Et cetera.

The book I am making for you is nearly half full. Another week and I'll send it. It has some very good poetry in it, and pictures too, I think.

Harry and Ed and Lauren leave for Miami next week, Ed to visit friends, Harry to visit Carol Clifford, and Lauren for the trip. My heart goes with them. I wish to God I could come to you. But I know that for us I can do the most good by being here, and possibly the most harm by coming there. I love you so much, Sandy, so much.

Dick just came in, grinning, and sat down to read his Rabelais. It's time to eat. I'll write again this afternoon, and maybe I will get ten or twelve letters from you today. Good morning, and thousands of love from your husband.

I love you forever,
Ted

Late April, 1962

I don't have any O'Neill books. I'm sorry. I read all his works and a lot of books about him a few years ago, and liked him, but I gave all my books about him to my students. But you should be able to get some of his things from the library. My favorites were *The Iceman Cometh* and *The Great God Brown,* but I liked nearly everything. His life was amazing, and he is representative of a type of Irishman known as the Black Irish. We'll talk about him later.

Today I'll send *Steppenwolf* for Leslie. I also have *Magister Ludi,* Hesse's great epic work, and two of his very early works. Maybe Leslie would like those, too. Also, you might mention a book to her called *Lord of the Flies,* by William Golding (I think). Dick read it yesterday, and said it is very good. It is about children from another point of view than Salinger's. Leslie should also like anything by William Styron (*Lie Down in Darkness, The Long March, Set This House on Fire*).

I haven't read much by Quasimodo. I have heard that the only translations of him are bad ones. But that might not be true. Tell me what you think if you read his poems. I like the two Russians Pasternak and Mayakofsky very much, especially Mayakofsky, who is zany like Kenneth Koch and Groucho Marx. I also like the French poets André Breton and Paul Eluard (I'd like to read his book on Picasso), and of course Rimbaud and Baudelaire, and Mallarmé and Verlaine. Dear, my imitation of "The Drunken Boat" is exactly that, an imitation. I have tried to stay with Rimbaud's imagery and language as much as possible, and have only deviated where I thought I could write closer to his and my meaning by using something in English which had the same meaning I thought he had in French, but different words (because meaning depends on color and sound too). My last stanza may have a different meaning than his, but my whole poem and his are very close, I think.

In my Lorca imitation the same thing is true. Basically I have translated what he wrote. But structurally there is much difference. More an English structure than a Spanish poem based on Arabic form as his was. The main thing about my imitations is that they should be able to be enjoyed without reference to the original, but with reference to the original one should be able to see that they are basically the same poem. I am learning my craft this way, and that's why I call them imitations, but I am also trying to *make* good poems.

I made another imitation of Rilke last night, two in fact, and I'll enclose one, which I like very much. We'll talk more about the technique I use when we are together. Do you like this?

DEDICATION

This is my life:
——To seek the holy
wherever it may take me
until, by this light
I may plunge my roots
deep into life——
thus through pain
to ripen
far beyond life
far beyond time.

after René Rilke

Rilke seems more and more to me to be a very great man. Honey, I thought I'd make a list for you of some American novels which I really admired at one time or another, and which really helped me understand what writing is, and what American writing is, and some of what America is and was. Maybe you'll want to read one or two of them. *In Dubious Battle* by John Steinbeck is really a good book about America in the Depression. I liked it a whole lot. John Dos Passos's early works are also very good, especially a trilogy which includes *Adventures of a Young Man,* and *Number One.* Hemingway's *Farewell to Arms* seems to me to be as good a novel as any American of that period wrote. It is a minor masterpiece, I think. Sinclair Lewis is somewhat dated now, in some ways, but he has great vitality, and his book *Arrowsmith* is an amazing book about the medical profession, almost a burlesque. Have you read Tom Wolfe's *Look Homeward, Angel?* It was the bible of my early twenties and I am still enchanted by it. It has some of the best writing about children, and about America, that has ever been done. I haven't read Faulkner much, but I liked his first novel, *Soldier's Pay,* as much as anything of his, and thought it was very good. Of all the Americans you might like William Saroyan best. He has an obscure book called *The Adventures of Wesley Jackson,* which is marvelous. *Miss Lonelyhearts,* by Nathaniel West is also a fascinating book. And almost all of Scott Fitzgerald's work is classic writing in its way, particularly *The Great Gatsby,* and his essay called *The Crack-Up.* Fitzgerald's short stories are also great.

And if you want to do something for me, everyone tells me that Ray Bradbury, a science fiction writer, is really a great writer. I'm dubious, but people I respect rave over him. Maybe you could read something of his and tell me what you think. I don't want to go on with this literary rambling, but there are some books I liked a lot, books I'd like to talk to you about sometime.

I have to stop and get back to work. But first, about Carol Clifford: she and Harry are just friends. He has another girlfriend, too, and has no intention of getting pinned down yet, for (he) has promises to keep / and miles to go before (he) sleep(s). So he and Eddie brought her here, she's staying at Eddie's until she gets a job. She's a nice kid, and says hello to you. She says you look beautiful with your hair long, and that she'd like to see you. Are all you Florida girls happiness girls? She's another happiness girl, who usually drives everybody crazy by trying to make everybody happy. But she's nice.

I hope my telegram arrived for our anniversary. I'm going to send this special delivery, so you'll get mail from me sooner, and I'll write again this afternoon. I love you.

Your husband forever,
Ted

[Undated]

Help me, Sandy. You held my hand, rode in the night with me, slept in my arms, cooked for me, cried over me. No one else there did any of those things. Tell me you know that you know me. That you know that whatever they say about me, you know it doesn't matter. Tell me that you know that I love you. That you know that I can and will take care of us. That you know that I will do nothing to make you unhappy. Tell me, please, that you know we are good together, that it is right that we be together.

Sandy, I always stand up straight, head cocked to one side, arrogant defiance on my face, when anyone pushes me. I tell them I *know* what's right. I tell them I've got the answers. Because I know that if I give them an opening they'll cut me down. As they did when we went to Miami, even though I knew better.

But with you, it's different. I'm not playing games, not fighting. I'm just a boy, trying to be good, trying to have a good life, trying to love. I'm as insecure as anyone, as subject to doubts, to fears and tremblings, as you are. That's the me I want *you* to see, as well as the other side. I am a big tough competent smart sonofabitch, but I'm a little boy who needs love, too. It isn't easier for me than it is for you, although it would be if I were in there instead of you. I don't have lots of people to turn to here. There is no one. All I have is you. Believe me, all I have is you. My friends here, and they are few (only Dick, really) are busy with themselves. My mother is someone who loves me, but not someone to turn to. I turn to myself only. And now, since early February, to you. You, the first person I have ever gone to in this way. I need you to reassure me, Sandy, to take my hand, to love me, in the same way you feel you need me. Whenever you feel surrounded, hemmed in, nearly defeated, I am still with you, my love is with you. And I feel those feelings often, too. I know then that your love is with me. But I need you to know that I feel that way. I need to be reminded, to be told, too. In spite of my poses (so necessary at times) I'm fighting for myself just as you are. In a fight the appearance of confidence is absolutely important. But every fighter knows that his opponent is just as insecure and worried inside as he is. I am just as afraid inside, just as lonely, as you. All these people here, all this city, only make it worse. There's no one here for me to busy myself fighting with. I sit, I wait, I write to you, I worry, sometimes I cry by myself, when no one is watching. When I'm watched I tell a joke, or shake my fist at fate. Only you, my wife, my love, my life, do I show my tears. They are something special, and only for myself and for you. I love you very much, Sandy.

I send you all my hope, all my love, I am your husband, you my wife,

    forever.
        Ted

Letters from Sandy

Dear Ted,

I hope this doesn't sound melodramatic. But I keep fearing that they will try to make me forget you. They give me some strange pill three times a day. The first does make me sleepy & I dozed on & off and had strange dreams about panels of doctors questioning me there were many but I have forgotten them now. I am still working on TAT (Thematic Aperception Test) tests. I wish I could finish them but I am tired of making up stories. I only have five more to go. I guess the quicker I finish them the better.

I haven't cried today. I guess the pills are to keep me calm. This too is false calmness not from within just what my father argued against. Maybe they think I'll be more receptive. They can't visit me for a few days all I want to say to them is if you love and trust me let me out of here to build my life with Ted. I know we can do it & that's all that is important.

I am reading the *Odyssey* with real joy and interest it is so good. I try to read when I am not writing these letters. I don't want to completely idle away these days. I have almost finished *The Plague* but I was so upset that I think I'll go back 20 pages and start there. I have this place & the doctors related to *The Plague* in my mind. It is like death to be sentenced here. Each day of my life is so important that I hate to waste one away from you and the world. They will never understand this. They only want to find my immaturities. They have no confidence in the goodness and maturity that I am endowed with they will not ask people who know me at school. They only use their judgments & those of doctors whom I cannot trust because I do not believe wholeheartedly in their method.

You are right even now in an age of enlightenment the saints and poets suffer on the cross.

Love my darling,
Sandy

Darling Ted,

I have just signed a paper saying I would voluntarily stay here. I really didn't want to because I don't want to be here but it seemed the only thing to do. Perhaps as the doctor says it shows I am cooperating. He also said that they did not know where you are. I hope you have left town as they believe & are in New York. When I tell them that I understand why you left they may not believe me. Perhaps even I would like you to be here so that you could come to me when I can have visitors, but it is better for you to be in New York so that you can write poetry read and live life.

I don't know how long I will be here the doctor has to get to know me and all as soon as I am released I will come to you.

I am trying to get a radio because music is necessary in my life. Although you know I need nothing material but you & being practical food & shelter & books for you to read. Perhaps we don't even need those.

The pills they gave me were tranquilizers but the doctor is stopping them so that I can read. It is another perfect day outside. Soon they may let me go into the yard. I told Dr. Skigen that I would not run away. Also I have no money.

I put my ring on the other hand because I was getting a rash I will change it back as soon as it is better What are you doing now wherever you are? And Tom & Dick write and tell me what you want. Remember the letters might be read before they are given to me.

All my love darling.
If only I were with you again.
Sandy

Ted,

I don't know if this is what they do for everyone but I am getting permission to go to the garden tomorrow for Occupational Therapy. They have a potter's wheel & I will make things for our apartment. I found a book called *Unpopular Essays* by Russell. At least I might get a lot of reading done. The doctor thinks that he and I might get along he also says don't plan for the future. He probably wants me to say that this marriage was wrong of my own accord. I never will I think of you always when I look out my window or am reading.

Love & kisses
Sandy

February 28, 1962

Dear Ted,

If only I were here observing, this would make an amazing experience. But now everything only makes me nervous and jumpy.
This morning I had breakfast with the rest of the patients. A
young boy sat across from me. He was calm but obviously way out
in another sphere. He wondered aimlessly around the halls.
Wanting and not wanting breakfast. He sat staring silently at his
tray. They tried to make him eat but he said he felt sick. Then he
asked the two aids and myself our last names. After which he
replied none of you gave the right answer. I brought *The Plague* to
the table and he stared at it too. The nurses aids treat me like the
others, asking me if I am going to eat some cereal etc. If only I
were sick it would be fine.

What are you doing my love? I want to see you so. It is terrible
to stay in a place like this and not to know how long. What do I
have rights for and when I will see you again, they are investigating you too. Where and how I do not know. I cannot talk to
my family anymore.

You know that I had faith in everyone. They will not harm us
because we are good and they are not. But you are far wiser than
I and anticipated the hostile tricks that people resort to and fear
and maybe hatred.

It is worse than anything, rather than better than nothing, to
be in a strange room in an alien place without the one you love to
hold your hand and look into your eyes.

I should now tell a joke that is "in earnest in the womb of time"
but all I can think of is "We must all tell the truth like men of
courage and character." I also tell myself to "shape up." It is hard
they all tell me to have composure and relax. But how can I when
I know nothing about what is happening. I cried all last night &

the nurse kindly came in & said not to cry & asked what was wrong. How can they expect that to help when even your soothing voice & look do not help immediately.

I wish the doctor would come. I hope he realizes that a normal person in a situation like this is under strain.

What are your thoughts my love. I know you must be full of anger. But what else. It's funny but you probably will not even be able to get this letter until I go. I hope they let me see you. I will write more only I must say

La vida es sueño
Y los sueños sueños son.
Life is a dream
And dreams are dreams
                    Calderon

Love forever
Sandy

My darling,

I have just finished *Saint Joan*. Shaw is so right. The world is not ready to let even people like us live in happiness let alone Saint Joan or Christ or Socrates.

I was looking in the mirror. I have circles under my eyes. I am eating too much candy and food. I fear that I will get fat. I exercise a bit every day.

My Greek book just came I am going to try to work. I hope that I can concentrate.

Tell Dick and Tom I will cook them a tremendous breakfast as soon as I come.

For you I will give love and happiness and laughter.

Love
Sandy

I feel a part of your new poem.

The head of the hospital is coming to see me.

My darling Ted,

Another day and another night will pass without you. I felt pretty bad this morning. Always after seeing the doctor I am sad. But later I think it all over and my love and all the authors and great men reconfirm our thoughts.

Remember when you said "What if I never come back or see you again?" I said I will always think of my knowing you as good. I will never regret anything—skipping classes, the afternoon spent in the park instead of studying. I am trying to feel that way now. But then I did not think of the future with you. Now I see what we could and will have and I am greedy and impatient.

There is so much that I haven't seen or done. And I want to be a teacher and inspire children with the love of life and learning and laughing and people. You know that I sometimes think that I will not be able to but even at Newcomb thinking about it I knew I could. I want to be with you and continue filling myself with poems and you and New York and life so that I can be a teacher or at least for a little while and then for our children if we have them and for our friends.

I wanted a letter today but I knew you were thinking of me.

I love Shaw, I am in the middle of *Man and Superman*. I am going to stop with him after that.

I found something about love of life in *The Brothers K.* I am going to show it to the next doctor. Maybe he will see that I am not going to destroy myself and you aren't. I seem to be struggling for both of us instead of just me. You will be part of my whole self forever.

I think I would like to read more of Ibsen.

I talked to the Negro maid today. She is a great lady. She ran away with her first husband at the age of twelve and was married to him for twenty-seven years. He then died. She is good. She thinks the whole business is silly. I wish you could meet her. I wish you could be here. These people need much hope. You show people that sometimes dreams do come true if the dreamer works hard and believes. If he has faith and courage.

Mother sent me some good food today. I have only seen her once. Naturally we both got upset. I am going to try to be good. Sometimes it is hard.

There is one lady here she reminds me of a dowager empress. She has a very straight back.

I long for good music. I can't even find rock and roll I like. The classical music is sporadic. No more for now my love. You know I always add notes.

Love
Sandy, spouse of Edmund

Tell Dick I think of him and his guitar poems.

Some new slang for you I learned in here
fecal scroll = shit list
music roll = toilet paper

March 7, 1962

The doctor said today, when I asked him, that I was disturbed. I am upset all the time now.

Did I tell you my parents made a photostat of Ron's letter to you about the investigation. God damn them I am furious. I can't even get mail out of this place. The doctor is an imbecile, and will not tell them it is o.k. I hate getting angry at the nurses but they are the only ones that are there at the time. You know that I want to make others happy and feel good but they will corrupt me. I don't have enough strength. Oh Ted I wish you were here to hold me and talk. Help me to understand this world.

I don't want to burst into torrents of tears when everything is wrong but what else is there to do. Screaming will get me nowhere, no one can feel as you and I do and the others like us.

The maid is mailing this—it has not been read by the doctor. I would run away but I am afraid if they caught us we would never see each other again.

I will try to have patience.

[Unsigned]

Dear Ted,

This is another secret letter. I am sometimes even afraid to write them because Eva, the maid, scares me by saying that they read everything at night. I know they don't because I wake up when anyone comes in the room.

I want to get away and come to you but right now I don't know how. I am not sure of the implications of the court order and how long it is valid or about hearings etc.

If I can cooperate enough to get out of the hospital it will be easier, I will try. It is hard for me not to get mad and pester the doctor with my and your beliefs. Eva says to play it cool and act as if I don't care. I will try.

Also don't know if the detectives are still watching you. If they are, they will know what is going on and we could not do anything.

When I get out I have a few ideas on ways to get to New York. If the court thing is off. First, however, I think I would need enough to take the plane. I am going to try to hoard money. Also withdraw my money from the bank with a specific purpose but always take a bit extra. I have no one here to borrow from or ask to help. Leslie could not stand the pressure.

Don't do anything positive, just tell me things that might help me in planning. A hard thing is getting my clothes away. Even a handful.

It might be three or four weeks or more. We must learn to have hope. Writing these letters is so much . . . .

When I got today's . . . I went completely wild. I practically flew through the ceiling.

The doctor's stupidity is too much for me. I might be here even longer because Dr. C takes so much time to get here. I shouldn't have mentioned that Dr. S was not like Freud. I do dumb things sometimes.

I love you so much darling we'll work something out. So far we have had only to think of money matters and escapes. When will it end. Have you thought of a job. I don't care if you get one or not. Write poems.

Love
Sandy

Dear Ted,

It's already afternoon and I haven't written to you yet. I have been busy all day and thinking of you. This morning we went to the yard and it was warm in the sun. I sat for an hour and I thought I would faint. It got so hot but I want to get a healthy look. I finished *Daring Young Man*. I am going to read some parts again. Oh! to be with you. Someday I would like to meet Saroyan.

I hope you will not be mad but I started *Rebecca* by Du Maurier. She reminds me of Conrad only not so intense. Her book so far is atmosphere. The second wife is painful in her ineptitude and shyness although I am sure she is a good soul. I want to finish it so that I can start *Bread and Wine*.

My family came this afternoon, bringing food clothing and a plant. They looked around sort of noncommittally at all your presents and asked if I hear from you. I said you write every day. They didn't say one other word about you and I. We didn't say much at all. I knew there was not much to say anymore. My father was going to start a speech about how we are only parents and now we have to wait for the doctor. He didn't though.

I am going to read *The Little Prince* again. It is so good, also full of love and hope.

They brought the pictures of me in color. I will send one every day.

I am going to have to promise to cooperate fully in order to get out.

Love
Sandy

Your mother sent me pictures of the whole family.

Darling Ted,

It is Friday March 9th. I just wanted to begin this letter before going to play cards. The doctor was here this morning and I told him what I was saving for Dr. C. He had only a few minutes before rushing to another patient. I don't think he took it all in. He keeps asking me to help him to understand. I have been trying for almost two weeks now. It leaves much to wonder at.

I found Saroyan again in the *Daring Young Man* book. This is another thing for the doctors to read to help them understand. After hearing Saroyan's voice and seeing his picture it is great to read more. The voice and face are a part of the book now. You and I are a part of the book

(This part from Saturday March 10th. The doctor made me erase something. I always feel bad after he comes. He will not let me send all the presents.)

I am sending surprises if I can ever get a box and the doctor's O.K. I hope you are getting my letters.

I think I'll read a book called *Bread and Wine* have you read it? Is it any good? If not I'll try to find something else.

I don't know what Leslie thinks about this because I haven't heard from her.

Tell New York to slow down a little until I come. I am so afraid I'll miss something even if it is the sand pile to play on.

It is cool and windy today. All the venetian blinds rattle in my room. I was trying to think of a good metaphor. But I'll let you.

I miss music and I miss you. I want to watch you listen to Leadbelly or some wild jazzman (Sandburg wrote a poem "Jazzman"). I want to dance to them and teach you to feel it not only in your feet but your whole self!

Each of your letters is more than a blessing. They are you and filled with you—the pictures of you and great men—the earnest jests—all of them. You are the most handsome and thoughtful fellow. I like you best now. Joe caught you perfectly as I remember you. The only other way would be hair askew, eyes open and your teeth pulled down. Maxine loves Joe's sketch of you. Could Joe make a sketch for her? Anything. She would like one very much.

Tell Joe I would write him separately but I am saving stamps. The news is for him too. The postcard he sent is fantasy. And I like it.

I am glad our bunny is Sleazus, although it seems kind of a funny name for such a small soft furry thing.

My parents are no longer going to Europe, my mother says. I was part of it so they cancelled that too.

Tell Joe also kisses for the art catalog. Soon my room will have a bit of all that New York offers. I like the *Sleep Walker* and lots of the others. All My Love.

Tonight I started a new project and made a new friend, Ann Lyons, she has been very sick but is a good person. We were talking about you and I and her and reading and religion and I told her that Jesus was one of the men you admired and that you like the Gospels. We are going to read some chapters of them every night. I began tonight. It was beautiful although I don't believe it. She also said a prayer for us and my parents and the doctors and the nurses. I cried because I feel she is good and this is the highest thing she can do for us. I'll tell you more about her later.

Love and good night—dream peacefully
Sandy

Darling Ted,

Today is especially bad since it is our anniversary. I think of you and celebrating and being together. I am reading *Quintessence* and can't concentrate. Reading isn't everything as you know. I didn't realize cruelty could be so subtle. If my husband enforced such rules on me, I would divorce him. I wanted to send you a telegram but I am sure I need the doctor's permission and he would say it was too extravagent (I cannot spell this word). All I can think of is it's our anniversary and we are so far apart.

Ernie Pinto and I played cards. He keeps looking at my ring and telling me how nice it is. He also repeatedly says that it's too bad that I'm married and asks if I have children. He doesn't have a very good memory.

I received two letters from you. I hope you find a place to live. I was very upset tonight and really almost in hysterics. Ann Lyons comforted me she started crying too. She is separated and will be away from her children for perhaps another year. I hate to make other people cry. You know that I can at least bring momentary happiness to some and to you even longer. Ann doesn't give advice except to say believe in G-d and Jesus. I don't want to start now because it would be a false belief.

I was very silly tonight after the episode. The doctor came and I asked him when Dr. C would see me and he said sometime. I was insistent but he doesn't listen very hard. Also I pretended to walk out the door with him and made all these jokes about sex interpretations to the girls. I have to be silly sometimes even though I am not really happy. Ted, I can feel your pains and strengths but I still worry, my letters are not very hopeful. All I ask is that you love me as you have.

I don't like to reprimand you but you are much too extravagant. I love *Suzuki* and it has given pleasure to lots of people here. But if you would save some money we might need it.

Ann whom I really believe in and who thinks we should be together right now thinks that a permanent job would go a long way in convincing my parents. I guess she is right but I don't ever want to force you. But no job is ever that permanent.

I hate the detectives for making everyone nervous and jumpy. My parents are wreaking more havoc than they realize.

I wish I had a lawyer friend on the outside that could give us information on the court order, etc. It would help.

Your mother sent another letter. She tried to write you but had the wrong address. I am sending her Joe's.

Everyone has faith and says that if we love each other things will work out. We do love each other but I have no patience and I hate injustice.

If you see Bill Gross send him my love. He was a boy I had a crush on for two years but he always made fun of me. Does he like Columbia? He thought it was hard. Thank Eddie for me. Tell him it makes me happy to know that you had a roof on your head. Yes, I know Carol, Clifford is her last name. She is a person I always wanted for a friend but never quite got. She writes and is a lot more intelligent than I. I'm prettier though.

THOUGHTS I HAD THIS AFTERNOON

God damn I hate the idle chatter of others
The laughing
The forced formal automatic questions
The relations and interrelations of their thoughts and ideas
As I lie in the bed the voices annoy me.
I think of you and I and
Dick and Tom and of Marge.
I want to hear their voices.
These voices in idle conversation have meaning.
They give pleasure—the sounds the words the laughter.

I am waiting for you and the voices.
Voices I love
Laughter and joy
I grow impatient and try to wait
I cannot
But I cannot scream either

You know I just write these. They are not poems only thoughts. I
take pleasure in writing them in verse form.

My darling husband,

Today was a pretty good day. I got dressed early and tried not to eat too much breakfast. Saw the doctor. But I never seem to make any dents in his hard heart. I waited anxiously all day for Dr. C but he did not show up. I don't see why he doesn't come. I will have a master's thesis prepared on my mental health. There is not one person in this hospital with the exception of the doctors that would not let me go to you this instant.

I received so much mail today. A letter from you. Your love is so real. I can feel your words and see you fencing in the charro jacket. And walking through the museum, eyes wide saying, "That's great!" or the equivalent.

I had never heard of Sabi—it sounds good. I know what you mean. I am glad Harry can fence. I have wanted to learn for about three years but can never find anyone to teach me. We can learn together. I miss Dick and the guitar. Music is hard to come by here. I wore the scarf all evening and I am boiling. What language is on the tapestry. The goddess at last is here. She is so beautiful.

Your letters are beautiful. Even most of life is beautiful with the exception of a few people. These few can do so much harm.

I have started *The Prophet*. But must get some more books. I have become lazy and I read less now than before. I really want plays by Ibsen but don't send any, I'll get them here.

Tonight we had bingo and I played. I won six candy bars. Will try to send you some. I may not be able to. I only gave a dime for prizes too.

I am so hot I wish I were in New York in the cold and with you, in a room somewhere, anywhere.

All my friends here get depressed a lot. Their problems are

not simple and the solutions will take a long time. In a place like this everyone's doctor and getting out are the main topics of conversation.

Leslie wrote me a letter and sent me a pen-and-ink drawing. It looks like a bride, or at least she is wearing the kind of dress I would like to be married in.

Today while reading letters again I found another picture of you. This time in the snow. You look so serious and stern. I love you in every mood no matter what you wear. Dr. S says he thinks you are my knight in shining armor. I said you are very real and not perfect but I just hadn't told him your faults. Lenny was more of a dream and unreal than you. If they keep us apart too long you will be a knight. I will always remember you as a flesh and blood living man. No knight would be poor, or swear or let me get in here because he would be invincible. You are in many ways, but not like a knight. I love you no matter what you are.

The corner where I put the goddess is the only place of peace and serenity in the room. She is standing on the tapestry.

My newest worry is the court order. Everyone says they are 90 days. They did not even give me tests for drugs. Something seems wrong there.

Karen hasn't written yet and I haven't heard from or seen Mimi. She is too young to come to a place like this. I guess she is O.K.

I got a letter from Kathy (your sister-in-law) she sounds sweet. She sends you her best. She says she is dieting.

Leslie is reading a play by Ionesco (in French). Can you tell me a few words about the Theater of the Absurd? She is now working for her father and going through civil-service processing. What a waste of potential and all that. I haven't seen her or talked to her. They have me in sort of semi-isolation. Only my parents are allowed and they don't help much.

I am not doing Greek. Someday I might be inspired.

I have a new friend on our side. She said they started out poor, no job, only love and will and courage. It's enough. You have potential for anything.

No more for now.
Love eternally
Sandy

My darling,

I just met the new male patient. He is a writer from New York by
the name of Barry Weiss. He doesn't know you or Joe. He lived
on 11th Street. He doesn't like poetry much and is very wary of
your type, he says. He is cynical. He loves Henry Miller and says
he can only read 25 or fewer pages at a time and then he must stop.
He has sad eyes. Thinks writers can only write in aloneness and
desolation.

Every minute I was talking to him I thought of you. He is like
another tie because he just came from New York. My love I want to
be with you so much. Dr. Caldwell has not come yet. I wait and wait.

Ann is singing now and her voice comes all the way to my room.
Life has people and goodness and sadness wherever you turn.

Have you ever heard of William Burroughs. I just got your
letter. I want to be with you on the Brooklyn Bridge in a poncho
with my patched slacks, just looking.

Your mother sent me a copy of the wedding announcement. If
you don't have one, I'll send this to show.† It has four big errors.
Your mother's letters are so trusting and full of faith and love. If
only a few more people had it. Also received a letter from Kathy,
your sister, but she forgot the last page. I guess she was a little
mixed up.

I am going to try to move in with Ann tonight. She will be a
good roommate and wants to be sure that she gets someone she is
compatible with. She will also give me privacy. The bed is better
and the toilet arrangement made so that I will not have to hold
the door with my foot.

I read "Kaddish" and "Howl" and "Thank You" and "Fresh Air"
and scattered other poems today. Nothing else.

I have so much excess nervous energy. I don't know what to do.
Oh Ted just to walk the streets with you would be enough, to talk
to you and hold your hand.

My mother wrote me a letter trying to tell me of their love and that I should let them help me. It began "It is 4 a.m. on Thursday. It seems I am with you in spirit." It continues in this vein. I am not ever with her and I know if she were with my spirit I would not be here. I wish I could love them now. But you are the strongest love I have. If I love both the same I will have neither.

Ted, have you read *Cain's Book* by Trocchi. I also want to know what you think of Tennessee Williams. Have you heard of *Oahspe*? It is a book and the basis of a way of life. Find if you can and read. I don't know anything about it. But it should be fascinating.

Dr. Skigen came again tonight to tell me that you called. I didn't get too excited but my heart is filled with joy. I hope you can come so much and that we can see each other. This is another hope for the future. Let it come soon. If you have to change plans I will understand. Bible reading stopped. Dr. Skigen doesn't think it's a good idea.

Night again, it comes and goes—I am waiting for you my love. Maybe it will be sooner than I think.

Love forever
Sandy spouse of Edmund

P.S. Tonight I seriously watched T.V. for the first time. *The Bell Telephone Hour* has music of love. Played Greig piano concerto, parts of *Tosca* and a ballet. All of it was you and me. Then saw a program about Mrs. Kennedy's trip to India. Saw beautiful India, some good old men's faces and heard Indian music.

Good night
Sandy

Darling husband,

It is Monday and I have been here three weeks. Tomorrow another anniversary. And then another and another. Dr. Skigen was in this morning. He said you were surely coming. He also said that you could see me if I promised not to try to escape from here. He thinks that they will not put you in jail. I really don't know because they have shown they are capable of anything.

Last night we moved furniture in the living room and this morning the day shift changed it. They are not very aesthetic. I am waiting for some books to read. People are so slow.

Leslie's flowers are open wide and dying now but they are very beautiful now. I would like roses every week. How extravagant I can be. In here I only spend money on stamps and candy sometimes.

I just got the wonderful letter from you about your love and Frank O'Hara. Don't come here if you feel you can't and don't do anything you don't want to. I am sometimes so lonely. I ask a lot but you are always with me. Don't get a job if that's not what you want.

Your letter was most . . . there is no word to describe it. With your love I can be patient. I can hardly wait until you meet Frank O'Hara. I had been wishing this past week that he would write you or something and it happened how wonderful.

Today one of the old mixed-up men came in my room three times. The second and third time I was out. The second excursion found him undressed. I am glad I wasn't there to observe.

Barry talked to me a little, he thinks perhaps you are just an ordinary beatnik. He doesn't know you. I wish you could give him a good going over. Send me *Tropic of Cancer* if you can. Barry did give me some candy and apricots so I can't hate him. He has a few good qualities. He doesn't think I have the stuff it takes.

Ann leaves soon and soon others. She is going to write the melody of her song and the first two verses. She says you can write the rest. She wants to meet you but I guess she will not.

Am enclosing an article about beatniks. It's funny and not so biased. Could you send a copy of "Traditional Manner" and "Biographers"?

Congratulations my love—kisses and Joy and my happiness for you.

I could shout your goodness.

Love forever
Sandy

I send my love to Dick and Tom and Joe and Andy and everyone. I wish them to share my joy.

My Darling,

I have been thinking about you and us all day. Perhaps in our need for love and for each other we have found each other. There are so many people in this world and only so few we truly love. I have always asked how do you know that you love someone? Now I know and I too cannot explain it. I will be strong for both of our sakes.

Please put something on the foils you great hero. I like soft smooth skin not great gashes.

Please write to Ron or visit him and tell him I hope he is soon out of the hospital. I for one know how terrible they are.

Don't know of Joe Williams or of Jimmy Rushing—now I at least know their names.

The pictures are marvelous. You do not look like Elizabeth Barrett Browning in this one. But it is you. This whole – situation – is – not – so – serious – as – you – think – look. It makes one laugh. Dick's is almost himself in the flesh. His glasses are so big. Lauren is very handsome and fine looking. His mouth is a little more sensual or sensuous than yours. Your pictures look like the Line-Up right there on my dresser.

I am almost done with the Edmund Wilson book. Parts of it remind me of the Keats poem "The Eve of St. Agnes"; lush and rich and full of color and food. The characters are rather "characters," some seem very romantic. I seem to tire of things easily. I am getting tired of his way too. He doesn't say much, his pictures are lush and beautiful. A dream world to me.

I like Garcia Lorca very much and I couldn't translate any better. Barry has already borrowed *Big Sur*. I wasn't ready to read it. Anyway I have Ibsen yet.

Just finished listening to *Petrushka* on T.V. with Leonard Bernstein. I like it very much. I felt like dancing but couldn't. I'm not crazy enough to pull that off.

Someday we can hibernate and listen to all sorts of things away from people talking and interfering.

Only Mr. Beam would get me a book of stamps, mixed 24 one-cent and 24 two-cent. He also told me that a booby or boobie is a real bird. He caught a baby booby once. I listened to him, mouth open. He has grand stories just like you.

Read "The Drunken Boat" again and I like it of course I can't be too critical of it as a free translation because I can't read French. I'll read it again tomorrow. I like the "Spooky Winds" especially where you put it. The last two stanzas seem much different than the others—tone I guess.

My love the nights and days are sometimes short and mostly long. I am waiting.

Love,
Sandy

(kiss)
The kiss is for pure sentimental mush and because I love you.
I don't have any bright orange paint to sign my letter with.
Happy Anniversary for tomorrow.

Dear Ted,

Much excitement just now. We were in the yard and I was talking to Mr. Beam when we turned around and there was Ernie over the gate. No one saw him but finally two attendants ran out and Norman. What a row. Mr. Beam and I thought it was pretty funny. Too bad, really Ernie is in a bad way. Norman was doing exercises; bare chest filled with back brace and bellowing like an ox. He has feet problems and wears Little Abner shoes.

Someone has said positively that there is some illegality. Please dear for you and I, go to Legal Aid and have someone look up Florida law. Even if you can't do anything else.

Another boy is upset too. He almost had a fight with the attendants. He was going to use the chair as a lion tamer. I was standing in back of him but quickly got away. I was very nervous after that. This is quite a wild place.

I just finished reading *Tropic of Cancer,* Barry loaned it to me. I did underestimate it. But still don't think it is the greatest book. Some parts I liked a lot. I will read them again. He does have great vitality and life. It makes me want to be out even more. Mr. Beam said he met him but maybe he means Arthur Miller. He says that there is something wrong with him somewhere.

Barry is as rotten as ever. He may leave. I hope so.

I got a letter from your mother—I always say "your" but she is our mother now. She has a quotation, "touch of the poet," I think too. I want to meet her badly.

Nothing else exciting. It's a month now almost since I've been here. Jokingly I tell people to expect me to be here a year or so. I am permanent. They will have to give me a suite and lots of book-shelves. I hope someone sees a couple of things before then.

For now—

I love you more than ever,

Sandy

Dearest Ted,

No letter today and now I know how if feels to get letters every day and then to miss one day. I know you were thinking of me and I can picture you working in your room. If you haven't gotten them yet two letters may have gone to Joe's last Monday. Today a letter from Margie. She sounded confused about the whole thing. I wrote back. There isn't too much to explain and you probably told her enough to make the situation clear. Joe and Anne wrote a joint letter all in red ink. Does Joe like red? They spend wonderful hours at museums. Joe sent a picture. He is not what I expected. His hair is beautiful. He was wearing so many layers of clothes. It must have been cold. He looks like someone. I don't know who. I am proud that he got a picture accepted. I wish you all would become successful in a big burst of recognition.

Ted it must be wonderful to go to a museum and look at a few paintings only and not rush frantically through and know that tomorrow that you can come back again.

My parents came today bringing fruit and some books and clothes. We did not get angry but talked quietly about Mimi and the hospital. They don't look happy. But no one is now.

I have started *Big Sur*. It is great. I do have faith and courage. We too someday will be able to live our life. This book so far isn't as wild that's why it's easier for me to take. Anyway he was a lot older. Life gets quieter after 50 or 60 I guess. I am glad he likes children. You know that I usually would rather talk to them. Their conversation and reactions are not automatic or stereotyped. Big Sur is a fantastic place. Yet it is real just as you are real.

I hate to see other people saying good-bye to their husbands. I have no one now who will listen when I cry. I sometimes am not even civil to people. Nasty Barry left today. One disturbance gone. Barry keeps saying at least you'll have time to catch up on your reading. How ironic all the books are yours or ours. He read your copy of *Meditations in an Emergency*. Didn't say anything about it. Also said some of the lives of the new poets were interesting.

Music blares at all hours—I don't even like it. It is cold here the wind blows hard. You underlined an album of Shankar, what is it? Indian music. If every man would think of life as Henry Miller—not live the same exact way how good things could be.

My darling, they will be good someday for us.

Good night and love
Sandy spouse of Edmund

March 31, 1962

Doctor Skigen hasn't come to read this yet so I'll add today's letter. Thank you for the book. My reading matter has become more well-rounded. I am still entranced by Miller. Entranced and reinjected with faith. He is great. Your letter was sad because I want so much for you to be writing but I can't do much now. I certainly don't want you to be locked up or anything. It doesn't torture me too much that you are out and free. At least one of us is and you share everything you see and do with me.

It's funny, seasons are changing and Easter is coming and we thought we would be together for all of it. It's a sad world when lovers cannot be together for changing seasons and spring and stars and sitting on doorsteps because it's too hot to stay inside.

Today I received a package that came to Margie's for me. It was a bridal package from some organization. The contents— Cheer, Joy, Prell, teabags, Kraft dinner and Bufferin and grape jelly. Also a 30-day free trial to the *Houston Post*. If I had known I would have asked Margie to have it. I am going to send her the coupon for the *Post*. Also asked Dr. S if I can send the others to you. He will no doubt say no.

I like the poem and some few of Herrick's other verse. Though their subjects and style go with a certain mood and time and gaiety. I just noticed that many times he has a solemn note of advice or warning to give.

I played pool today but was embarrassed because I am so bad. The table is lousy too but that's no excuse.

Tonight has been pretty bad. I acted very silly and I am afraid some things are going to be written on my chart. I ate six pieces of French toast, pretended I had an invisible pass, and generally giggled all evening. I have all this excess energy and life that is being wasted and I can't even act silly without worrying about a doctor's analysis of reversion to childhood. You and I could have such fun and joy together and wouldn't have to worry about bars or locked doors. Oh well, I will have to wait.

Can't stand it too much but I guess if I act silly it relieves tension or something. Maybe too many people don't know about acting natural and stupid sometimes.

Darling, I love you
Sandy

The end of *Big Sur* is like a prayer.

My darling Ted,

The mail came early today. All of your treasures are so joyously received that I want to devour everything right away. But I can't so I read your letters first. You are right about the project. I should have one. I am not very good at them though. I get tired and bored. I will try to think of one. Shaw is the best yet because he is so diverse. In translation I would think that I would like to do *Platero y Yo* by Jiménez. I stopped here, the lady across the hall is so sick. Here is exactly how I felt then centered on today's horror.

    I always write things immediately.

Over the singsong repetition of the 23rd Psalm
A woman shrieks
I thought she died two hours ago
but no, lying on a stretcher stiff and lifeless they brought her back.
Now she screams in pain.
Now she cries.
Sometimes little weak cries
Others long piercing
And I frantically
walk down the corridor to get away but they follow me
Back in my room I eat Girl Scout cookies
To choke my horror
But the cat quiet moaning continues
And Maryanne wishes she would die
and I, I wish I were with you.

This sounds like something by somebody I don't know who, maybe it's you.

    I read *Dear Dorothea* once. I like it. Some good advice therein. It would be good to follow just one idea through his other works and see if they change. Also follow other thinkers' ideas in comparison with his. Like Ibsen on duty. I'll read it again and say something more critical.

I read the revision of "The Drunken Boat." I feel so good that you dedicated it to me. I wish you were here so you could explain the various changes. Some of them affect the flow and rhythm and style a lot. Later we can do it. Many of the good parts you left the same. I am going to read them a few more times.

Because you write longer letters than I, I am including a picture† of my room even though you didn't ask for it.

I spent a lot of time today talking to Mrs. Hech and Mr. Beam both are great people. I watched part of a Tarzan movie. Mr. Beam said Edgar Rice Burroughs is the most-bought American writer. He told me to tell you. Also that you should write an epic about Tarzan and make much money. New person to ask you about: Flannery O'Connor. What about Robert Lax and a magazine he publishes called *Pax*.

I'll write you more tomorrow, my darling, my love in loneliness.

Love Sandy

April 1, 1962

My darling Ted,

April 1 today is the fool's day and no one played tricks on anyone today. I guess the joke is on those of us in here. We had a joke for someone, but Mr. Beam forgot. Did the Handy Boys do anything wild today like paint the lions in front of the New York Library?

I just finished watching the world championship for ice skating. It was very beautiful. Anything fine or beautiful reminds me of you and things we could be doing. Ice skating is so graceful and smooth and fast. Can you skate? I can barely stand. I am always so afraid that I will fall. When is your birthday in November. I forgot. Also why are you on crutches in your army picture. I thought you said you had malaria.

I got mad at the doctor today. I can't yet understand his stupidity. I wish I wouldn't get mad it doesn't help. He doesn't listen and I don't like being angry.

I have started being very cold and indifferent to the others and to everyone. I don't want to be either but all I can think about is the cruelty and injustice. I don't want you to worry either but who else do I have that understands fully and completely? Who else understands tears of love and sadness and longing and yes laughter? My parents only understand fear and anxiety and hate.

I am reading *Listen, Yankee*. It is very convincing. The personal tone even strengthens the pleas. If it is all true, Cuba is right I think. I am reading more Ibsen now too. Last night there was a hysterical British comedy about a man giving blood to the blood bank—Gardener was the comedian. I thought of you.

Mr. Beam has made some more jokes. One was influenced by a mortuaries ad. He is really good for humor.

They had a program about cancer on tonight and someone is

singing a patriotic song about America. I can't stand it. Life, liberty and pursuit of happiness—HA!

Mrs. Hech, the dowager, left today. She sent, via another patient, candy and a special pack of M&Ms for me. I'll miss her. She has spirit and will and independence. At 84 she was still young. I am sending it to you because I am eating too much, my love, and I can't control myself. Silly again tonight and it wasn't happiness but frustration.

Do you realize only six of the same patients are here that were here when I came and Mr. Beam leaves soon and Sylvio never will.

I see your image all the time—best when you are reading poetry or asleep. I wish I could think some profound thoughts but I only think of you.

Good night, my love
Sandy

Dearest Ted,

I had all sorts of other things to write you but tonight my parents came.

The private detectives have handed in their reports and the doctors theirs.

They are putting the annulment papers in tomorrow. I asked them if they would harm you if you came down, and my father said he might even try to kill you if he saw you or lock you up. The doctor has recommended treatment with an analyst or psychiatrist and I would live at home. They have accused you of much. Mainly of being schizophrenic and not realizing it or trying to do anything about it. Also you are a moocher and live off of others; Anne, Pat, Margie, your mother. They have evidence, letters etc. and what they have said about you. They also said you were not given your master's degree, not even awarded it, but your letter of non-acceptance was a front and so many more things.

I wish you would write a letter telling me about all the truth about you. No matter how bad you may think it to be. Ted, even though I believe in you and your love for me, they have created doubts. I am not even sure I will believe either of you.

I do believe your love and many of the things you have said to me because I have seen myself the truth in life and the communication we have had is real.

The most dubious thing is your sincerity about a job. Could you now get some kind not for them but for me, part-time, half-day? Then you would read and write the rest of the time. Say it is for you and I. Save some of the money—try to live without handouts all the time.

On my side I will try to be strong and brave and good.

When I am 21 and after treatment then, so my parents say, I will be free to do as I please. They have fulfilled legal responsibility.

They do not want to accept or bear any shame that a son-in-law like you may bring them.

I want to see you so badly before the annulment. Because I may not see you for a long time. I am distraught and completely confused. Everything is very bleak.

If this situation you cannot take, I will understand completely. I hope that you are strong but your strength is different.

I love you with all my heart, as you know. But so much at once overwhelms me. I will never think the annulment and confinement were *right and just!!* My darling, write to me as always and I will write to you.

Things were so happy when we were only concerned with providing for ourselves and joyous plans for the future. Our future is much more distant now.

Love and good night
my darling—
your memory is with me always.

Sandy spouse of Edmund

Being a wife is no easy matter and I have not even begun. Do you want to tell your mother or should I. I will write to her anyway because I love her.

Nothing like this has ever happened to me.
Nothing you do now is for them only me.
Coming down here for any length of time is out of the question now.
In two weeks the papers will be through.
Only two or three days will be practical now.

Dearest Ted,

Before I forget there may be two letters at Joe's I sent last week. If you don't have them you could see if they are there.

I haven't done too much this day yet. In the morning Mr. Beam revised yesterday's poem some more. I don't have a copy. Anyway the poem by that time was no longer me. His title, "Today at the Penthouse." We are going to publish a book of poems about our impressions here. If you were here you could contribute too. Maybe we could fit one or two of your poems anyway.

I went carefully over "The Drunken Boat" the final version is more idiomatic and modern and concise—less 19th-century I guess. We can talk about the fine details later. I think it's good to know the reason for picking certain words over others in translation. Some sound better but there must be other reasons.

I finished reading *Hedda Gabler* I do like Ibsen very much.

Mary-Anne comes to visit all she does is complain about her doctors and nurses and talk about past operations. She never eats, she talks in such a loud voice. I wish someone around here were quiet and peaceful like you. It is so loud and grating here. No peace. Also I have a stiff neck. The bed gets worse. Finally a new bed: it is just as bad but I sink in the middle so I will not fall off, only get a spinal curvature.

Finished *The Wild Duck*. There is a kind of naturalness with Ibsen even with pistols and ducks as symbols.

I am getting a hot fudge sundae now. I am getting fatter. I can't find much satisfaction in anything except reading and candy. I will be a horse. I try to skip bread and starches at mealtimes.

I read Lorca every day. He is good—sounds beautiful—very simple, lyric, and clear. Have been reading in the *New Yorker* about a beautiful grand modern cathedral. We must remember it in case we ever go to Europe.

This is a short letter. I could fill pages with love.

Your wife
Sandy

A Book of Poetry for Sandy

(selections)

Dear Sandy

here's your book, started in
March, finished in October, 1962.

I love you.

Your husband
forever,

ted

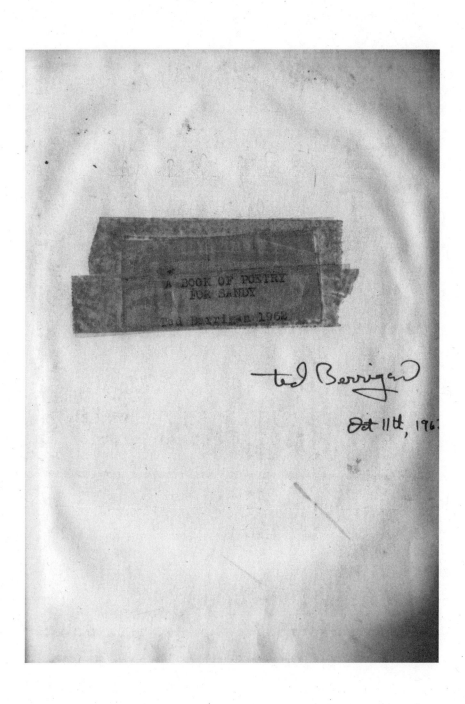

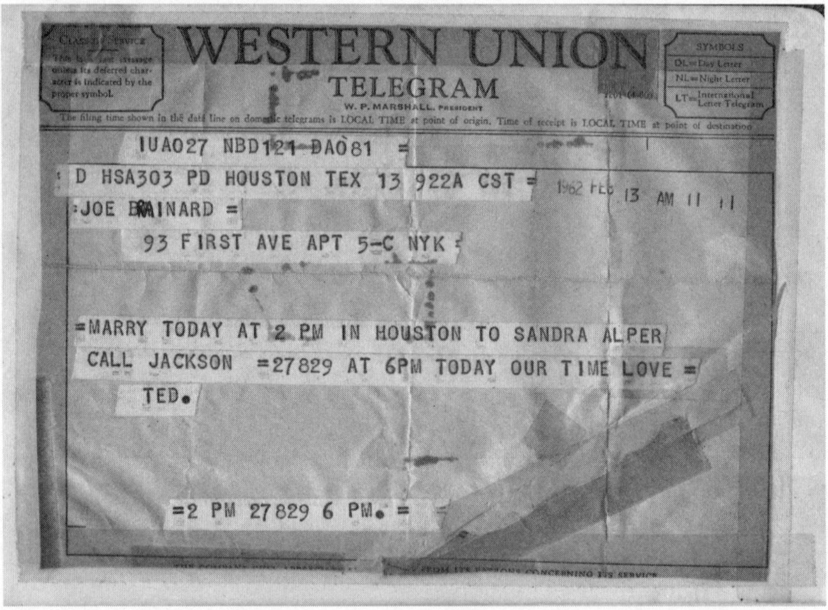
WESTERN UNION
TELEGRAM
W. P. MARSHALL, PRESIDENT

CLASS OF SERVICE
This is a fast message unless its deferred character is indicated by the proper symbol.

SYMBOLS
DL=Day Letter
NL=Night Letter
LT=International Letter Telegram

The filing time shown in the date line on domestic telegrams is LOCAL TIME at point of origin. Time of receipt is LOCAL TIME at point of destination

IUA027 NBD121 DA081 =
D HSA303 PD HOUSTON TEX 13 922A CST = 1962 FEB 13 AM 11 11
JOE BRAINARD =
93 FIRST AVE APT 5-C NYK =

=MARRY TODAY AT 2 PM IN HOUSTON TO SANDRA ALPER
CALL JACKSON =27829 AT 6PM TODAY OUR TIME LOVE =
TED.

=2 PM 27829 6 PM. =

Sandra Alper Becomes Bride

Dr. and Mrs. Lewis Alper of Miami, Fla., announce the marriage of their daughter, Miss Sandra Kay Alper, to Mr. Edmund Joseph Berrigan Jr., son of Mrs. Edmund J. Berrigan Sr. of Gordon Avenue and the late Mr. Berrigan.

The ceremony was performed in the chambers of Judge W. C. Ragan in Houston, Tex., on Feb. 13 at 2 p.m. A reception was held at the home of the bridesmaid, Miss Marge Kepler in Houston.

After a trip to Tulsa, Okla., and Miami the couple has taken up residence in New York City.

The bride, a graduate of Coral Gables High School, attended the H. Sophie Newcomb Memorial College for Women, Tulane University.

Mr. Berrigan, an alumnus of LaSalle Academy, received both his B.A. and M.A. degrees from Tulsa University.

From the Providence Journal-Bulletin

Sandy March, 1962
in her Wedding dress
Miami, Fla

Margie Kepler
Summer 1960

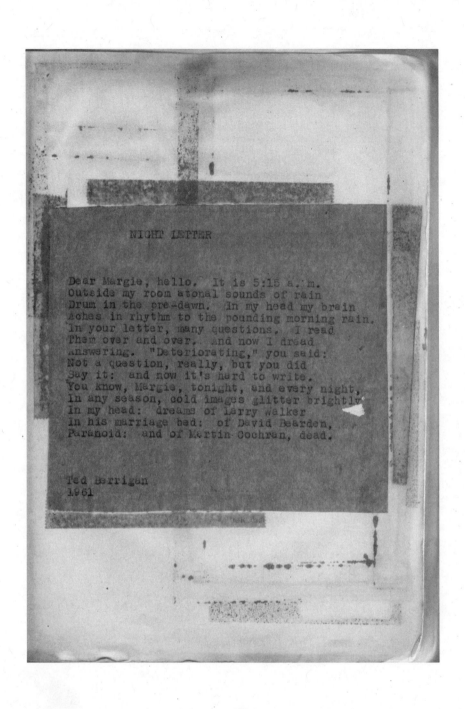

NIGHT LETTER

Dear Margie, hello. It is 5:15 a.m.
Outside my room atonal sounds of rain
Drum in the pre-dawn. In my head my brain
Aches in rhythm to the pounding morning rain.
In your letter, many questions. I read
Them over and over. And now I dread
Answering. "Deteriorating," you said:
Not a question, really, but you did
Say it: and now it's hard to write.
You know, Margie, tonight, and every night,
In any season, cold images glitter brightly
In my head: dreams of Larry Walker
In his marriage bed: of David Bearden,
Paranoid: and of Martin Cochran, dead.

Ted Berrigan
1961

Ezra Pound

Old Father,
I am very young.
I am afraid.

Teach me to run,
for I would learn to fight.

Sing would I, many songs,
and many candles
burn.

Teach me to fall,
for I would learn to stand

Old Warrior, guide me
now. Help me believe
The necessary lies.
~~Teach me to shoot~~

I would preserve my love.

Ted Berrigan
March, 1961

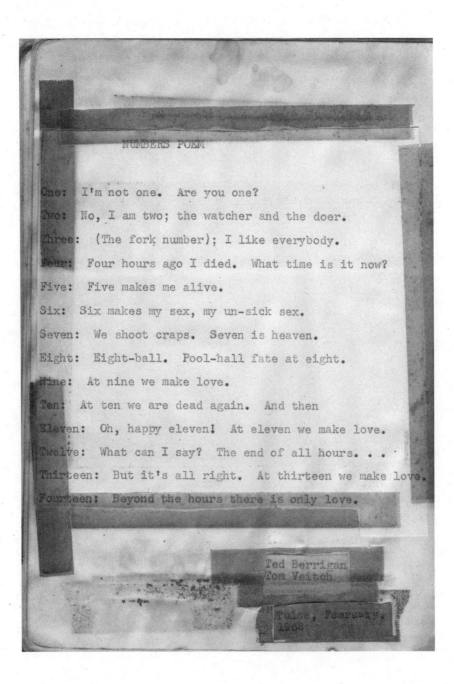

NUMBERS POEM

One: I'm not one. Are you one?

Two: No, I am two; the watcher and the doer.

Three: (The fork number); I like everybody.

Four: Four hours ago I died. What time is it now?

Five: Five makes me alive.

Six: Six makes my sex, my un-sick sex.

Seven: We shoot craps. Seven is heaven.

Eight: Eight-ball. Pool-hall fate at eight.

Nine: At nine we make love.

Ten: At ten we are dead again. And then

Eleven: Oh, happy eleven! At eleven we make love.

Twelve: What can I say? The end of all hours. . .

Thirteen: But it's all right. At thirteen we make love.

Fourteen: Beyond the hours there is only love.

Ted Berrigan
Tom Veitch

Tulsa, February,
1968

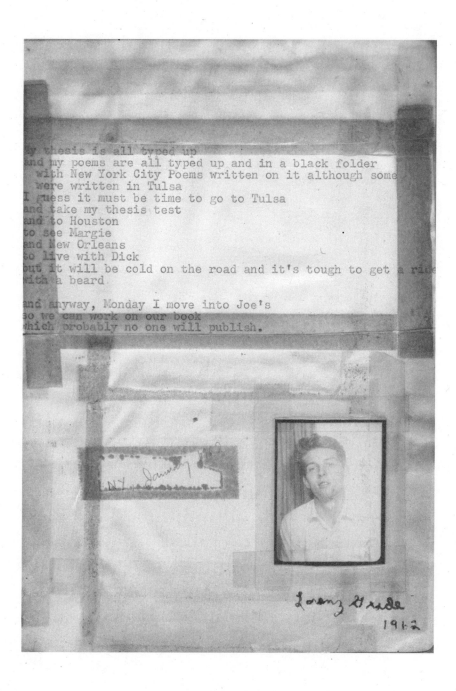

my thesis is all typed up
and my poems are all typed up and in a black folder
    with New York City Poems written on it although some
    were written in Tulsa
I guess it must be time to go to Tulsa
and take my thesis test
and to Houston
to see Margie
and New Orleans
to live with Dick
but it will be cold on the road and it's tough to get a ride
with a beard

and anyway, Monday I move into Joe's
so we can work on our book
which probably no one will publish.

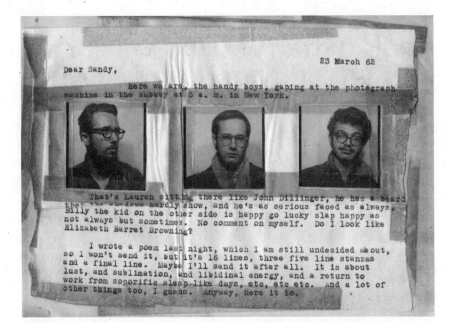

23 March 62

Dear Sandy,

           here we are, the handy boys, gaping at the photograph machine in the subway at 5 a. m. in New York.

      That's Lauren sitting there like John Dillinger, he has a beard that the shadows hardly show, and he's as serious faced as always. Billy the kid on the other side is happy go lucky slap happy as not always but sometimes. No comment on myself. Do I look like Elizabeth Barret Browning?

      I wrote a poem last night, which I am still undecided about, so I won't send it, but it's 16 lines, three five line stanzas and a final line. Maybe I'll send it after all. It is about lust, and sublimation, and libidinal energy, and a return to work from soporific sleep-like days, etc, etc etc. And a lot of other things too, I guess. Anyway, here it is.

"DEAR CHRIS

it is 3:17 a. m. in New York City, yes,
it is 1962, it is the year of parrot fever:
in Brandenburg, and by the granite gates, the
old camalyas streel into the streets; yes, it is now,
the season of delight. I am writing to you to say
I have gone mad. Now I am sowing the seeds which shall,
when ripe, master the day, and portion out the night.
Watch for me when blood flows down the streets. Pine-
apples are a sign that I am coming. Dress the snowman
in the Easter sonnet we made for him when scissors
were in style. For now, goodbye,
and all my love, The Snake."

                              Ted Berrigan
                              NY/January 1962

ted Berrigan
Sept 10th, 1962

Joe Brainard
Sept. 1962

Pat Mitchell
NY / 1962

Dick Gallup
NY / 1962

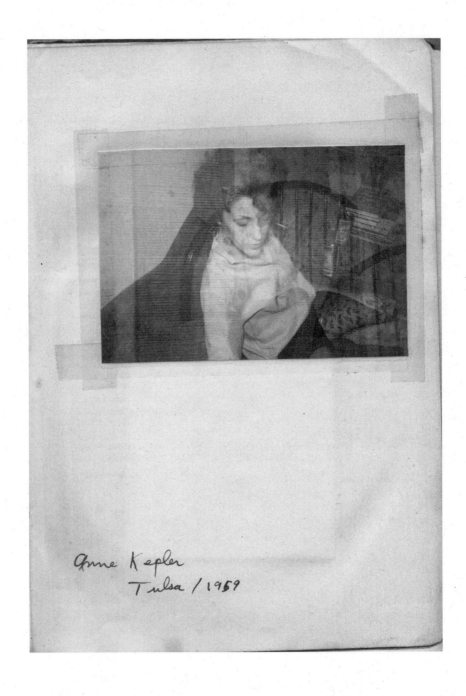

Anne Kepler
Tulsa / 1959

Ross Padgett
Tulsa / 1960

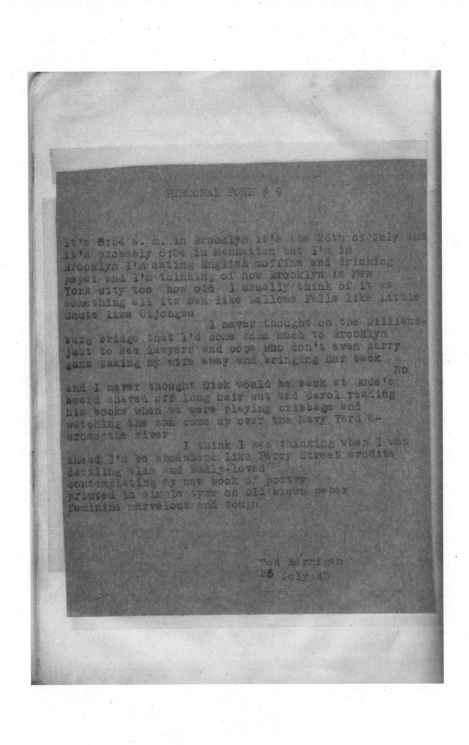

PERSONAL POEM # 9

It's 8:54 a. m. in Brooklyn it's the 26th of July and
it's probably 8:54 in Manhattan but I'm in
Brooklyn I'm eating English muffins and drinking
pepsi and I'm thinking of how Brooklyn is New
York city too how odd I usually think of it as
something all its own like Bellows Falls like Little
Chute like Uijongbu
                        I never thought on the Williams-
burg Bridge that I'd come so much to Brooklyn
just to see lawyers and cops who don't even carry
guns taking my wife away and bringing her back
                                                    No
and I never thought Dick would be back at Gude's
beard shaved off long hair out and Carol reading
his books when we were playing cribbage and
watching the sun come up over the Navy Yard a-
cross the river
                        I think I was thinking when I was
ahead I'd be somewhere like Perry Street erudite
dazzling slim and badly-loved
contemplating my new book of poetry
printed in simple type on old brown paper
feminine marvelous and tough

                                        Ted Berrigan
                                        26 July 62

THE WESTERN UNION TELEGRAPH COMPANY

RECEIPT

NOR 2801 BROADWAY NY

MAY OFFICE 1962 DATE

RECEIVED FROM RICHARD J GALLUP

1962 MAY 4 PM 1 44

ADDRESS 520 W 113 ST APT 307

THIRTY TWO AND NO/100 NOR NEW YORK 32.00

Account for the month of _____ 19___

☐ Telegraphic Money Order

☐ Telegram or Cable

☐ Deposit on Collect Telegram
   Returnable after 24 hours

☐ Account No. _____
   FOR REMITTANCE

TO EDMUND J BERRIGAN

Address WILL CALL

Place MIAMI FLO

MONEY   Chgs $ .65

ORDER   Tolls $ 7.60

CHARGES Tax $ .16

PAID   TOTAL $ ___

THE WESTERN UNION TELEGRAPH COMPANY

BY _____

*Dick, Cord, and Lorenz
send us money to run from Miami*

ted Berrigan
Tulsa / 1960

A Ted and Sandy Chronology

- Sandy enrolls at Sophie Newcomb College, fall of 1960.

- Sandy meets Dick Gallup, an undergraduate at Tulane, fall of 1961.

- Early February 1962, Ted and Tom Veitch take a drive-a-car from New York City, destination New Orleans. They stop in Washington, DC, so Ted can see if his first book, *A Lily for My Love*, is in the Library of Congress. When he finds that it is, he steals it, in order to destroy it. Ted and Tom drive through West Virginia to Yellow Springs, Ohio, where they visit a girl Tom knew from high school. Then they continue on to New Orleans, to visit Dick.

- Sandy and Ted meet around February 7, 1962, in New Orleans through Dick.

- Dick withdraws from Tulane. He and Tom get a drive-a-car for delivery in Chicago. Ted and Sandy take a bus to Houston on February 11 or 12.

- Ted and Sandy are married on February 13, by Judge W. C. Ragan in Houston. Spend the night at Marge Kepler's.

- Then several days in Tulsa, at Ron Padgett's parents' home. Dick and Tom rendezvous with Sandy and Ted in Tulsa. At the University of Tulsa, Ted completes his orals and is awarded his M.A. degree (which, shortly thereafter, he refuses to accept).

- Around February 20 the couple fly from Tulsa to Miami to visit Sandy's parents, Louis and Dorothy Alper, who paid for the flight.

- Dick and Tom deliver another car to Miami, staying in a maid's room attached to the garage of the Alpers' house.

- A few days later, Sandy's parents obtain a court order committing Sandy to the Jackson Memorial Hospital's mental ward in Miami. Police immediately escort her to the hospital.

- The Alpers have the Dade County Sheriff run Ted out of town. He goes to Savannah. There, Ted's letters to Sandy begin. The first one, written from the Savannah YMCA, is dated February 27.

- Dick and Tom pick Ted up in yet another drive-a-car, a new Cadillac. The three return to New York City.

- In New York, Ted begins a poetry and art scrapbook for Sandy in March 1962, finishing it on October 11 (though later he added some annotations).

- Sandy spends March, April, and early May in the hospital, until she gets a good-behavior pass to visit the public library alone. There she joins Ted, who has slipped into town, and they flee, helped by the $32 wired to Ted on May 4 by Dick, Carol Clifford, and Lorenz Gude.

- The two go to St. Louis (apparently staying with a friend of Ted's, perhaps with his former army buddy John Luyendyk), then go on to Chicago, which seems dark and gloomy and where they can't figure out where to stay, so they hitchhike toward the West Coast. Their ride drops them off in Denver. Sandy gets a job in a dry cleaners. Ted, caught shoplifting in a supermarket, has to outrun the store employees. The two eventually make their way, by bus or hitchhiking, back to Tulsa.

- In Tulsa, Ted introduces Sandy to Lauren Owen. With Lauren and a young woman (possibly named Patsy), Sandy and Ted make their way, perhaps by drive-a-car, to New York.

- Sandy and Ted settle in a cheap rooming house called the Galatea, located near Columbia University on West 113th Street, where Dick already has a room and where Ted had stayed with him in April. In a letter (postmarked June 12, 1962) to her Coral Gables High School friend Leslie Klupt in South Miami, Sandy mentions that she has learned to shoplift. Leslie shows the letter to her mother, who in turn shows it to Mrs. Alper. For a second time, the Alpers hire a private detective agency to find Sandy and gather more incriminating information against Ted.

- Summer of 1962, around mid-June, Sandy is again whisked away by police, first for a night in the Women's House of Detention in Greenwich Village, then to Bellevue's mental ward. After two weeks there and two weeks at the Euphrasian Girls' Home (in Manhattan's east side), and after a court hearing in Brooklyn on July 26, she is released and her parents finally give up the fight. Ted's "Personal Poem #9" (dated "26 July 62" in the poetry scrapbook he made for her) mentions "I never thought . . . / that I'd come so much to Brooklyn / just to see lawyers and cops who don't even carry / guns taking my wife away and bringing her back."

- In November of 1962, during the stay on 113th Street, Ted begins to write the series of poems that become *The Sonnets*.

- In June of 1963, Ted and Sandy move to New York's Lower East Side, where they live for the next five years. From a literary point of view, it is a very fruitful period for him, though fraught by constant financial pressure. They have two children, David and Kate, in a marriage that lasts until 1969, when it finally falls apart in Iowa City, where Ted is teaching in the Iowa Writers' Workshop program.

—R. P.

Glossary of Names

NOTE: *This glossary includes friends and acquaintances of Ted's or Sandy's, mostly his. Not included are well-known literary figures, such as Frank O'Hara.*

LOUIS and **DOROTHY ALPER** (b. ?) Parents of Sandy Alper. Dr. Alper was a respected physician in Miami.

MIMI ALPER (b. 1951) Sandy's younger sister.

SANDRA ALPER (b. 1942) Born in Detroit, moved to Miami at age 13. Attended Sophie Newcomb College in New Orleans, where she met Tulane student Dick Gallup. In her sophomore year, after a courtship of a week, she married Ted Berrigan in Houston, thus setting in motion the events described in this book.

JOE BRAINARD (b. 1942) Tulsa high school friend of Ron Padgett and Dick Gallup who met Berrigan in 1959. Brainard moved to New York in late 1960. When Berrigan followed a few months later, he shared Brainard's storefront apartment on East 6th Street, until the summer of 1961.

CAROL CLIFFORD (b. 1942) Barnard student who had been a classmate of Sandy Alper's at Coral Gables High School. Became Ted's girlfriend while Sandy was in Jackson Memorial Hospital, unbeknownst to Sandy. In 1964 she married Dick Gallup.

HARRY DIAKOFF (b. 1942?) Columbia student in the class of 1964, along with Lorenz Gude, Ed Kaim, Bill McCullam, and Ron Padgett. In high school Diakoff became a serious scholar of the work of Ezra Pound.

DICK GALLUP (b. 1941) Poet whose family moved from Greenfield, Massachusetts, to Tulsa over the 1949–50 holidays. Dick and his family lived directly across the street from Ron Padgett and his family. After attending Tulane University for two and a half years, he withdrew from school and moved to New York in the spring of 1962. In 1964 he married Carol Clifford.

KAREN (b. ?) Sandra's roommate at Sophie Newcomb.

LORENZ GUDE (b. 1942) Columbia student and Bellows Falls (Vermont) High School friend of Tom Veitch. Gude's freshman dorm room was on the same floor as Ron Padgett's. Gude bore a close resemblance to Arthur Rimbaud.

ED KAIM (b. 1942) Columbia student and friend of Ted's, Kaim had, coincidentally, been a classmate of Sandy Alper's at Coral Gables High School in Florida.

ANNE KEPLER (1942–1965) Accomplished flutist and Tulsa high school classmate of Joe Brainard and Ron Padgett, she came to New York to study flute in 1961. Ted met Anne in 1959. She died in a fire.

MARGE KEPLER (b. ?) Anne Kepler's cousin whom Ted met in Tulsa in 1959 or 1960. Ted always thought of Marge as his first truly personal sexual experience.

LESLIE KLUPT (b. ?) Sandra's high school friend. Ted may have met her.

BILL MCCULLAM (b. 1942) Columbia student. Dorm roommate of Ron Padgett during their freshman year.

PAT MITCHELL (b. 1937) Ted's fellow student at the University of Tulsa who began dating him in 1957. In 1961 she discontinued her graduate studies and, in the summer, moved to New York, where Ted had moved in January of that year. In 1963 she married Ron Padgett.

RITA (b. 1930) Sandra's older sister, married, who lived in New Jersey.

RON PADGETT (b. 1942) Poet who met Ted in a Tulsa bookstore in the spring of 1959 and who came to New York to study at Columbia in 1960. He married Pat Mitchell in 1963.

TOM VEITCH (b. 1941) Fiction writer, comic book author, and free spirit, in 1962 a recent Columbia drop-out. In February of that year Tom and Ted drove to New Oreans, where the latter met Sandy Alper.

—R. P.

Notes on *A Book of Poetry for Sandy*

In March of 1962, Ted started taping poems, illustrations, and photos, as well as two telegrams, into a blank sketchbook as a gift for his young wife, who at the time was being held in the mental ward of a Miami hospital. The black notebook, which measures 6 inches wide and 8 3/4 inches tall, has a flexible leatherette cover. Ted filled its two hundred pages, completing the book on October 11, months after he and Sandy were reunited. In the following few years he entered some additional remarks, usually noting the subsequent deaths of people in the book.

Although most of the tape has yellowed and fallen off and many of the items have come loose, the scrapbook is still complete, page for page.

The contents are as follows (bold-face entries appear in this book.)

- **Front endpaper: "Dear Sandy, here's your book, started in March, finished in October, 1962. I love you. Your husband forever, Ted."**
- Title page: A Book of Poetry for Sandy / Ted Berrigan 1962.
- **Page 1. Telegram from Ted to Joe Brainard announcing Ted and Sandy's marriage later that same day.**
- **Ted and Sandy's wedding announcement, clipped from the *Providence Journal-Bulletin*.**
- *The Conjurer*, painting by Hans Hoffman.
- Four lines from Baudelaire's "Le Voyage": "True voyagers alone are those who leave / just to be leaving; hearts light as balloons, / they never shrink from their fatality / and without knowing

why, say, 'Let's get going!'" Translated by C. G. Wallis.

- **Photo of Ted taken in Providence in March 1961.**
- **Photo of Sandy wearing her wedding dress, taken, according to Ted's note, in Miami in March 1962. A very similar picture later in the scrapbook is dated by him February 1962. The February date seems more likely.**
- Photo of William Carlos Williams.
- "A Letter to William Carlos Williams" by Kenneth Rexroth.
- Untitled ink sketch still life signed "Brainard 62."
- "Now Kindness" by Peter Viereck.
- Painting by Mark Tobey and a photo of him.
- "Song" by Theodore Spencer.
- Painting by Morris Graves and a photo of him.
- "To My Sisters" by Theodore Roethke.
- Photo of Theodore Roethke.
- "The Waking" by Theodore Roethke.
- Portrait of Frank O'Hara by Alice Neel.
- "To the Harbormaster" by Frank O'Hara.
- Photo of Willem de Kooning.
- "Overlooking the River" by Frank O'Hara.
- Photo of Franz Kline in front of one of his paintings.
- "Initiation" by Rainer Maria Rilke, translated by C. F. McIntyre.
- Photo of Robert Lowell.
- "Man and Wife" by Robert Lowell.
- Photo of Delmore Schwartz, with Ted's annotation "died July 1966 age 50."
- "Will You Perhaps Consent to Be" by Delmore Schwartz.

- Photo of Conrad Aiken.
- "xviii" from *Preludes for Memnon* by Conrad Aiken.
- *Jardin d'amour* by Hans Hoffman and a photo of him, with Ted's annotation "d. 1965."
- "Praising, that's it!" from *Sonnets to Orpheus* by Rainer Maria Rilke, translated by C. F. McIntyre.
- Photo of Hart Crane.
- "Indiana" by Hart Crane.
- Photo of Ezra Pound with Ted's poem addressed to him, beginning "Old Father," dated March 1961.
- "Francesca" by Ezra Pound.
- *Untitled Abstraction* by Mark Rothko.
- "The River Merchant's Wife: A Letter" by Rihaku, translated by Ezra Pound.
- **Two photos of Margie Kepler, summer 1960.**
- **"Night Letter" by Ted, 1961. Ted rearranged the lines of this syntactically normal poem and turned it into "xviii" in his *Sonnets*.**
- Picasso's *Manager*, 1917, and a photo of Wallace Stevens.
- "Disillusionment of Ten o'Clock" by Wallace Stevens.
- Unidentified original ink drawing (perhaps by James Bearden).
- "The Tennis Court Oath" by John Ashbery.
- Photos of Kenneth Koch, Frank O'Hara, and John Ashbery.
- *The Wedding* by Marc Chagall.
- "To You" by Kenneth Koch.
- Interior by Henri Matisse.
- "A Sort of a Song" by William Carlos Williams.
- "From a Book of Poetry" by Kenneth Koch. This uncollected poem begins "Oxcart bramble stinkweed and L 'fust fust'."

- "Lines on the Mermaid Tavern" by John Keats.
- Self-portrait by Rembrandt van Rijn.
- "The Argument of His Book" by Robert Herrick.
- *Time and Duration* by Max Ernst.
- "To His Coy Mistress" by Andrew Marvell.
- "You, Andrew Marvell" by Archibald MacLeish.
- *Guitar, Glasses, and Bottle*, 1914, by Juan Gris.
- "Thoughts of a Young Girl" by John Ashbery.
- *Self-portrait*, 1921, by Juan Gris.
- "23rd Street Runs into Heaven" by Kenneth Patchen.
- Photo of Kenneth Patchen.
- "The Second Coming" by William Butler Yeats.
- Photo of Arshile Gorky and his painting *The Betrothal*.
- "Which Is My Little Boy?" by Tennessee Williams.
- *The Agony* by Arshile Gorky.
- "Little Horse" by Tennessee Williams.
- Photo of D. H. Lawrence.
- "Hatred" by Frank O'Hara. Ted added: "Frank died July 1966."
- *Woman in Blue (Second State)*, 1912, by Fernand Léger.
- Photo of Henri Matisse by Edward Steichen, 1909.
- Photo of Jackson Pollock and his *Blue Poles*.
- Photo of Willem de Kooning and a painting, with Elaine de Kooning's portrait of Frank O'Hara taped on top of it.
- *Val's Birthday Gift*, 1952, by Henry Miller.
- "The Whip" by Robert Creeley.
- Two-page spread of a painting by Jackson Pollock.
- Photo of Larry Rivers standing next to his painting *The Last Confederate Soldier*.

- "The Way" by Robert Creeley.
- Movie still of Charlie Chaplin and Jackie Coogan peering around a corner fearfully at a policeman.
- Poem written by a nine-year-old boy: "The two lights hung high / Through the night, how they glitter / He's yelling, 'To arms!' / Everyone gets his rifles / The revolution is done."
- Self-portrait by Alfred Pinkham Ryder.
- "Words for Love" by Ted.
- **"Prayer" by Ted, dated December 1961.**
- Uncollected "Poem for Biographers" by Ted, beginning "They were waiting for me when I came home." Part of this poem was used in *The Sonnets*.
- **"Numbers Poem," an unpublished collaborative work by Tom Veitch and Ted, written in Tulsa, February 1962.**
- "What are you thinking . . .", an uncollected poem, some of whose lines made their way into *The Sonnets*. Dated Denver, May 1962.
- "Goodbye to Ron, Bonjour to Pat, Hello to Marge and Dick and Joe and Anne," parts of this poem by Ted resurfaced in *The Sonnets*. Dated New York, January 1962. Probably written at 81 Horatio Street, where Ted was sharing an apartment with Pat Mitchell and Ron Padgett.
- **Photo booth picture of Lorenz Gude, 1962.**
- Two photos of Ted, the first taken in Korea in August 1955, the second taken by Joe Brainard on East Sixth Street in New York in March 1961.
- Photo of Ted by Joe Brainard, taken on same day as the one above.
- Photo of Ted by Ron Padgett in Providence, February of 1961, across the street from his mother's house.

- "Lines from across the Room," an uncollected poem dedicated to Anne Kepler, by Ted in March 1962 in New York. A few words from this poem found their way into *The Sonnets*. Ted noted: "Anne died in a fire."
- **A letter to Sandy dated 23 March 62, with three photo booth pictures taped into it: Ted, Lauren Owen, and Dick Gallup. This short letter accompanied Ted's poem "Cosmic Apples," dated July 1962. Lines from this uncollected poem about Ted's youth were used in *The Sonnets*.**
- Photo of Oswald Spengler.
- "The Pocketa, Pocketa School," a poem, as Ted noted, "done by an IBM machine," meaning a computer. The poem reads: "Few fingers go like narrow laughs. / An ear won't keep few fishes, / Who is that rose in that blind house? / And all slim, gracious blind planes are coming, / They cry badly along a rose / To leap is stuffy to crawl was tender." The title refers to something Ted was fond of quoting, "pocketa pocketa beep," from James Thurber's *Secret Life of Walter Mitty* (or perhaps from the film of the same name). The sound suggests that this poem was created by a computer using certain words furnished by Ted.
- **"Dear Chris," a poem by Ted dated NY/January 1962. This poem, lightly revised, became "LXXVII" in *The Sonnets*.**
- "Three Airs" by Frank O'Hara.
- Photo of Ted, June 1961.
- "Le Voyage" by Charles Baudelaire, translated by C. G. Wallis.
- Photo of George Bernard Shaw, 1898.
- "In place of Sunday Mass We Sanguinize," poem by Ted dated 29 April 62. The first line, "My beard is a leaping staff" seems to refer to Wallace Stevens's "His beard is of fire and his staff is a leaping flame," but also to the photo of Shaw on the facing page and to Ted's own beard. In 1962 wearing a beard was often

a public statement that one was an outsider.

- *Two Figures* by Edwin Dickinson, as Ted noted, "contributed by Joe Brainard."
- "From a Poem by Taliessen" (sixth-century Welsh writer), beginning "The wind without flesh."
- Photo of Pablo and Jacqueline Picasso, "contributed by Joe Brainard."
- "Protected by Hoffman, Matisse," an unpublished poem by Ted, dated 24 June 62.
- *The Next to Last Confederate Veteran, 1959,* by Larry Rivers.
- "How Much Longer Will I Be Able to Inhabit the Divine Sepulcher . . ." by John Ashbery.
- Photo of Henry Miller and his wife Eve in Paris, 1959.
- Photo of James Agee, c. 1947.
- "Poem Read at the Marriage of André Salmon" by Guillaume Apollinaire, translated by Roger Shattuck.
- Line drawing figure study by Joe Brainard, 1960. The model was Marge Kepler.
- "Farewell to Arshile Gorky" by André Breton, translated by Denise Hare.
- "The Level of Every Day," poem by Ted, dated March 1962. Bits of this unpublished poem were used in *The Sonnets.*
- **Photo booth picture of Ted, September 10, 1962.**
- "Spring" by Thomas Nashe.
- **Photo booth picture of Joe Brainard, September 1962.**
- "Poem in the Traditional Manner" by Ted, dated January 1962. Ted noted: "Published in *Locus Solus* #V, October 1962."
- "Jumping from Pottawottamie" by Ted, dated April 1962. Parts later used in *The Sonnets.*

- "Lines for Lauren Owen," poem by Ted, dated January 1962, and later lightly revised and used as "XLVI" in *The Sonnets*.
- "Poem in the Modern Manner" by Ted, dated 1962, became one of his sonnets.
- "In Time of Fever," an unpublished poem by Ted, dated August 1962. Parts used in *The Sonnets*.
- Two photos of Pat Mitchell taken in New York, dated 1962 by Ted. Pat is certain they were taken in the summer of 1961.
- "A Poem of the Forty-Eight States" by Kenneth Koch.
- Photo of Lauren Owen, Tulsa, 1959.
- "Poem" ("Another has come to the silver mirror") by David Bearden, 1960.
- **Photo of Dick Gallup, New York, dated 1962.**
- "Voltaire at Ferney" by W. H. Auden.
- "Love Calls Us to the Things of This World" by Richard Wilbur.
- **Photo of Anne Kepler by Ron Padgett, Tulsa, summer 1959.**
- **Photo of Ron Padgett, Tulsa, 1960.**
- "Wind" by Ron Padgett, taped over Shakespeare's song "Full fathom five thy father lies" from *The Tempest*.
- "In Memory of My Feelings" by Frank O'Hara.
- Photo of James Dean, New York City.
- "Orange on Plate," drawing by Joe Brainard.
- "Rain Dance," unpublished poem by Ted, dated 19 Sept 62.
- Photo of Jan Muller.
- *The Accusation* by Jan Muller.
- Photo of Marcel Duchamp.
- Photo of Willem de Kooning.
- Portrait of Ezra Pound by Orfeo Tamburini, 1935.

- Portrait of Ezra Pound by an unidentified artist.
- Three photos: Ezra Pound at 20 (1908); Ford Madox Ford and Ezra Pound, 1932, in Rapallo; and Ezra Pound and his daughter Mary, Venice, 1935.
- "The Unbelievable One," unpublished poem by Ted, parts of which he used in *The Sonnets*. Dated 23–30 Sept 62.
- Photo of Edgar Allan Poe.
- "Sonnet," poem by Ted that, lightly revised, became "xvii" in *The Sonnets*. Dated 18–31 July 62.
- "A Sonnet for M'sieu Hillyear," unpublished poem by Ted, a few words of which reappear in *The Sonnets*. Dated July 1962.
- "Homage to Mayakofsky," unpublished poem by Ted, parts of which appear in *The Sonnets*. Dated 2 Oct 62.
- **"Personal Poem #9" by Ted, which became "xxxvi" in *The Sonnets*. Dated 26 July 62.**
- Portrait of Apollinaire by Jean Metzinger.
- "Anniversary," unpublished poem by Ted, lines of which appear in *The Sonnets*. Dated 5 Oct 62.
- *Three Cards*, 1913, by Juan Gris.
- Photo of Frank O'Hara and Larry Rivers working on *Stones*.
- "The Minstrel Boy" by John Ashbery.
- *Portrait* by James Whistler.
- Portrait of Percy Bysshe Shelley.
- Poem by Ted later titled "From a Secret Journal," dated 15 June 62. Used as the ninth poem in *The Sonnets*.
- "Answering a Question in the Mountains" by John Ashbery.
- The cover of *Evergreen Review* no. 3, showing Jackson Pollock sitting on the running board of an old car.
- **Receipt for a Western Union telegram showing that Dick**

Gallup in New York wired $32 to Ted in Miami on May 4, 1962. Ted noted to Sandy: "Dick, Carol and Lorenz send us money to run from Miami."

- *Portrait of a Chess Player*, 1911, by Marcel Duchamp.
- *Nude Descending a Staircase #2*, 1912, by Marcel Duchamp.
- Final page: Photo of Sandy Berrigan, February 1962, in Miami. At bottom of page, Ted's note: "Book completed 11 Oct 1962 Ted."
- Back endpaper: photo of Ted sitting on his bed in Tulsa, 1960. Behind him is his book collection and a still life drawing by Joe Brainard. He is beginning to grow his first beard.

—R. P.

COLOPHON

Dear Sandy, Hello was designed at Coffee House Press, in the historic
Grain Belt Brewery's Bottling House near downtown Minneapolis.
The text is set in Caslon.

FUNDER ACKNOWLEDGMENTS

Coffee House Press is an independent nonprofit literary publisher. Our books
are made possible through the generous support of grants and gifts from many
foundations, corporate giving programs, state and federal support, and through
donations from individuals who believe in the transformational power of
literature. Coffee House Press receives major operating support from the Bush
Foundation, the McKnight Foundation, from Target, and from the Minnesota
State Arts Board, through an appropriation from the Minnesota State
Legislature and from the National Endowment for the Arts. Coffee House
also receives support from: three anonymous donors; Allan Appel; Around
Town Literary Media Guides; Bill Berkson; the James L. and Nancy J. Bildner
Foundation; the Patrick and Aimee Butler Family Foundation; the Buuck
Family Foundation; Dorsey & Whitney, LLP; Fredrikson & Byron, P.A.;
Sally French; Jennifer Haugh; Anselm Hollo and Jane Dalrymple-Hollo;
Jeffrey Hom; Stephen and Isabel Keating; the Kenneth Koch Literary Estate;
the Lenfestey Family Foundation; Ethan J. Litman; Mary McDermid;
Sjur Midness and Briar Andresen; the Rehael Fund of the Minneapolis
Foundation; Deborah Reynolds; Schwegman, Lundberg, Woessner, P.A.;
John Sjoberg; David Smith; Mary Strand and Tom Fraser; Jeffrey Sugerman;
the Archie D. & Bertha H. Walker Foundation; Stu Wilson and Mel Barker;
the Woessner Freeman Family Foundation in memory of David Hilton;
and many other generous individual donors.

To you and our many readers across the country,
we send our thanks for your continuing support.

Good books are brewing at www.coffeehousepress.org